Interruptions

STUDIES IN SPIRITUALITY AND THEOLOGY 4

Lawrence Cunningham, Bernard McGinn, and David Tracy
SERIES EDITORS

INTERRUPTIONS

Mysticism, Politics, and Theology
in the Work of Johann Baptist Metz

JAMES MATTHEW ASHLEY

University of Notre Dame Press
Notre Dame, Indiana

Library of Congress Cataloging-in-Publication Data

Ashley, James Matthew, 1958–
     Interruptions : mysticism, politics, and theology in the work of
Johann Baptist Metz / James Matthew Ashley.
          p.   cm. — (Studies in spirituality and theology ; 4)
     Includes bibliographical references and index.
     ISBN 0-268-01185-0 (alk. paper)
     1. Metz, Johannes Baptist, 1928–   . I. Title. II. Series.
BX4705.M545A74   1998
230'.2'092—dc21   98-9193
                                                                           CIP

CONTENTS

INTRODUCTION

This work originated as a dissertation on the evolution of theological anthropology in the thought of Johann Baptist Metz.[1] Like many others, I was struck by the sudden change in direction that Metz took in the mid-sixties, away from the transcendental Thomism of his mentor, Karl Rahner, and into the long and difficult development of what he came to call "political theology." While many emphasized the discontinuities, I thought it worthwhile to try to illuminate the discontinuities in terms of what I believe to be deep and significant continuities: among others, his critical commitment to the Enlightenment and its understanding of the subject, guided by the ideal of *Mündigkeit;* his belief that these Enlightenment themes have emerged not in spite of the spirit of Christianity but due to it, and, consequently, his advocacy of an aggressive dialogue between modernity and Christianity; his use of argumentative strategies very much like Rahner's; and, finally, his enduring interest in spirituality. While the discontinuities in Metz's thought are striking and important, I argued that the shifts he made derived from these deeper commitments, which could only be sustained, in Metz's view, by changing dramatically the ways in which they had been articulated and satisfied in the theology he learned from Rahner.

The initial premise bore fruit, especially for understanding the "what" and the "how" of Metz's theological development. I showed that the central, organizing question in Metz's mature work is no longer the *Seinsfrage*—the question of being and of meaning, threatened in a secularized, one-dimensional world. Rather, it is the *Leidensfrage*—the question of catastrophic, massive and systemic suffering in a world supposedly come of age, allegedly possessing both the will and the resources finally to put an end to such scourges. In Gutiérrez's well-known formulation, this is the question of the nonperson, rather than that of the nonbeliever. But Metz continued to apply the transcendental, phenomenological strategies that he learned from Rahner, and indeed, from Heidegger, to ask about how the human being must be constituted such that she or he raises, indeed is defined by, *this* question. The phenomenological tools by which Metz endeavored to disclose this ontological structure now came to include the resources of revisionary Marxists like Ernst Bloch and the members of the Frankfurt School. In this way Metz arrived at a set of "existentials" (memory, solidarity, narrative) that makes it clear how human beings are constituted by this question, as well as how it is that they are only thus constituted by means of a profound and grace-filled relationship to the God of Abraham, Isaac, Jacob, Job, and Jesus Christ. This underlying anthropology serves the same organizing function for Metz's mature thought as the anthropology developed in *Spirit in World* and *Hearers of the Word* does for Rahner's. It unites the diverse concerns that have occupied his writing over the past three decades: his dialogue with Marxism and with Judaism, his posing of the theodicy question as *the* question for theology, his insistence on the integrity and importance of apocalyptic traditions in Christianity, his raising of the "time question" in general, and finally his incessant and passionate resistance to postmodernism—both theoretical and practical, both in the academy and in the broader social, political, and cultural milieu of central Europe.

I am still satisfied with those results; indeed, the substance of that argument can still be found in the middle chapters of this book. The question that persisted, however, was the question of "Why?" Why did Metz take the path that he took? The straightforward response, one furthermore that is suggested by some of Metz's own statements, is that he became convinced that Rahner's transcendental theology was incapable of answering the question of suffering, that it could not overcome the strangling constraints of privatization that modernity had placed upon Christian faith and theology, that it could not give an account of the hope in the future that sustains Christian praxis, that, for all its talk of historicity it was, in the final analysis, ahistorical, idealist, even gnostic. On this reading, Metz abandoned the transcendental paradigm because of its constitutional inability to meet the challenges of doing theology in a still—or post—modern world.[2]

This hypothesis has some value as an initial heuristic mechanism for looking at Metz's development and at his relationship to Rahner. But, as simple and attractive as it is, it will not bear close scrutiny. It forces one to make an either/or judgment which does justice neither to Rahner's theology nor to Metz's. On the one hand, one might judge that the criticisms listed above are correct, but only by denying that Rahner himself responded in any substantive way to the challenges that emerged in the post–Vatican II years. This position simply cannot be sustained; furthermore, it cannot explain why Metz has continued to hold up Rahner's theological praxis (if not "transcendental theology" as a method) precisely as a model of how to respond to the Church's present dilemmas.[3] From the other direction one could assert that Metz is wrong, that he is either unaware of or refuses to acknowledge the ways that Rahner's theology continually developed in response to the changing needs of Church and world. On this reading, even Rahner's early foundational works had implicit resources for dealing with the issues that Metz has raised, and these resources were explicitly utilized in the last two decades of Rahner's work.[4] A more plausible variant, given Metz's continuing high regard for the theological praxis of his teacher, starts from Metz's own admission that his theology is a "corrective theoogy." On this reading, Metz's contribution lies in pointing out certain unresolved problems, or areas in need of further development, in Rahner's thought; but Rahner's system is in fact open to the kinds of development that Metz wants.[5]

Such a view does seem able to do justice to the continuing and deep respect that existed between the two men, even after their theological paths diverged. But can this view account for the strength of their disagreement, particularly over the issue of demythologizing apocalyptic symbols and narratives in Christian theology, the issue that came to dominate their arguments in the last years of Rahner's life? In addition, this position has a corollary which also has its difficulties. The corollary asserts that Metz's "political theology" lacks sufficient grounding in a foundational anthropology to be a "practical fundamental theology" and hence stands in need of Rahner's theological anthropology. In other words, Rahner's theology can encompass the tasks that Metz sets for his own political theology, but the converse is not true. My own conclusions were, first, that one can, in fact, construct the essential features of the anthropology that underpins Metz's political theology, and, second, that this anthropology is coherent and at least worthy of consideration as an alternative to Rahner's. If these conclusions about the degree to which Metz used by transforming transcendental method were correct, if it was indeed true that Metz had come up with a different set of existentialia, and consequently a different anthropological base, then "corrective" seems too weak a word for characterizing his relationship to Rahner. Their differences were real and substantial. Then how *should* we evaluate the roots of their disagreement?

My thesis is that the difference between Rahner and Metz should ultimately be located in the different spiritualities that nourish their respective theologies. This interpretation, which will be defended in more detail in the last chapter of this book, has the virtue of building on the central concern for spirituality that characterizes the theological biographies of both men. This is certainly true for Rahner. Surely, he must be counted among those theologians who have most helped to close the gap between spirituality and theology in this century. It is a testimony to the profundity of Metz's grasp of his teacher's theology that he has identified Rahner's greatness not in the brilliance of his arguments, or in the comprehensiveness and versatility of a theological system, but in his respect for the mystical experience of all persons, especially of the everyday believer, and in his insistence that this must form the starting point and context of justification for the theologian's retrieval of the doctrinal riches of the Christian tradition.[6] For his part, Metz not only joined Rahner in insisting on spirituality as a starting point for theology but was one of the first to press explicitly the further claim that this includes showing that and how spirituality or mysticism has an inherent and inalienable correlation with political commitment and action.[7]

Rahner voiced his agreement with this position but, again, clearly felt that his own theology could fulfill this requirement.[8] Are we back at an impasse? No. This is precisely where I believe that some progress can be made. The differences between the two can be located by a more careful consideration of what "mystical" means for each. The growing body of work done by scholars in the field of the history of spirituality has shown that "mysticism" is not a univocal term, even within the confines of Christianity. If one changes the "mystical" side of the mystical-political relationship, then will not the "political" side shift as well, and will not the theology which attempts to disclose, elaborate, and justify that relationship also change?

My conclusion was that yes, they would, and that the relationship between the theological developments of Rahner and Metz provided a case in point. The theologies of *both* Karl Rahner and Johann Baptist

Metz have developed in relationship to particular spiritualities. For both, one of the animating drives of this development was the desire to bring out more fully the political implications of the experience of God that is expressed and nurtured through specific spiritualities. The difference lies in the particular spiritual traditions out of which each theologized. I argued this briefly and tentatively in the concluding chapter of my dissertation, leaving many issues and questions unanswered. This book is an attempt to work out this thesis in a more comprehensive way, focusing on Metz's theological development. I have undertaken it not only to round out my own understanding of Metz's thought but as a more interesting way of giving a comprehensive presentation and analysis of his thought than through the more academic approach of focusing on the category of "theological anthropology." More interesting, first, because it locates the heart (in all senses of the word) of Metz's development, and allows one to understand its dramatic shifts. This is well worth doing, not only because Metz is a serious and creative thinker, but also because he is among that first generation of theologians who mastered their craft immediately prior to and during the Second Vatican Council and consequently had as their task not the work of breaking ground for the council or serving as midwives for its results, but of charting a course for Catholic theology during the difficult years that have followed it. As another generation of theologians begins to take on this task, they would do well to consider the efforts of their predecessors.

Second, this approach to Metz is more interesting because it provides an illuminating case study in a topic that is receiving increasing attention in theology today: the relationship between spirituality and theology. Reflection on this relationship was initiated and developed earlier in this century by figures like von Hügel, Chenu, Leclercq, von Balthasar, and Rahner. The concomitant explosion in scholarship on the history of spirituality and mysticism has vastly deepened our knowledge, complicating the task but also laying the groundwork that would enable us to make the requisite distinctions and nuances. But much remains to be done; indeed, it is my conviction that one of the most important tasks for theology today is understanding this relationship. The theoretical progress that has already been made will be enriched by careful case studies of men and women, past and present, in whom this relationship is present in a clear and provocative way. As I shall attempt to show below, Metz is one of these figures. It is with that in mind that I offer this study.

As the title suggests, therefore, I will argue that Metz's thought has been driven and "interrupted" at key junctures by a deep and disturbing consciousness of God's presence to the world of late modernity. The contours of this presence can be limned by considering one particular tradition in spirituality: that of apocalyptic spirituality. Metz was predisposed to this form of experiencing God's presence by traumatic, "interruptive" experiences as a youth during the Second World War. The memories of those experiences still haunt him. As he studied theology during the fifties and early sixties, they spurred him to press Rahner's theology toward a greater openness to "interruption" by the social and historical dimensions of the human. However, it was his encounter during the 1960s with Ernst Bloch and Walter Benjamin, who advocated, albeit idiosyncratically and for quite different purposes, a retrieval of apocalypticism, that led to the decisive interruption of Metz's career. Adopting this often repressed, or suppressed, tradition in Judaism and Christianity not only allowed Metz fully to recognize the force of his early memories, but also crystallized his dissatisfaction with Karl Rahner's theology and set him in search of a new set of categories and concepts for theology. This search reached maturity with the publication of Metz's most important book, *Faith in History and Society*.[9] For the last two decades Metz has been working out the further implications within the ever-changing terrain of late modernity (or postmodernity, if you will) for society, for the academy, and for the church, of this correlation of transcendental theology with apocalyptic mysticism.

With this in mind my first task must be to establish some initial parameters for understanding the relationship between spirituality and theology (chapter 1). Then I will embark on a presentation and close analysis of Metz's theological career, paying close attention to the tensions and ruptures which have guided it (chapters 2–4). This will bring me to a presentation of Metz's mature thought, in which the centrality of spirituality, indeed, of apocalyptic spirituality, will be clear (chapter 5). As further corroboration of this conclusion I will return to the relationship between Rahner and Metz and then close with some reflections on how this case study illuminates the fields both of theology and of spirituality, and on the further work that needs to be done (chapter 6). For it may very well be objected that I have not so much explained Metz's development, including its divergence from Rahner's, as I have displaced it to the realm of spirituality and the history of spirituality. But I believe that this displacement of explanatory locus is an advance, since it opens this issue up to the study of spirituality and its relationship to theology. My hope is that this book will provide some warrant for my conviction that the ensuing dialogue has been and can continue to be fruitful not only for understanding Metz, not only for understanding his relationship to Rahner, but for charting the course of Christian theology into the next millennium.

As for any extended project, I have incurred many debts in carrying this one through to completion. The final stages of writing the dissertation, along with the initial research that led to its revision for this book, were suppported by a generous grant from the Institute for the Advanced Study of Religion at the University of Chicago. The University of Notre Dame granted me a sabbatical leave and the Boston College Center for Ignatian Spirituality supported me as a visiting fellow while I completed the process of seeing the book through to publication. The Institute for Scholarship in the Liberal Arts provided funds for creating the index. I am grateful to all of these institutions for their support.

It has been almost nine years since I first approached David Tracy and asked him to serve as director for a dissertation on the work of Johann Baptist Metz. Since then he has given unstintingly of his time, his encouragement, and his wisdom, accepting me not only as a student but as a friend. Both a great theologian and a man of profound faith, if there is anyone who has taught me the truth of the epigram with which the first chapter begins, it is he. For all of this I am, and will always remain, deeply grateful.

Many others among my teachers at Chicago had a hand in this work as well. I will always be indebted to those who taught me the craft of theology; I wish to thank in particular Bernard McGinn and Anne Carr, who introduced me to the riches of the Christian mystical traditions and to liberation theology, respectively. Professor McGinn graciously permitted me to participate in his graduate seminars on the history of mysticism as I was finishing the dissertation and beginning to envision the further project. His classes proved crucial for nurturing the first beginnings of the ideas that led to this revision. The same must be said of conversations with my fellow students at the University of Chicago Divinity School. At the risk of forgetting others, I would like to thank here Gaspar Martinez, Mary Doak, Lois Malcolm, and especially Mark A. McIntosh, whose worthy book precedes my own in this series.

Lawrence Cunningham, of the University of Notre Dame, accepted the thankless task of first reading through the dissertation and then through every chapter of the revision. Where I took his advice, as I almost invariably did, the work has been greatly improved. The editors and staff at the University of Notre Dame Press have also made the laborious process of preparing a manuscript for publication as close to enjoyable as it can be.

There is one person who has endured not only the writing of the dissertation but its revision as well. She has done so with the unfailing wisdom, patience and grace that are second nature to her. This book is for her: my wife, Anselma Dolcich Ashley.

1

THE RELATIONSHIP BETWEEN SPIRITUALITY AND THEOLOGY

If you are a theologian you truly pray. If you truly pray you
are a theologian.

Evagrius Ponticus

A TURN TO SPIRITUALITY?

Spirituality is in the air today. Whether it be the proliferation of
New Age spiritual technologies or the retrieval of classics of medieval
spirituality onto compact disk or music video, the fascination with mysticism and spirituality has spawned an unending stream of texts, video
and cassette tapes, art works, workshops, conferences, and retreats.
Considering cumulative publishing trends over the past decade, Phyllis
Tickle observes that "what books currently are establishing about our
landscape is, first and foremost, a burgeoning and generalized absorption with spirituality and religion today."[1] Most major publishers, book
clubs (like the Book-of-the-Month Club) and booksellers have established categories in "spirituality," encompassing works on everything
from angels to the spirituality of quantum physics.[2] Surely this interest
in spirituality is among the most compelling signs of the times that
North American theologians need to interpret.

On the one hand, it shows that even in the midst of the wealth
and privilege of the world's last remaining superpower, our hearts are
still restless. The interest in spirituality offers Christians new footholds
and resources for pursuing the perennial mission to evangelize their
culture. On the other hand, this new fascination with spirituality is not
without its pitfalls. There is a very real danger that this turn to spirituality will only hinder Christianity in its attempts to find a productive

1

way out of the paralyzing privatization which has so often been its fate in secularized modern societies. Spirituality seems even more prone than religion to fall victim to what Philip Rieff has diagnosed as "the triumph of the therapeutic."[3] It is eminently commodifiable. It can be marketed to individuals who can sample its pleasures in the unassailable but isolating privacy of their own homes. Could it be that after family, hearth, and home have shown their inability to protect us against the onslaughts of modernity, spirituality has become the new candidate for a haven in a heartless world? This, at any rate, seems to be the gist of sociologist Robert Wuthnow's sobering remarks on the role that spirituality plays in American life:

> Our spirituality is often little more than a therapeutic device. Having a relationship with God is a way of making ourselves feel better. Faith is a way of massaging our feelings. We pray for comfort but do not expect to be challenged. We have domesticated the sacred by stripping it of authoritative wisdom and by looking to it only to make us happy.[4]

Theologians must not ignore this important but ambiguous dimension of the contemporary scene in North America and Europe.

But the concern with spirituality is not just a sign of the times for popular culture. Early in this century the renaissance in patristic theology and the recognition of the consequences of the separation of theology and spirituality that began in the High Middle Ages, gave birth to groundbreaking work in the study of classic traditions of spirituality.[5] In Roman Catholicism, this endeavor was supported by the considerable resources of religious orders, which took up the task of rediscovering and implementing the spiritualities of their founders. A number of ongoing multivolume works like the *Dictionnaire de Spiritualité* or *The Classics of Western Spirituality* have greatly enriched our access to the diversity of spiritualities in the history of Christianity.[6] From rather modest beginnings, academic programs in spirituality have flourished, so that now a number of universities offer doctoral programs in spirituality. Moreover, this interest in spirituality has not been confined to Catholicism, or even to Christianity in general, as, for instance, Gershom Scholem's lifelong study of Jewish Kabbalah (viewed at first with suspicion or amusement) shows.

Moreover, this development has not been confined to historians. Many Roman Catholic theologians of the generation that helped prepare the way for Vatican II were also distinguished by their concern to overcome the gap between spirituality and theology. Theologians like Karl Rahner, Hans Urs von Balthasar, Marie-Dominique Chenu, Jean Leclercq, and Yves Congar not only lived lives of great holiness, following the traditions laid down by the founders of their respective religious orders, but made it their particular concern to make that holiness (or spirituality, in our terms) an integral part of their theological production.[7] The generation that followed has been, if anything, more insistent. Indeed, after thirty or more years of grappling with the task of doing theology on modernity's ambiguous terrain, many Catholic theologians have turned to spirituality as a uniquely important resource. This is true across the disciplines of theology, and across different theological paradigms. That this is true of the German, Johannes Baptist Metz, is the argument of this book. But not just for him. David Tracy can stand for many in his assertion of the importance of recovering spirituality for the practice of theology today:

> I think that theology will be better off the more theologians attempt to recover a relationship to traditions of spirituality and thus undo the separation of theology and spirituality that developed after medieval scholasticism, which made a distinction between the two without separating them. Unfortunately that once helpful distinction became a fatal separation, one that intensified in the ever-wider split between theory and practice in most modern thought. Surely an absolutely crucial part of the undoing of that separation would be, in theology, spiritual attentiveness to the presence of God in all of life, including theological thought.[8]

Perhaps most striking today is the insistence on the relevance of spirituality in the broad spectrum of contemporary liberation theologies—a relevance precisely to the transformative-liberative intention that its representatives claim must orient theology today.[9] An early landmark, both for liberation theology and for the recognition of the need to bring together *theoria* and *praxis,* theology, spirituality, and political commitment, was the issue of *Concilium* which introduced the "mystical-political" as a fundamental category for Christian faith and theology.[10] It is remarkable how many liberation theologians have felt the need to supplement, or even correct, purely conceptual theological work with a return to the spiritual fonts of the communities their theologies are meant to serve. In 1971 Gustavo Gutiérrez pointed out the need for a "spirituality of liberation" in his first major work, and followed this work up with an attempt to locate and describe such a spirituality and to root it in the Christian tradition.[11] James Cone, one of the founding fathers of black theology, tells us that after he wrote his two ground-breaking books—*Black Theology and Black Power,* and *A Black Theology of Liberation*—he recognized the validity of the criticism that while these works argued the need to break free from the concepts and categories of North Atlantic white theology, in fact they did not succeed in doing so: "I was still held captive," he admitted, "by the same system that I was criticizing."[12] His first move in response to this criticism was to turn to distinctively African-American spirituality, which he did in *The Spirituals and the Blues.*[13] A similar insistence on the need to embrace the distinctive spirituality of the community for whom one claims to be practicing theology also gave rise to Hispanic theology.[14] Feminist theology in North America has followed a similar path.[15] Indeed, it may be that feminist theology has been the first to make effective use of the new resources being opened up by historical research into forgotten or suppressed spiritual traditions, for example, that of the great women mystics.[16] The importance of spirituality to Third World liberation theologies can best be indicated by noting the topic of the third general assembly of the Ecumenical Association of Third World Theologians (EATWOT), in Nairobi, Kenya, in 1992: "Spirituality of the Third World." EATWOT's president, K. C. Abraham, summarized the meeting's results in these words:

> The Nairobi Conference firmly declared that Third World theology should be decisively shaped by the spirituality of the marginalized— women, indigenous people, Minjung and Dalits. *Spirituality of the Third World* articulates this creative and life-affirming spirituality that is at the very center of the life and struggles of the poor.[17]

In sum, spirituality is an increasingly important element in theology today. It is my conviction that the vitality and integrity of Christian theology in a community making the difficult but unavoidable transition from a monocultural, Eurocentric Church to a polycentric, global Church, depend on establishing the proper relationship between spirituality and theology—or, perhaps better, articulating the one that already exists—in a fruitful, self-reflective, and self-critical way. Yet this task is a daunting one, replete with its own particular difficulties and pitfalls.

Not least, as we shall see in the next section, is the fact that there is no consensus among its diverse advocates as to what "spirituality" is and means. Furthermore, theologians may be wary (or weary) of being told that there is yet another foundational realm into which they must "turn" or root themselves as a part of their theological work. In the past few decades theologians have been advised that they need to make the critical turn (the turn to praxis), the turn to history, the linguistic turn, the interpretive or hermeneutical turn, the turn to the subject, and, more generally, the turn to experience. Added to this there is the continual need to re-turn to Scripture. Why add yet another, potentially more sweeping, field of study which theologians must take into account?

Finally, there is a legitimate concern that emphasizing the importance of spirituality—whether defined as the individual holiness of the theologian or as a historically identifiable tradition—will further fragment the theological world. Is not spirituality an intensely personal, if not irrational at least a-rational, and finally noncommunicable phenomenon? Is there not the danger that when one appeals to a particular spirituality as a crucial element of a theological position, the evaluation of that position will become insurmountably subjective? Either I accept the spirituality—and with it the theological position—or I do not. What of disputes between theologies rooted in different spiritualities? Do we not run a parallel risk to the problem posed by the increasing privatization of religion: just as individuals increasingly have their "private" faiths, their "Sheila-isms,"[18] so too will communities, and finally individuals, have their own private spiritualities and theologies? While most would no longer defend an aspiration that theology be rigorously *wissenschaftlich,* this kind of balkanization of theology surely does not do justice to theology's mandate to give a reasoned, reasonable account of the hope that is in us—not just to the like-minded and like-spirited, but to all who ask it of us.

For their part, not all the advocates of the "new" discipline of spirituality welcome the attention of theologians. In part this is because of the recent history of the relationship, in which spirituality was reduced to being a ward of neoscholastic theologies. Spirituality was relegated to a subdivision of moral or pastoral theology, to be viewed with suspicion and policed by the dogmatic theologian. Partially in reaction to this, and partly in response to hegemonic claims of European and North American theologies, the *topos* of spirituality has been used by many liberation theologians to assert the authority of the local community (often of marginalized persons) over and against a "theology" being imposed from above. Often, those who advocate spirituality in this way define it as a virtually polar opposite to theology, mapping the pair spirituality/theology into some combination of a set of (to my mind) unhelpful disjuncts: feeling/thought, intuition/logic, concreteness/abstractness, bodiliness/intellectuality, feminine/masculine, popular/elitist, spontaneous/dogmatic, and so on. In these terms, the attempt to reflect on spirituality from an explicitly theological perspective, drawing on the doctrinal resources and the philosophical elements of the Christian tradition, cannot but be viewed with great suspicion.[19] Even among those advocates of a historical or phenomenological approach to the study of spirituality who avoid this sort of dichotomization, there is a concern that the theologians will reassert some a priori theological grid on the field of spirituality, occluding or suppressing whatever does not fit that grid.

Despite all of these difficulties, a "turn" to theology is not only unavoidable for a theologian today but potentially is at least as fruitful as the other possible turns on the theological *itinerarium*. This is not to deny the other turns but to place them in a context where historical work on the Christian tradition can be brought to bear on them. What better way to reflect on the role of experience (in ways that do not covertly import our modern, Cartesian expectations about what "experience" is and what is authorized by appeals to experience)[20] than by careful attention to attempts by Christians past and present to record and teach their experience of God, as found in the classics of Christian spirituality? What more exemplary instances for investigating the constitutive role of language in faith and theology could there be than the ways that Christians (and Moslems and Jews, for that matter) press language to its limits, sometimes against its own grain, to speak the unspeakable? Would not the "turn to praxis" benefit from reflection on the arena in which the difficulties over using the Greek concepts of *theoria* and *praxis* within Christian theology have received the most sustained attention: namely, in debates over the relationship between the *vita activa* and the *vita contemplativa*, in the history of Christian spirituality? Careful attention to the relationship between spirituality and theology does not offer easy answers to the difficult problems raised by the other turns of this century. Neither does it offer an edifying excuse for avoiding them. All of the difficulties that have been highlighted by the other turns will show again in this one, and the various methodologies developed to make the others will no doubt prove useful for this one as well. What a turn to spirituality does do, in sum, is to locate a fruitful locus for posing the needed questions correctly and interrelating them productively.

Will this turn further the fragmentation of theology and render it insurmountable? The risk cannot be denied; but it will be averted not by denying the relationship between spirituality and theology, but by finding ways of fruitfully articulating it. After all, the problem of adjudicating differences between theological positions rooted in different spiritualities is not one only now suddenly looming on the horizon; it has been present in Christianity at least from the Middle Ages on. The differences between a Bonaventure and an Aquinas, between the Dominican advocacy of the primacy of the intellect, and the typically Franciscan advocacy of the will, certainly reflect different argumentative strategies, choices of philosphical conceptuality, and decisions regarding which elements of Scripture and tradition to emphasize, and how. These differences should be examined. However, one cannot get to the root of these distinctive theological approaches without understanding their commitment to, and living out of, the Franciscan and Dominican rules—the former with its practices fostering devotion to the concrete particularity of the poor and crucified one, and a focus on love; the latter with its center on preaching and teaching the Word, and its concomitant emphasis on truth as *the* central transcendental for articulating the presence of God, and knowledge as the central descriptor for human beatitude.[21] Is not the *De Auxiliis* controversy of the sixteenth and seventeenth centuries understandable, at least in part, in terms of the different spiritualities (Jesuit and Dominican) of its opponents?

Whether or not one concludes that such a turn in theology will result in its fragmentation depends in large measure on the standards of rationality and commensurability demanded of different theological systems. Here we would do well to consider recent developments in the history and philosophy of science. Thomas Kuhn's now classic (if still controversial) *The Structure of Scientific Revolutions* argued in essence that the "rationality," as well as the synchronic and diachronic commensurability of different scientific systems, cannot be completely determined without considering a host of factors that relate to the concrete social and historical contexts of the scientific communities that produce and sustain those systems: the institutions and practices by which a given community of scientists initiate new members, determine relevant questions, allocate resources, set up and evaluate research programs, and adjudicate debates.[22] Kuhn always insisted that this does not mean that scientific disputes and revolutions are irrational or in the final analysis reducible to political processes, but that the "rules" by which they are carried on cannot be reduced to any canon of univocal, universally applicable logical rules.[23] Similarly, the realization that theologies, and debates between theologies, depend in part on particular spiritualities need not lead to historicism, relativism, or radical skepticism about the validity of theological systems and their results. It does mean, however, that just as an alliance between careful historical work, sociological and anthropological investigation, and philosophical probings has brought to light a more complex but also more fruitful understanding of how the arguments and results of science are related to the underlying "lived scientific experience," so too does an alliance between different approaches to spirituality, theology, and philosophy promise a deeper comprehension of how theologies are born and develop, as well as of the relationship between the practice of spirituality and the various ways of articulating and understanding that practice, whether they are overtly theological ways or not.

SPIRITUALITY: A DEFINITION

Clear definitions of spirituality and theology would seem to be essential at the outset of any attempt to bring the two subjects into creative interrelation. But the definition of spirituality in general, and the self-definition of the discipline that studies spirituality in the academy, have given rise to vigorous debate.[24] One approach emphasizes spirituality's embeddedness in the broader complex of Christian faith and theology, arguing that a spirituality's significance must be worked out in terms of explicitly theological discourse. Another focuses on the anthropological depth-dimension, and thereby tends to define spirituality as a phenomenon which crosses religious and cultural borders. A third approach considers spiritualities in their concrete sociohistorical contexts, emphasizing careful historical work.[25] The definitions will vary according to the distinctive focus of the approach, and it is probably neither possible nor desirable to come up with one definition that could count for all of the approaches. Yet, insofar as the cognate disciplines of each approach—theology for the first; philosophical and cultural anthropology, as well as psychology, for the second; and the historical sciences for the third—are not hermetically sealed from one another, we should expect significant overlap. The point of a definition, my own included, should be, on the one hand, to facilitate mutual communication between the approaches on their common concerns, and, on the other, to bring into focus one's own concern. Since my particular concern is to disclose the interrelations between spirituality and theology, my definition will be formulated accordingly. I hope, however, that I will not ignore data provided by other approaches.

I will begin with the common observation that while Christians have always done and reflected on the sorts of things that we today would gather under the category of "spirituality," it is not until well into Christianity's second millennium that *they* would so organize them. The origins of the *term* spirituality go back to the Pauline corpus, but it does not appear there as an abstract noun.[26] The "spiritual person" (*pneumatikos,* rendered *spiritualis* in Latin) is the one who lives according to the Spirit of God. As has been frequently noted, "spiritual" and "spirit" intend modal descriptions of the *whole* person. The difference between *sarx* and *pneuma* does not map into some anthropological division (say, between mind and body), but refers to the quality of the actualization of the whole of a person's life, including both what we today would call spiritual or, perhaps, intellectual powers and bodily faculties. Even when the noun form, *spiritualitas,* began to appear in the fifth century, and became more common as the early and High Middle Ages progressed, it still retained its connection to the Pauline, modal-adjectival, usage. But two other usages gained currency which can help us understand the birth and development of what we today call spirituality. First, spirituality began to be contrasted with corporality or materiality, often (as in Aquinas's case) reflecting the incorporation of Aristotle's anthropology, which has a greater affinity to such a dualistic rendering of human existence in general.[27] Second, "spirituality "was used in delineating ecclesiastical jurisdiction, denoting those who exercised such jurisdiction (a "spirituality" of bishops) as well as the property over which they exercised it. The second usage calls particularly to mind the phenomenon of secularization, which also had to do with jurisdiction, and had its beginnings in the High and late Middle Ages.[28] Both shifts point to the growing complexity of European social, cultural, and intellectual life.

Growing urban centers created and nourished a growing and literate middle class, which occupied an increasingly diversified matrix of economic roles in the expanding European economy. The needs of this class, and the general growth in complexity in European society, explains, at least in part, the exfoliation of new forms of life which arose out of the search for the authentic *vita apostolica* during this period. The Fourth Lateran Council tried to reign in this process in 1215 by prohibiting the institution of new religious orders, but this decree did not, indeed could not, affect the underlying causes of this growth and diversification of "spiritualities." It continued, often in innovative ways, leading to quasi-religious foundations and groups which were looked upon with increasing suspicion from the vantage point of traditional centers of ecclesial power in monasteries and cathedrals. Accompanying this change was a growing interest in individual "spiritual experience" (again, as we would call it today). While it is probably too much to say that the High Middle Ages "discovered" the individual (at least as understood during the Renaissance and Enlightenment), there is evidence of a growing interest in the individual and his or her interior landscape—an interest which was increasingly slaked by itineraries of the soul and methodologies for prayer, autobiographical accounts of visions, as well as by the growing phenomenon of spiritual direction, particularly of the laity.[29]

In a crucial respect another important development for which we remember the High and late Middle Ages ran counter to this one. The birth and triumph of the university and its theological innovation, scholasticism, meant the increasing hegemony of theology as rational science, with its techniques of *lectio, quaestio*, and *disputatio*, structured into the *summa*. These techniques could not easily accommodate the growing interest in recounting and elaborating one's personal and interior experience of God. But alternative forms of theology that were perhaps more sensitive and responsive to this need developed outside of the university, and because of that, increasingly outside of the boundaries of theology, as the university was coming exclusively to represent it. The genres and concerns of texts produced in "monastic theology," as Jean Leclercq named it, as well as the increasing flood of materials in the vernacular, were to some degree marginalized. These materials enjoyed theological legimitacy only with the imprimatur of academic theology, which for its part increasingly claimed the right and responsiblity of policing the realm of theology.[30] Vernacular theology in particular was closer to the joys and sorrows of the growing class of educated laity in medieval Europe and saw the first large-scale emergence of women's voices in Christian theology. The linguistic fluidity of vernacular theology, as well as its greater presence to the urban populations which were experiencing most profoundly the dislocations of the late Middle Ages, explain in part its daring innovations, as well as its explosive growth, notwithstanding the suspicion of ecclesiastical authorities and scholastic theologians who had been able to monopolize the university and to make themselves the spokesmen of orthodoxy during the thirteenth and fourteenth centuries. Monastic and vernacular texts were the primary carriers of what would come to be called "spirituality," although they increasingly lost their legitimacy as theologies or enjoyed it only at the pleasure of the universities. Here we find the origins of a split between different genres and the institutional sites of their production, a split which eventually would become expressed terminologically as one between "theology" and "spirituality."

As I have already suggested, many of these developments bespeak the onset of the secularization of European Christendom. By this I mean the growing differentiation of separate spheres of activity, with their correlative institutions and modes of discourse, organized not around the medieval delineations—between this world and the next, and, within this world, between the religious and the secular—but around multiple organizing axes, the two most important being the growing market economy and the increasingly powerful nation-state.[31] A situation began to come into being which many of us can recognize today: men and women find their lives divided into multiple roles—citizen, consumer (of goods and services, but also of "culture"), worker, intellectual, parent—each of which is associated with increasingly distinct constellations of institutions and different ways of organizing time and space, different sources of authority and legitimating logics, often in conflict with one another, and almost never in harmony with the traditional, religiously centered patterns of organization. Rather than being the organizing axis of the human city, Christianity had to find room in a city that was organized around different axes. In this regard, Michel de Certeau's insight about the origins of "mystics" as an autonomous field of discourse and practice seems applicable for spirituality as a whole. Speaking of the human city constructed by modernity, he says:

> The One is no longer to be found. "They have taken him away," say so many chants of the mystics who inaugurate, with the story of his loss, the history of his returns elsewhere and otherwise, in ways that are the effect rather than the refutation of his absence. While no longer "living," this "dead" one still does not leave the city—which was formed without him—in peace. He haunts our environs.[32]

To be sure, it would be another three or four centuries before the term "spirituality" completed its migration to refer to a relatively autonomous constellation of practices and topics, often considered apart from, indeed in tension with, theology and its locus (the university). But, what I am suggesting here is that the decisive shifts in the underlying "plate tectonics" of European society were already well underway by the thirteenth or fourteenth century. Spirituality, in its modern sense, arose as a result of and a response to the same complex social, cultural, and intellectual shifts that produced modernity. Yet it was and is an ambiguous response. It could function as a "compensation device," a way of dealing with the desacralized and in many ways dehumanized milieu of the modern age, without getting at its roots, or addressing its destructive consequences.[33] It could, however, also be a way of living in the presence of the One whose presence is keenly sensed as an unsettling absence, a way of living that allows that sense of absence to nurture a constructive and, if necessary, deconstructive attitude and practice on modernity's complex terrain. This ambiguity is precisely the reason why liberation and political theologians, Johann Baptist Metz not least among them, have a particular concern to incorporate "spirituality" within their theological projects.

Having given this overview, albeit brief, of the history and origins of "spirituality," let me venture a definition. As I understand it here, a spirituality comprises two complementary aspects. First, *a spirituality is a classic constellation of practices which forms a mystagogy into a life of Christian discipleship.* By defining a spirituality as a constellation of practices I am emphasizing the fact that a spirituality is something (or things) that one *does.* Whatever else Ignatian spirituality is, at its heart is a set of spiritual *exercises* and a regimen of daily practices (like the examen of conscience). Benedictine spirituality has at its heart a rule of life that sets down a specific set of practices. Dominican spirituality is built upon a set of practices that revolves around teaching and preaching while renouncing the monastic practice of stability. This definition attempts to draw our attention to the historical particularity of a spirituality. Spirituality's practices are carried out against a definite cultural and institutional backdrop and make sense (in the active and passive sense: see the second aspect, described below) in a specific way against that backdrop. Thus, an approach to spirituality which operates from this definition will draw heavily on the third of the approaches I listed earlier: the historical-contextual approach to studying spirituality.

I insert the modifier "classic" intending both the more common-sense understanding of the word and the more specific meaning it has attained in the hermeneutical school that culminates in Hans Georg Gadamer and Paul Ricoeur, and has been appropriated theologically by David Tracy.[34] A classic constellation of practices is one that has achieved a certain perennial status: it has endured, been taken up again and again, renovated, revivified in new cultural contexts and new institutional settings. It has a perduring capacity to capture our attention and both enrich and challenge the ways we live and understand our lives. As Tracy argues, the classic does not exercise its claim to attention at the price of abstraction from its historical particularity but precisely to the extent that we give ourselves over to that difference and allow it to draw us, however briefly and tentatively, outside our limited horizons. So too with a spirituality. First embodied and formulated by a founding figure (or small circle of such), a constellation of practices becomes a classic over time when it proves its ability to transcend the particular historical and social context of its birth and continues offering a rich and animating mystagogy into a life of discipleship in contexts that present different resources and challenges to such a life. On this view, a given spirituality admits of various degrees of participation, depending on the degree to which the entire constellation of practices is embraced (not everyone is ready to kiss leprous sores), and the degree to which those practices that are embraced are integrated into and transform the broader set of dispositions and practices with which the person interacts with his or her environment.

I am suggesting that a spirituality is a classic constellation of practices which forms a mystagogy into a life of Christian discipleship. By this I am adding a normative-critical dimension to my definition. The term "mystagogy" can be used in a variety of senses; my primary analogue here is the period of the liturgical year, between Easter and Pentecost, when the newly initiated are invited to deepen their appropriation of the life of *imitatio Christi* into which they have entered by the sacraments of initiation. This is done by individual and communal prayer, reflection on Scripture, and particularly by participation in the liturgy. The period is also understood as a time for the broader Church to recommit itself to the ongoing process of putting on Christ, drawing inspiration from the newly initiated. In calling spirituality a mystagogy, then, I am making at least the following theological claims about what spirituality is or should be. First, whatever it is or does, ultimately a spirituality is instrumental to an encounter with God, an encounter which is consummated to the degree that it becomes incarnate in a life of discipleship. Second, a spirituality should incorporate one more deeply into the body of Christ. A spirituality should be a profoundly ecclesial reality. Just as for the liturgical period of mystagogy, a spirituality is for the individual adherent, helping her or him to enter more deeply into the mystery of Christian discipleship by becoming more fully incorporated into the body of Christ. But it is also for the wider Church, inspiring all of its members (to be sure, often by prophetic challenge, as was the case with St. Francis)[35] to a deeper appropriation and realization of that same mystery.

The second and complementary aspect of a spirituality is the particular way of speaking and thinking—in song, poetry, sermon, and even in theological and doctrinal assertions—about God, about the ultimate meaning of human life, and so on, which both nurtures but is also nurtured by the set of practices which make up the spirituality. Again, various adherents of a spirituality will embrace this broader vision, with its symbols, narratives, rhetorical strategies, metaphysical speculation, and so forth, in varyings ways and to different degrees. There are certainly many deeply spiritual persons who have embraced and integrated a given set of practices into the rest of their lives in a way that suffuses the whole with the light of Christ, and yet are relatively inarticulate when it comes to the vision that is connected with these practices.[36] This leads me to suspect that the practice of spirituality (the first element of my definition) is the more primary dimension. Yet since a spirituality is a mystagogy into a following of Christ, who is alpha and omega, the Lord of creation and history, it will have an inherent tendency to "spill over" into all areas of our lives, and thus will naturally move toward some degree of "articulacy." Furthermore, if a spirituality is to endure over time it must produce a set of traditions, written and oral, which can be used to induct new adherents into the spiritual practices in the proper way. The important point here is that these traditions have as their primary intent inducting the person into the practices that make up that spirituality, giving him or her the materials upon which he or she can exercise him- or herself. In short, they are materials for *spiritual exercises*. This is true even when these materials also provide (or appear to us at any rate to provide) descriptions or analyses of extramental physical, metaphysical, or even divine realities. To separate these materials from their context as materials for enlivening and deepening spiritual practice is to risk fundamentally misunderstanding them.

Pierre Hadot has made this point very forcibly with regard to the writings of the philosophical schools of classical antiquity and the Middle Ages:

> [N]one of these philosophical productions, even the systematic works, is addressed to everyone, to a general audience, but they are intended first of all for the group formed by the members of the school. . . . Above all, the work, even if it is apparently theoretical and systematic, is written not so much to inform the reader of a doctrinal content but to form him, to make him traverse a certain itinerary in the course of which he will make spiritual progress. This procedure is clear in the works of Plotinus and Augustine, in which all the detours, starts and stops, and digressions of the work are formative elements. One must always approach a philosophical work of antiquity with this idea of spiritual progress in mind.[37]

Hadot argues that it is this dimension that modern philosophers and historians of philosophy forget when they approach classical texts. They attempt to judge (and often thereby reject) the texts on the basis of their internal coherence and their fitness for describing reality, rather than on their utility in initiating members of a school into a comprehensive, and comprehensively transformative, way of life. Of course, this is a quite modern problem—indeed obsession. It represents a truncation or bifurcation of philosophy, which Hadot argues we must learn to overcome. "Ancient philosophy," he writes, "proposed to mankind an art of living. By contrast, modern philosophy appears above all as the construction of a technical jargon reserved for specialists."[38] If one replaces the noun with "theology," it will become apparent that the dilemma of creatively interrelating theology and spirituality is mirrored in a broader dilemma that has confronted Western culture since the late Middle Ages.

Thus a spirituality comprises a constellation of practices along with oral and written traditions that are used to communicate it and which derive much of their persuasive force and coherence within the way of seeing the world that these practices develop (more on this shortly).[39] Consequently, we can infer the presence of a given spirituality when we have enough knowledge about a person so that we can assume that he or she was heavily invested in its practices. Or, more germane for this investigation, when we lack this biographical data but the person is also an author we can look for the distinctive tropes and rhetorical strategies that characterize such a spirituality's teachings. Given this admittedly difficult and tentative inference to the presence of a spirituality, we can ask, paraphrasing Hadot's discussion of Plotinus and Aristole, whether an author's theological demonstration derives its evidential force not so much from abstract reasoning as from an experience which is at the same time a spiritual exercise.[40] But this brings us to the relationship between spirituality and theology.

THE RELATIONSHIP BETWEEN SPIRITUALITY AND THEOLOGY

Defining theology is an issue no less contested than defining spirituality! But, entering *that* debate far exceeds the compass of this work. Here I can only try to be clear about what I hope is a reasonable definition of theology, and show how the relationship "looks" in its light. By theology I mean here the disciplined and self-critical attempt to construe all of reality—God, the human person, society, human history, and the natural cosmos, individually and in their interrelations—in the light of the symbols and narratives of the Christian tradition, in dialogue with other disciplines in the academy that attempt to understand reality, but finally in the service of believers who are trying to live with integrity in that reality.[41] Like spirituality, theology so defined is a distinctively modern discipline. It is (depending on your point of view) enlivened, challenged, or encumbered by the ambiguities of our modern world, ambiguities which beset all three of the publics or audiences to which the theologian is accountable: society, church, and academy.[42] Theology must endeavor to respect not only the particularity of the traditions it serves, but also to create and evaluate mutually critical correlations with what we otherwise know or think we know which can be publicly presented and defended.[43] It strives to unleash not only the disclosive power of Christian symbols and narratives, but also their transformative force, in ways that are faithful to the history of their origins and use, intelligible and credible to ourselves and to those in other traditions with whom we share our world, and in ways that empower us to live and act hopefully in often hopeless situations.[44]

Of course, at this point I have already decided my argument to some degree by these definitions, since by them theology already suggests the second dimension of spirituality. So, in one sense, my task in this section is to render explicit the relationship that is implicit in these definitions. I will do this by making use of the admittedly permeable division between systematic and fundamental theology. Briefly, in systematic theology, classics of spirituality offer new, creative, often provocative formulations of the symbols, doctrines, and practices of Christian faith. From the perspective of fundamental theology, a given spirituality defines the horizon or, perhaps better, the atmosphere within which theology is undertaken and which permeates its methods and results. Let me elaborate on these two avenues along which the turn to spirituality can enrich theology.

First, then, the use of images, symbols, and narratives from the classics of spirituality can illuminate specific issues and problems in systematic theology. As I have said, spiritual teachers work out in various ways a vision of reality, of the world, human existence, human history and society, and God, which recommends, nourishes (but also is legitimated by) the spirituality's practices. They do this in creative, often provocative or even scandalous, ways, selectively using, stretching (to some, abusing) the religious symbols handed down within the Christian community. This is the case for the daring images of God and the Trinity in the Rhineland mystics, which have born theological fruit even into this century (in Karl Rahner's thought, for example). In a similar way, Hans Urs von Balthasar set up imagery of the dark night in a mutually illuminating relationship with scriptural and doctrinal reflections on the passion of Christ.[45] The experience and portrayal of Jesus as mother in many medieval women mystics has served a similar function for feminist theologians.[46] As these examples show, daring articulations can breathe new life into theological systems that have become too closed in on themselves and too obsessed with the drive to logical consistency and technical articulation—"technical jargon reserved for specialists." They can serve as correctives to theological constructs, when, for instance, the latter emphasize only the distance and kingship of God, and not also God's nearness and tenderness. Karl Rahner recognized this role of the spiritual classic when he described it as a "'creative,' original assimilation of God's revelation *in Christo*, . . . a new gift by God's Spirit of the ancient Christianity to a new age."[47]

This way of speaking of the relationship between spirituality and theology might create the impression that theology is the discipline which receives and reflects upon the models, images, and practices of spirituality "from the outside," from a "neutral" and thus authoritative perspective. I suggested that this has been precisely the claim increasingly made by theologians vis-à-vis spirituality, as the gulf between the two opened up from the High Middle Ages on. While there is need for theological reflection at some "distance" from spirituality, as I shall argue below, there is nonetheless another dimension to the relationship that makes it much more complex than this. I have already hinted at this second and complementary dimension in reference to Hadot's discussion of philosophy and spiritual exercises. Marie-Dominique Chenu articulated this dimension of the relationship over fifty years ago in these words:

> The fact is that in the final analysis theological systems are simply the expressions of a spirituality. It is this that gives them their interest and their grandeur. . . . One does not get to the heart of a system via the logical coherence of its structure or the plausibility of its conclusions. One gets to that heart by grasping it in its origins via that fundamental intuition that serves to guide a spiritual life and provides the intellectual regimen proper to that life.[48]

Most theologians are now comfortable with the recognition that theology is a "second step," that it does not generate results out of its own resources and cannot authorize them simply on the basis of logical coherence and argumentative precision, but, rather, relies on the experience of the Church (both present, and as retrieved from the past). Indeed, the complexity of this reliance is the reason for all of the various "turns" which are pressed upon the theologian today. Chenu seems to be pointing to a similar sort of derivative character for theology. But how should we understand Chenu's reference to a "spiritual life" and "the intellectual regimen proper to that life" as the heart of a theological system? My suggestion is that we consider how the constellation of practices that makes up a given spirituality also makes those of its adherents who are theologians, in the modern sense I defined above, attentive to the world in a certain way, opens up the world to them in a certain way, so that when they attempt to articulate this presence systematically, so as to formulate a theology, they draw on the store of religious symbols, concepts, and theologies handed down to them and deploy those resources rhetorically in correspondingly selective ways.

An analogy with developments in the philosophy of science might help make my point. As I noted above, at least since the debate incited by Kuhn's controversial book on scientific revolutions, philosophers of science have by and large come to recognize that there is no fully neutral, purely raw and uninterpreted data (experience) to which one can appeal in order to authorize scientific theories apodictically or adjudicate disputes between rival theories. Scientific arguments and results cannot be legitimated solely in terms of logical coherence or by appeal to some interpretation-free facts independent of the scientific systems under consideration. Rather, they are justified against the broader background of the life-world of the scientific community: its often tacit beliefs, attitudes, convictions, aversions, and practices, into which scientists are initiated by lengthy and arduous exercises, which are intended to actualize and/or transform their ways of being present to the world and of constituting it as an object of investigation. Even a practice as trivial as the way that scientific results are recorded and reported is significant for eliciting and sustaining a particular way of perceiving the world, as Frederick Ferré notes:

> There is a ritual way of writing up experimental reports. . . . The ritual is to write everything in the passive voice, with all references to the experimenter eliminated, if possible, but if not, at least transformed into the third person. . . . The ritual of scientific writing style systematically impersonalizes. Why? I suspect that neither clarity nor precision would need to be sacrificed in a laboratory report that used first-person active language; but the mood, the tone, the subliminal feel would be very different. And so would the symbolism, which now works to *cultivate a consciousness* in which the peculiarities of

individual subjectivities count not at all. The persons who do or see or measure don't matter; what matters, as symbolized and reinforced by the ritual language, are the objective events, the recorded observations, the performed measurements.[49] (Emphasis added.)

The point is that the scientific mode of perceiving the world is not the unproblematic, "natural" way of being present to the world; rather, it is laboriously elicited, sustained, and reinforced by a specific constellation of practices to which a scientist commits himself or herself when he or she commits to the scientific community. One necessary element (to be sure, not the only one) of the structure of scientific revolutions is the development of a coherent set of practices for sustaining a new way of being attentive to world, as well as the sociological mechanisms necessary to initiate new adherents into those practices. In this context it is suggestive to recall that the origins of modern science in the late Middle Ages have much to do with the origins and growth of a new spirituality: Franciscan spirituality, with its practices revolving around and sustaining what Ewert Cousins has called "the mysticism of the historical event."[50]

Analogously, theological arguments and results cannot be legitimated solely in terms of logical coherence or by appeal to facts (be they facts of experience, of tradition, or of Scripture). Rather, it is the broader world of the Christian community—constituted by the relationship to God through Christ that is discipleship—to which the theologian belongs that allows the world to show up the way it does. Theologians are formed and initiated into this life-world by academic *and* spiritual exercises (and let us not forget that, at least at the origins of academic theology in the medieval university, these were not strictly distinguished). In the process theologians are transformed, they become attentive to self and world in new ways, allow reality to be present to them afresh and differently. This presence lies at the heart of the theology by means of which they try to articulate and justify their understanding of God, of oneself and others, and of the physical world. This is, I believe, what Chenu was getting at. *Any* theology of breadth and depth has, either explicitly or implicitly, a constitutive relationship to a spirituality, and it cannot fully be understood without taking this into account. Disagreements between theologians and theological schools are often due, at least in part, to the different ways in which they are attuned to the world—these in turn arising from the different spiritualities which incarnate over time their response to God. Such differences cannot be overcome or even fully comprehended by purely logical considerations; they require a sort of transformative shift of attention (not illogical or absurd, but perhaps alogical, indebted to imagination and empathy) that is analogous to what Thomas Kuhn had in mind when he talked about paradigm shifts.

Baldly put, then, the claim here is that a theologian's grasp of his or her system is incomplete until and unless he or she has grappled with the particular spirituality of which his or her theology is an expression, and which gives this theology its "interest and grandeur." Does this mean that a theologian must have a spiritual life, must embrace a spirituality? Affirming this would really only amount to saying that a theologian must be a believer, with the added proviso that being a believer, following Christ, never occurs in the abstract, but always in the concrete as a specific set of practices by means of which one grows into the inexhaustible riches of discipleship (i.e., a spirituality). Of course, it would be ridiculous to assert that one needs to be a Dominican to appreciate the theology of Aquinas, or a Jesuit to appreciate Rahner. There are, after all, many degrees and ways of embracing or appreciating a spirituality. Indeed, my argument for a "turn" to spirituality is a recognition of this fact, and an appreciation of the specific results and methodologies that the study of spirituality can offer to help the theologian find ways to enter into other spiritual traditions, short of actually becoming a disciple.

Nor does this claim necessarily imply that theologies are only valid within the horizon of the spirituality which gave birth to them. Theological concepts and arguments may (and do quite often) not only slip free of the particular spirituality which originated them, but break free entirely from any appeal to spirituality. An extreme, but significant, instance of this is found in Heidegger's relationship to Eckhart.[51] What does seem evident at this point is that theologies will mean and function differently when correlated with different spiritualities.[52] This can be a fruitful encounter, a way in which theology can enrich a spirituality by deepening its own self-understanding, relating it to a broader cross-section of the Great Tradition that is different from the one which it might adopt of its own accord, as well as by relating it to other sorts of practices in which we engage and other fields of knowledge.[53]

This suggests that just as spirituality nurtures and challenges theology, the converse is true. Theology can enrich spirituality as well. The above analysis will make a theologian wary of *imposing* theological concepts forged within one spiritual tradition upon another. But a given spirituality may nonetheless be enriched by considering it anew and differently, using theological concepts that arise from a different mystagogy into the inexhaustible riches and mystery of God. Clearly, our history is replete with ways in which theologies and spiritualities have interacted productively. This was certainly the case for the relationship between Meister Eckhart's mastery of scholastic theology and his powerful advocacy of a particular way of living the mystical life in his sermons and exhortations.[54] As I have already noted, a similar relationship held true of Bonaventure's commitment to the spirituality of his master and his mastery of the Neoplatonic tradition, as well as of scholastic argumentation. For a more recent case, think of the fascinating interplay between phenomenology and mysticism—Husserl and Theresa of Avila—in Edith Stein's life and work. Or consider (moving farther afield), the fascinating—at times baffling—interplay between Kabbalistic mysticism and Marxist philosophy in Walter Benjamin, a figure who, while most emphatically not a Christian, has had a signal impact on the development of political and liberation theologies.

These figures demonstrate the permeability of the boundaries between spirituality, theology, and philosophy. Our understanding of this permeability can be aided by the sort of careful "thick descriptions" offered by the historical-contextual approach to the study of spirituality, as well as by insights from psychology, cultural anthropology, sociology, and so on, offered by the anthropological approach. On the other hand, theologians can remind us that spiritualities are in their origins not ways to achieve purified states of consciousness, a more peaceful, integrated life, care of the soul, and so on, although these all may result. They arose in response to the call of the Spirit and they are taken up in order to live more deeply the mystery of discipleship. This makes a difference for how we study and interpret them.[55] Finally, theology can remind us that even the most self-avowedly secular descriptions of the human condition that we apply to spiritualities may very well have a theological history worth attending to.[56] For example, many definitions of spirituality use terms like "self-transcendence," "ultimate value and meaning," and so forth, which seem theologically and spiritually neutral at first blush. I do not intend to deny the legitimacy of these sorts of definitions, but it is important to note that these terms are themselves part of an intellectual (often overtly theological) tradition that takes its inspiration from one spirituality: Christian Neoplatonism in general, more specifically, the Eckhartian tradition.[57] This raises the question of what happens when one uses terms that bear an affinity to one particular spiritual tradition as a heuristic guide for recognizing and studying other traditions. My suspicion is that they will do quite well with some spiritualities, provide interesting insights, or even fruitful misreadings of others, but fail to recognize or adequately interpret others. Again, my intention here is not to proscribe definitions (my own included), or even to deny the need for definitions and methodologies that are as "theologically neutral" as we can make them. Rather, it is to point out the limitations of these strategies, with the hope that we have a growing body of research which can help us map out these limitations and use our definitions fruitfully within those limits.

METHODOLOGICAL CONCLUSIONS

Thus far I have argued that spirituality and theology interact with one another in complex but extremely important ways. Our understanding of a given theological system will be enriched by an understanding of the spirituality which inspires its particular vision of God, the world, and human beings. Grasping the spirituality that finds expression in a particular theology will help us to understand some of the crucial choices the theologian makes in deploying the resources of the tradition in order to meet uniquely contemporary challenges. Furthermore, understanding a spirituality in terms of the different theologies that it can engender and fructify can help us understand better the latent possibilities of the spirituality itself. The academic discipline of the history and phenomenology of spirituality provides potent tools and a wide range of historical data for pressing this sort of investigation. Finally, the challenges of our age to the Church and to theology make this task particularly pressing. In the remainder of this book I will try to show the fruitfulness of such an approach for understanding the theological work of Johann Baptist Metz, but before I do so I will make a few methodological remarks on how such an endeavor can be undertaken and, more specifically, how I will undertake it with regard to Metz's work.

How do we find access to a given theologian's spirituality and evaluate the impact it has had on his or her theology? If we had to rely on detailed biographical information on whether or not a given theologian was invested in and exercised the practices of a particular spirituality, then we would operate under fairly severe limits. Of course, it is increasingly frequent today that a theologian will explicitly name the spiritual sources of his or her theology.[58] Furthermore, if the theologian is a member of religious order, then it is also reasonable to infer at least some influence of that order's spirituality, in both its dimensions. But this is not the only way to try to answer the question. If a theologian has written explicitly on topics which make up the modern category of spirituality—on prayer, in some cases on sacraments—or if he or she has been involved in teaching or directing people in a given spirituality, then these will be obvious sources for identifying the spirituality which informs his or her thought. Furthermore, we can infer the presence of a spirituality even from texts and genres of "academic theology." This can be done by positive and negative means; preferably we should use a combination of both.

Positively, besides explicit references to spiritual masters of the past, we can look for adages, favored Scripture passages, or gleanings from the tradition that are typical of a classic spirituality. Here the work of historians of spirituality is invaluable, since this work is beginning to map out the richness of classic spiritualities, both in their particular depth and in their complex interweavings with one another, identifying the typical tropes of particular spiritual traditions and the ways in which they are employed. These allow us at least to identify elective affinities between a particular theological argument and a spiritual tradition. The more pervasive these elements are in a theology, the more they shape the contours of a theological argument or provide rhetorical force at key moments, then the closer one has come to "that fundamental intuition that serves to guide a spiritual life and provides the intellectual regimen proper to that life."[59]

Conversely, and more negatively, we can look for those stages or choices in a theologian's thinking which are underdetermined by the conceptual structure of his or her thought or the logical sequence of the arguments that justify the choices he or she makes. Here it is not a matter of explaining or licensing theological vagueness or logical incoherence by appeal to spirituality. Rather, after having identified as best we can the conceptual structure and the forms of argumentation which govern the progression of a theologian's work, and having found that these do not fully explain certain choices that the theologian has made, we can then ask whether there is a deeper reason, whether or not the theologian is attempting to articulate, in a properly academic mode, something that arises from a way of seeing the world that has roots outside the academy, that is, in a particular spirituality. This "negative" criterion may be more apparent in some theologians than others, particularly if the theologian has made a major shift in his or her theology at some point in his or her career. This, as I shall argue in the remainder of this book, makes Johann Baptist Metz's work a particularly apt case study for investigating the relationship of spirituality and theology. With other theologians the question may not be so much one of explaining dramatic shifts in conceptual and argumentative strategies as it is understanding their continuing commitment to particular strategies in the face of new situations and new challenges. Then we can look for the ways in which motifs that were muted and hidden in earlier work become more explicit, how the theologian redeploys conceptual resources from his or her earlier thought in new and innovative ways, ways unpredictable from a knowledge of his or her "system" but more easily intelligible from a knowledge of the spirituality which is inspiring and informing the theologian's praxis. This, as I shall argue more briefly in my final chapter, is a fruitful way of considering Karl Rahner's career and, finally, the relationship between Rahner and his always admiring student, Metz.

Turning explicitly to Metz, the matter to be explained, and explained by reference to the presence of a particular spirituality in his thought, is the dramatic shift he made in the 1960s, away from the transcendental method which he mastered under Rahner's tutelage and into the development of a new sort of theology: political theology. We can make use of a number of techniques identified above. Metz has been concerned with some classic topics in the history of spirituality (for instance, with "poverty of spirit"), and has written books of meditations on prayer, both individual and liturgical. As we shall see, he has been quite concerned with the future of religious life in the Roman Catholic Church, and has twice addressed superiors of men's religious orders in Germany. These will supplement our consideration of his writings in academic theology. In considering these materials, I will make use both of the negative and positive ways given above. On the one hand, I will need to establish as clearly as possible the parameters of the theological system and the conceptual resources that Metz has used. We need a sort of intellectual map of the terrain that Metz traversed, showing the conceptual paths open to him when he confronted the new challenges of a "postmodern" European society and the postconciliar Catholic Church, so that we can grasp the choices he made and understand the reasons he had for making them. Here, what I will show is that the dramatic shift he made in the 1960s can only be fully understood in light of his embrace of elements of apocalyptic spirituality which he learned by reading certain (secularized, to be sure) Jewish thinkers who had turned to those same sorts of resources in Judaism. The "negative" methodology will be complemented by the positive approach and by looking at his more explicitly "spiritual" writings. Finally, I will look for further confirmation by comparing Metz with his teacher, Karl Rahner, who certainly confronted the same challenges but responded to them by rooting his theology *more deeply* in the spiritual tradition in which he already stood: a particular, primarily apophatic and Neoplatonic, rendering of Ignatian spirituality.

Our first task, then, is to find some initial access to Metz's work, and to lay out a conceptual map that will allow the shifts and continuities in his work to emerge as clearly as possible. To this I now turn.

2

DANGEROUS MEMORIES:
THE DYNAMISM OF METZ'S THOUGHT

My purpose in this chapter is to gain an initial overview of the development of Metz's thought, which will prepare us for the more detailed treatement in the chapters to follow. After an introduction to the elements that make up Metz's work, I will make a first attempt to determine the spirituality which envelops and energizes it. Then I will develop a "map" of the various intellectual traditions, conceptual artifices, and argumentative strategies from which Metz would choose in order to bring that underlying spirituality more and more clearly to expression. This will give us an intellectual itinerary which will not only set the agenda for the following chapters but alert us to those crucial themes and issues at which the presence of this spirituality can be most clearly discerned.

READING METZ

Johann Baptist Metz was born on August 5, 1928, during the twilight of Weimar Germany. He served in the military for a few months at the end of World War II (a crucial experience, as we shall see), and after the war began his studies for the priesthood. He completed his doctoral studies in philosophy in 1952 with a dissertation on Heidegger, under the direction of Emerich Coreth.[1] He was ordained to the Catholic priesthood in 1953, and next year went to Innsbruck and joined the first circle of graduate students who gathered there around Karl Rahner.[2] Under Rahner's direction he completed a dissertation on Thomas Aquinas, *Christliche Anthropozentrik*.[3] During this period Metz was also intensively involved in the development of Rahner's brand of transcendental Thomism. He edited for republication the two foundational works in Rahner's metaphysics of knowledge and theological anthropology: *Geist in Welt* and *Hörer des Wortes*.[4] Metz contributed key articles to two dictionaries that Rahner edited: *Lexicon für Theologie und Kirche* (for which Metz was entrusted with the entry on theology), and the *Sacramentum Mundi* (with articles on apologetics, political theology, and miracles).[5] Metz took up a chair in fundamental theology on the Catholic faculty at the University of Münster in 1963, where he remained until his retirement in 1993. His activities during this period were varied. He was a cofounder of the journal *Concilium* and for many years served as director of its section for dogmatics. He served as a cofounding member of a Biconfessional Research Institute for the University of Bielefeld (a project which failed, due in part to ecclesial opposition). He served as consultant for the Papal Secretariat for Unbelievers from 1968 to 1973, and as consultant for the synod of West German bishops from 1971 to 1975.[6]

Metz has written prolifically, but after *Christliche Anthropozentrik* his preferred form has been the essay or short monograph. His major books, *Zur Theologie der Welt* (1967), *Glaube in Geschichte und Gesellschaft* (1977), *Jenseits bürgerliche Religion* (1980), and *Unterbrechungen* (1981), are, in fact, collections of essays, addresses, and interviews.[7] These short works had diverse audiences (popular lectures and journals, academic conventions, ecclesial meetings). Furthermore, the brevity of these essays necessitated a schematic style of presentation. For these reasons, it is difficult to interpret or weave them into a "system" which one could then name "Metz's theology."

There is more to this stylistic change, however. The major shift in Metz's thought, which began in earnest with his arrival at Münster, coincided with his abandonment of the systematic, metaphysical approach of his first decade of theology, in search of a postmetaphysical, postexistentialist, postidealist theology. When he began reading the work of Max Horkheimer and Theodor Adorno in the sixties he discovered kindred intellectual spirits. Adorno's assertion that "the whole is the untrue," and his consciously antisystematic style, fit Metz's own developing style. He became more aware of the impact of the social location of the thinker and of the conditions under which thinking was carried on; the old style of thinking came to seem closed in on itself, sterile, cut off from the lived history of endangered subjects.

Whatever the reasons (and I shall return to them in more detail below), the title of one of his later books, which I have taken as the title of my own work on Metz, is indicative of his style and purpose: *Unterbrechungen*, interruptions. He intends to interrupt social norms and ideals (progress, efficiency, quantification—the norms that define what the Frankfurt School thinkers called "instrumental reason") that could operate quite well—indeed better—without concrete, living human subjects. He wants to interrupt the hypnotic spell laid upon Christianity in modernity, turning it into a "bourgeois religion" with a crippled sensibility for danger in the modern world. Finally, he wants to interrupt theological work that takes place far from the endangered subjects of history, to whom, and for whose sake, Christianity and theology should be directed.[8] These interruptions are often brilliantly evocative and suggestive; often they are fragmentary and frustrating. The insights presented in his work often seem like blinding searchlights turned on the landscape of contemporary society and theology. They briefly, dazzlingly, light up the scene; but by the time one's eyes have adjusted, the light is gone. One wants more.

Metz often speaks of his theology as *eine korrektive Theologie*. His criticisms of others, particularly other theologians, is never absolute, almost always qualified. Moltmann's work on the Trinity, for example, is "too speculative." Sometimes one can know too much, he tells us. But then, is speculation wrongheaded? Metz does not want to rule out theological argument.[9] Then how much *should* one aspire to know? This tendency is most evident, and most frustrating for the interpreter, in Metz's dealings with Karl Rahner, his teacher, from whom, Metz says, "I have learned everything I know theologically," "from whom we continue to learn even when we have to contradict him." Metz's own position is difficult to identify; indeed, one can be tempted to wonder whether he *has* a position in the sense of a systematically argued and warranted system. How then, can one re-present Metz's thought?

As a beginning I will suggest a device that Martin Jay uses in his excellent short summary of Theodor Adorno's work. This method involves the application of two important concepts from Adorno's own thought: the force-field, and the constellation.

> The first of these is the force-field (*Kraftfeld*), by which Adorno meant a relational interplay of attractions and aversions that constituted the dynamic, transmutational structure of a complex phenomenon. The second is the constellation, . . . a juxtaposed rather than integrated cluster of changing elements that resist reduction

to a common denominator, essential core, or generative first principle.[10]

I will imitate Jay's procedure and suggest that there are five major stars in the constellation of Metz's work, five vectors in the force-field that makes it up. The restlessness, the dynamic, sometimes disconcertingly volatile nature of his thought is derived in part from the "interplay of attractions and aversions" among these elements.

The first three elements are highly complex phenomena in their own right and could very well themselves be resolved into constellations of interacting elements held in unstable equilibrium. First, Metz is a Roman Catholic and, second, he is a *German* Roman Catholic. First, Metz's Catholicism. He was born and grew up in Auerbach, a village he himself describes as "arch-Catholic":

> One comes from far away when one comes from there. It is as if one were born not fifty years ago, but somewhere along the receding edges of the Middle Ages. I had to approach many things slowly at first, had to exert great effort to discover things that others and that society had long ago discovered and had since become common practice. . . . [F]rom a point quite removed I had to work my way into the academic and social discussion fronts, had to learn to comprehend things that supposedly my theology and I had already discovered and comprehended long ago, had to gain access to phenomena that my contemporaries seemed to master through clichés: enlightenment, pluralism, emancipation, secularization, the critique of capitalism, and Marxism. And I had to learn how difficult and problematic it was to connect these parameters of contemporaneity . . . with that religion already so familiar to me before I had begun reflecting on it.[11]

Metz ascribes his own "noncontemporaneity" to this Catholicism, to this "way of looking at things," this "psychological life-rhythm."[12] To be sure, insofar as this noncontemporaneity leads to isolation and withdrawal, it paralyzes and leads to sectarianism. Yet Metz will never fully condemn Catholicism's hesitancy at entering the modern age. As much as he criticizes late nineteenth-century Catholic theology for sealing itself off from the intellectual and cultural debates raging in Europe, this is not because it "failed to keep up with the times," but because it demonstrated a failure of nerve, a failure to trust that the substance of tradition was up to a thorough confrontation with modernity. Catholicism failed to put its essence at stake in the confrontation with modernity, and even its most creative initiatives (the tradition of social teachings beginning with Leo XIII, for instance) were stamped with an ad hoc character, were peripheral to the heart of lived Catholicism, and thus, in the final analysis, ineffective.[13]

Metz's Catholicism also expresses itself in his deep concern for the Church. Like his teacher, Metz is a theologian motivated by deep pastoral concerns. The explicit audience or public for much of his work is the Church. I mentioned some of his involvement with the Church above; he has also been very interested in religious life.[14] He helped compose one of the documents for the 1975 synod of West German bishops: *Unsere Hoffnung*. He has continually addressed himself to issues of Church reform, and suffered the disfavor of Church authorities as a result.[15] Finally, in the course of his career Metz's Catholicism has drawn him to think more and more in terms of the world church. The (Catholic) Church of the Third World, particularly that of Latin America, became increasingly important for his thinking during the seventies and eighties. In sum, there are many dimensions to Metz's Catholicism. Its richly textured fabric—woven from his rural Catholic upbringing, his priesthood, his university teaching on a Catholic faculty, and his growing consciousness of the world-wide catholicity of the Church—stamps all of his work.

The second point in the force-field of Metz's thought is his Germanness. But, as with his Catholicism, Metz's Germany is itself a tensive, conflicted reality. First, it is the Germany for which the Enlightenment is an "unfinished project."[16] But, if the German Enlightenment was unfinished, displaced from politics into philosophy, literature, and art, neither did it lead to the Terror. The evaluation of modernity by German thinkers is, correspondingly, quite different from that of thinkers in France. While German thinkers produced theories of an "iron cage" or a "dialectic of enlightenment," they were not (at least until recently) as deeply suspicious of the Enlightenment as French thinkers.[17] For them (if one might risk a generalization) the Enlightenment is still something to be saved and implemented, even if this means saving it from itself. Metz shares this attitude. His commitment to the Enlightenment and its ideals of *Mündigkeit* are clear and consistent throughout his career.

Metz's Germany is also the Germany of National Socialism. Weimar expired when Metz was only five years old. Most of his childhood was spent under the Third Reich, and he experienced at firsthand Germany's lockstep march to destruction. For Metz, as for so many intellectuals of his generation, one of the great problems is how the Germany of Goethe, Kant, and Beethoven could become the Germany of Hitler, Himmler, and Eichmann. Finally, then, Metz's Germany is the Germany of Auschwitz. Increasingly, beginning in the seventies, Auschwitz becomes one of the focal points for Metz's theology, the key historical "interruption" to his own thought.

Thus the third element of Metz's thought: Judaism. The affinities Metz feels for Judaism are due in part to the fact that the German Jewish experience concentrates the ambiguity inherent in the German Enlightenment.[18] Judaism shared, to be sure, in a much deeper way, the non-contemporaneity which Metz ascribes to his own Catholic beginnings. Of course, the difference is that the Jews suffered far more terribly for it. Indeed, as Metz himself notes, the fate which Jesus predicted for his own disciples is far more observable in the history of Judaism than it is in Christianity.[19] For Metz this fact betrays Christianity's failure. Furthermore, that Christian theology continued after Auschwitz as it did before evinces its complicity in the general failure of Christianity. It was the realization of this failure that Metz identifies as the impetus for the development of a new political theology, for the construction of a theology that could not remain unaffected by such a catastrophe.[20] It led him to reexamine the relationship between Christianity and Judaism, and to rethink the significance of the Hellenization of Christianity.

The other two points are more explicitly intellectual. First, the tradition of transcendental Thomism. Metz's relationship to this tradition is crucial to understanding his thought, even today, and requires careful explication. This will occupy us more fully in the next chapter, but suffice it to say here that this method, of which Metz became a thoroughly versed and creative practitioner, defined a way of thinking that continues to determine his intellectual manner of proceeding. For instance, Metz makes a crucial distinction in *Christliche Anthropozentrik* between the content of thought and the form of thinking (*Denkform*), analogous to the distinction between ontic and ontological levels of being and thought in Heidegger, or between transcendental and categorical in Rahner. This distinction, which depends on a certain philosophical anthropology, can still be found in Metz's thought today, as when, for instance, he tries to identify the distinctive way of perceiving the world (*Weltwahrnehmung*) that is appropriate to the biblical tradition of Israel.[21]

Finally, there is Metz's relation to Marxism. Early in the sixties Metz began participating in a series of dialogues with so-called "revisionary" Marxist thinkers.[22] He felt the challenge of these thinkers deeply, as well as the insight from Vatican II that "believers can have more than a little to do with the rise of atheism."[23] He soon gravitated toward this revisionary wing of Western Marxism, which challenged the ortho-dox interpretation of Marx being imposed in the Eastern block. First Ernst Bloch, and then the thinkers of the Institut für Sozialforschung—including the eccentric satellite of that school, Walter Benjamin—were crucial interlocutors in Metz's development. It was his dialogue with them that occasioned his break from metaphysics. Through them he entered that stream of the Enlightenment which emphasized practi-cal reason and *praxis* over speculation and *theoria*. Yet it should be noted that the Marxist thinkers who effected this change for him were precisely those who rejected a simplistic abandonment of all theory. Adorno and Horkheimer insisted on the continuing need for theory, an insistence for which they came under considerable criticism during the sixties (the period when Metz encountered them).[24] Activism without thought, in their view, was exposed to the danger of being co-opted by instrumental reason, and thus of compounding rather than solving the dilemma of modernity. The resultant ambiguity concerning the status of reason and theoretical argument (including that of negative dialec-tics) is mirrored in Metz's thought.

Besides this general shift in the style of thinking and presentation, Metz also derived from these thinkers many of the most crucial cate-gories and concepts of his thinking—from the primacy of the future in the sixties, to "dangerous memories" in the seventies and eighties. Yet he was, if anything, more concerned than the Frankfurt School thinkers (and it was their hesitation on this point that attracted Metz to them) about the co-option of Marxism by instrumental reason. He rejects any materialist understanding of history; indeed, he was most attracted to Walter Benjamin precisely because of the latter's critique of understandings of history as progress, whether derived from a belief in the omnicompetence of technology or from the belief in the revolution-ary potential of some particular class in history.

These five elements—Metz's Catholicity, his Germanness, Judaism, transcendental Thomism, and Marxism—form the force-field of vari-ously attracting and repelling points in Metz's life and work. They form a tensive field within which the key concepts of Metz's theology develop and function. Their diversity suggests that they do not come together easily, and Metz does not force them to do so. However "unsystematic" this makes Metz's thought, however inconsistent and frustrating at times, this openness to tension and ambiguity has its own virtues. These different elements express the conflicted reality within which Metz has carried on the vocation of theology in the second half of this century. His contribution lies in allowing their interruptive voices to speak and to disturb us, if we are willing to listen. His creative fidelity to them accounts both for the unresolved tensions in his thought, but for its fruitfulness as well.

An adequate representation of Metz's thought must encompass these points, showing how first one, then another, became the center of gravity, without, however, ever fully subsuming the others into a completely resolved system. The deficiency in many interpretations of Metz's work, as I read them, is that they prematurely close off the interpretation by reading him only in terms of one point of reference. Some readings of Metz fail to recognize the continuing importance of his early work on Heidegger,[25] others focus on his confrontation with Marxism.[26] Most adequate, relatively, are those readings which focus on his relationship to Rahner. As long as these readings grapple with both the discontinuities and the continuities, developing and shifting over time, in Metz's appropriation of the thinking of his beloved teacher, then they can implicitly encompass the other tensions in his work.

My own strategy will be to identify the sources of irritation and interruption in Metz's own thought. In fact, this is to give a preliminary reading of the underlying spirituality which nourishes and drives Metz's thinking. Concretely this may be done by identifying the "dangerous memories" that have enkindled his thought, even driving his search for the very categories in anthropology (memory and dangerous memory) and in fundamental theology (*memoria passionis*) that could do justice to the importance of the specific memories. This will give us a first look at the growing focus on the problem of suffering, particularly that of others, and the growing appeal to the resources of apocalyptic spirituality which make up the spiritual heart of Metz's theology.

As I have already suggested, my strategy will be to follow as carefully as possible the shifts in Metz's conceptual arsenal and in his argumentative strategies, but to do so on the lookout for a deeper forcefield which governs the attractions, repulsions, and shifts between the various stars in his "constellation." This deeper field is a particular spirituality. The next stage in this preliminary overview is to establish the contours of that spirituality. Then we must work up a map of Metz's intellectual journey, following the strongest thread of continuity through his work: his concern with the subject, which marks all of his work (as well as Rahner's) as a type of theological anthropology.

MEMORY AND THE OTHER

Only in the last decade has Metz begun to speak publicly of his own biography and its impact on his "speech about God." This is a little surprising, since Metz has long spoken of the irreducible contextuality of reason. Almost three decades ago he began to speak of "dangerous memories," memories which continually disrupt the smooth processes of reason, and in so disrupting, save it from a catastrophic self-absorption. Recently it has become clear that the category of memory not only functioned to remedy some structural difficulties in his system[27] but served to articulate an approach to Christianity that was deeply stamped by two dangerous, interruptive memories from his youth. At a conference in Boston, in 1987, Metz related these memories:

> The first event occurred when I was sixteen years old. At the end of the Second World War I was taken out of school and pressed into military service. It was in 1945. With barely any military training I was sent to the front, and at that time the Americans had already crossed the Rhine River. My whole company was made up of young soldiers of about the same age. One evening my company commander sent me back to the battalion headquarters with a message. Throughout the night I strayed through burning farms and villages. When I returned to my company the next morning, I found all my comrades dead. The company had been attacked by planes and tanks and was completely wiped out. I saw only the lifeless faces of my comrades, those same comrades with whom I had but days before shared my childhood fears and my youthful laughter. I remember nothing but a soundless cry. I strayed for hours alone in the forest. Over and over again, just this silent cry! And up until today I see myself so. Behind this memory all my childhood dreams have vanished.[28]

The other "dangerous memory" for Metz is Auschwitz. As Metz always says, only very slowly did *this* memory intrude into his theology.

> Somewhere and somehow I have become aware of the situation in which I try to do theology. It took much time, and this is due to the fact that my great teacher, Karl Rahner, to whom I owe the greatest debt and the best that I have ever learned in theology, never spoke in his theology about this catastrophe. . . . I slowly became aware of the high content of apathy in theological idealism and its inability to confront historical experience in spite of all its prolific talk about historicity. There was no theology in the whole world which talked so much about historicity as German theologies. Yet they only talked about historicity; they did not mention Auschwitz.[29]

One can begin to get a sense for the irritating, interrupting concern that has been driving Metz's theology from the very beginning. It is a concern for the suffering of others in history, for those negativities in it which obdurately refuse to be "systematized." Even more, it is a concern that we are coming to the point at which memories such as these no longer touch us. As we shall see, Metz believes that Western culture is becoming increasingly weary of such disturbing memories. Even in an age of instant communication, in which we are inundated with reports of the passion of the world, we are becoming increasingly unable to let them disturb us or move us to action. We are more and more becoming the voyeurs of others' suffering and consequently of our own dissolution as responsible subjects. We divest ourselves of responsibility for the suffering of others in history by means of elaborate theoretical "exculpation devices"—"anthropodicy" instead of theodicy. Others are dehumanized; they are counterposed to some authentic, revolutionary subject of history, whose coming into power justifies the suffering endured by the "inauthentic" or "immature and still developing" subjects. Or, the master-myth of modernity's understanding of time explains the "necessity" of suffering in history: the myth of progress (even as Metz finds it hidden within Habermas's developmental schemata). This "forgetfulness of the forgotten" needs to be interrupted. Yet Metz is worried that it is not only the broader culture which is increasingly lapsing into forgetfulness. Increasingly, it seems, the Church and its theology have little room for such memories. If we keep this concern in mind, Metz's theological journey may be thought of as the search for a Christianity and a theology in which such memories are not only allowed (perhaps in the back pews) but are *central:* "What happens if one takes these memories not to the psychologist, but to the Church? And what if one will not allow him or herself to be talked out of these memories, or soothed, but rather wants to believe with them?"[30]

Metz's theology is a journey in which he tries to find appropriate theological language to speak of these memories and the concern which they bring to light. What is crucial to understand for this case study in the relationship between spirituality and theology is that the reason why the "other" and his or her suffering becomes so central in Metz's theology is that he lives out of a general outlook upon life and history which is intensively, painfully aware of the suffering of the world, of the negativities of history. Indeed, this outlook is for Metz nothing less than a mystical stance which is prior to theological articulation and conceptualization, a stance which he has variously named a "mysticism of open eyes," a "mysticism of mourning," or a mysticism of "suffering unto God."[31] The question is how to travel the various argumentative paths available in the theological community and deploy its conceptual resources so as to give appropriate theological expression to this stance toward the world, this way (one way among others, as Metz admits) of "connecting one's life-history with one's faith-history."[32] This brings us to the intellectual context of Metz's work, and to that figure who is so important for all of German intellectual history of the past two centuries, including the work of Rahner and Metz: Immanuel Kant.

METZ, THE TURN TO THE SUBJECT, AND THE KANTIAN HERITAGE

In recent years Metz has taken to the concepts of "paradigm" and "paradigm shift" as a way of describing what is involved in the birth of his political theology.[33] In his view the modern situation is so characterized that theology can continue to carry out its responsibility to speak about God only by undergoing a profound shift in its methods. He views his own approach as an attempt to shift from the paradigm of "transcendental-idealist" theology. He describes the latter, exemplified above all by Karl Rahner,

> as the attempt to appropriate the heritage of the classical patristic and scholastic traditions precisely by means of a productive and aggressive

dialogue with the challenges of the modern European world: the discovery of subjectivity as a crisis for classical metaphysics; a critical-productive confrontation with Kant, German Idealism and existentialism on the one hand, and with the social processes of secularization and of scientific civilization on the other.[34]

Some understanding of "the challenges of the modern European world" and the theologies that attempted to grapple with them is essential for understanding the intellectual milieu in which Metz was trained. These intellectual shifts, that came to maturity in the seventeenth and eighteenth centuries as the defininig matrix for modernity, have frequently been summarized with the phrase "the turn to the subject."[35] Charles Taylor has shown that one of the key strands in this complex tapestry is the shift from a substantive to a procedural understanding of truth. Classically, truth referred to and depended on a broader cosmic order, so that human knowing was at a profound level essentially contemplative: "[C]orrect human knowledge and valuation comes from our connecting ourselves rightly to the significance that things already have ontically."[36] In modernity, however, beginning with thinkers like Descartes and Locke, we find that truth depends more and more on the performance of the knowing subject.

> [T]he modern conception of reason is procedural. What we are called on to do is not to become contemplators of order but to construct a picture of things following the canons of rational thinking. . . . The aim is to get to the way things really are, but these canons offer our best hope of doing that. Rationality is above all a property of the process of thinking, not of the substantive content of thought.[37]

This new approach to truth (and to the moral and the beautiful) found its most far-reaching systematization (especially for the German intellectual tradition) in Immanuel Kant. Awakened from his dogmatic slumber by Hume's work, Kant attempted to save philosophy from the deconstructive consequences of this shift, reconstructing the field of philosophy by asking the questions, "What can I know? What ought I to do? For what may I hope? What is man?" The first-person singular in these questions is not accidental. Further, Kant observed that "all these might be reckoned under anthropology, since the first three questions [answered, respectively, by metaphysics, morals, and religion] refer to the last."[38] In Kant, as much as in Hume, no certain knowledge (whether speculative, moral, or aesthetic) was to be had prior to a methodologically rigorous examination of the human person as knower and doer. Transcendentals no longer described predicables which could be ascribed to all beings. Rather, they pointed to certain general characteristics of human knowing, prior to and therefore constitutive of all knowing, which thereby provided legitimate warrant for making universal claims concerning truth, morality, and beauty. Transcendental analysis was no longer a metaphysical endeavor but an analysis of human performances of knowing, choosing, and valuing which would uncover this underlying structure of a priori conditions. Philosophical anthropology became in an unprecedented way the keystone for the modern edifice of knowledge, morals, and aesthetics. Could it also serve as a keystone for elaborating the religious?

Kant certainly thought it could. Others were not so sure. Could crucial religious beliefs, particularly concerning revelation, survive this reconfiguration? Most of nineteenth-century liberal theology endeavored to grapple with this problem. In diverse ways it tried to show that, correctly understood, the results of a transcendental analysis of human knowing and doing are consonant with the elements of Christian faith: that is, they neither directly contradict the Christian understanding of the human person and his or her destiny, nor render it superfluous ("positive" religion, to be transcended and left behind by a religion of reason). Even though its successors in our own century have been unrelentingly critical of this liberal project, it did not necessarily entail capitulation. Even Kant's *Religion within the Limits of Reason Alone*, is not a religion *of* reason. In this work on religion he carried on a fruitful, if also tensive and problematic, confrontation with the anthropology he had developed in his critiques, allowing, for instance, a concept of radical evil into his anthropology that did not fit comfortably with his other works.[39]

This was a risky strategy, to be sure. As figures as diverse as Ludwig Feuerbach and Ralph Waldo Emerson demonstrated, anthropology could consume theology and God could become a cipher for human fulfillment or self-expression. Anthropology as a methodological starting point seemed difficult to harmonize with the traditional contents of anthropology in Christian dogmatics. Witness, for example, the fate of the doctrine of original sin—Kant notwithstanding—in the nineteenth century. In making the first move of accepting the anthropologically centered starting-point of modernity it was not clear how and how much *specifically Christian* anthropological content could be preserved. The neoorthodox revolt can be seen in part as a recognition of this danger.[40]

Catholic theology took a different, more torturous path through the landscape of modernity.[41] At first, early nineteenth-century Catholic theologians took up these conceptual tools of modern philosophy to defend the meaning and integrity of the Catholic tradition. Figures as diverse as Louis Bautain, Anton Günther, as well as Johann von Drey and his successors in the Catholic Tübingen School, attempted to essay this project. No doubt these attempts (as with their Protestant parallels) were fraught with peril; but broader currents in European history were far more significant in determining their success or failure. Popes such as Pius IX, and even Leo XIII, stung by incursions into papal sovereignty during the eighteenth and nineteenth centuries, looked with increasing disfavor on all manifestions of modernity, including these intellectual ones. They felt and acted on the need to establish a united philosophical and theological front which would rescue Catholicism from the corrosive effects of modernity. Presented with the alternative system provided by the Neo-Thomist syntheses of Matteo Liberatore and Joseph Kleutgen, the Catholic attempts at a critical dialogue with modernity were labeled "modernist" and suppressed. Yet, what is striking about this history is that even the Neo-Thomists argued Thomism's (as they construed it) superiority *as a fundamental anthropology and epistemology,* as a better way of executing the "turn to the subject." They, just as much as their opponents in Tübingen, were responding to modernity on its own grounds.

The immediate result of this history was the enthronement of Neo-Thomism in Catholic thought and the stultification of other creative attempts to do theology in modernity. But a new generation of philosophers, historians, and theologians arose in the twentieth century who acted on the twofold mandate given them by Leo XIII: on the one hand to carry on research into the historical sources of Thomism and, on the other, to continue the creative confrontation of Thomism with modern thought. Both avenues opened up a new, more critical appropriation of modern thought. The historical work, carried on by thinkers like Etienne Gilson, Henri Bouillard, and Henri de Lubac, deconstructed the reduction of scholasticism to Thomas, and showed the "modern" provenance of supposedly scholastic distinctions like nature/supernature. Meanwhile, Pierre Rousselot and Joseph Maréchal continued the confrontation of Neo-Thomism with modernity, specifically, with Kant's epistemology and anthropology. Convinced of the value and power of Aquinas's thought, they attempted to show that with his system one could better the kind of transcendental critique of human knowing that Kant had attempted. This enterprise involved readings of Thomas that were distinctively modern (as "orthodox" Thomists were quick to point out). The outcome of these developments, internal to the development of Neo-Thomism, was an "explosion of pluralism" in the fifties that spelled the end of Neo-Thomism.[42] Although the "new theology" was ecclesially suppressed one last time in 1950 by Pius XII, with his encyclical *Humani Generis*, the future was with the new theological approaches, as Vatican II was to show.

Johann Baptist Metz's philosophical and theological apprenticeship took place during this last spasm of Neo-Thomism before the birth of a Catholic theology freed from ecclesial constraints and open to modernity. As we have seen, his training was done under transcendental Thomists, arguing for a more thoroughgoing *Auseinandersetzung* of Catholic philosophy and theology with modernity. His first published monograph, *Christliche Anthropozentrik*, argued that, far from being opposed to the spirit and letter of Aquinas's work, modernity's turn to the subject was in fact a natural outgrowth and culmination of the decisive shift in Aquinas's theology: away from Greek, cosmocentrically oriented forms and categories of thought, toward anthropocentric ones more appropriate for articulating and communicating the content of revelation. This work can be read as a broader apology for the type of reading of Aquinas carried out in Rahner's early work *Spirit in the World*.

Metz was thus firmly committed to the research program mapped out by Rahner's brand of transcendental theology: to retrieve and reconfigure the doctrinal resources of the Catholic tradition on the terrain ruled by modernity's subject. Ironically, though, the young professor at Münster was taking on this task just as the attacks against this subject were beginning to reach a crescendo, sounding together as an unruly chorus of voices which would eventually be grouped together under the elusive term "postmodernism."

Of course, this phenomenon can be traced back at least into the nineteenth century and the three paradigmatic "masters of suspicion" of the Enlightenment's self: Karl Marx, Friedrich Nietzsche, and Sigmund

Freud. Marx saw in modernity's "subject" an intellectual mirror-image of the entrepreneur, objectifying, instrumentalizing and exploiting nature (including human nature) for the sake of the accumulation of capital, or other ends separate from, and incompatible with, the ends of integral human fulfillment. If, after Max Weber, the disengaged self, along with its technical-purposive rationality, was still interpreted as the foundation of modern culture and society, it was a foundation for an iron cage, from which there was seemingly no exit. Philosophers of life, existentialists, and phenomenologists attacked the monstrous palace of reason (to use Kierkegaard's parable) built by philosophers, within which the modern subject is supposed to live but in which its builders, as living, thinking, existing human beings in the world, were not to be found.

For thinkers like Schopenhauer and Nietzsche, the depths of the self, celebrated by Romantics as the stuff of aesthetic self-expression and unity with nature, were deeply ambiguous and amoral. To use Joseph Conrad's deeply disturbing metaphor, the human heart was a heart of darkness.[43] To Nietzsche, positing the existence of a rational and ethical subject constitutes an attempt to ethically determine, define, and confine these depths. The self is thus an illusion, a Christian deception born of *ressentiment*, which truncates and cripples human beings, rather than fulfilling them. However much Freud tried to reestablish some form of rational distance from and control over these depths, after him the concept of the subject which expressed human beings' confidence in their ultimate self-transparency and autonomy was radically destabilized.

This confidence was further undermined by the so-called linguistic turn.[44] Philosophers like Ludwig Wittgenstein attacked with devastating effect instrumental theories of language which interpreted language as a means for communication on the part of a "transcendental" subject, always already immediately present to itself without benefit of language.[45] Heidegger's thought-paths carried out similar moves against the concept of the subject. On his reading, the emphasis on the human subject, and the metaphysical humanism that resulted from it, is an intensification of a forgetfulness of being that has plagued Western thought since it was born (perhaps stillborn) in Plato and Aristotle. In his "Letter on Humanism" and "The Question Concerning Technology," Heidegger savaged this tradition in an argument that bears strong family resemblances to the "iron cage" argument of Weber, as well as its various descendants in the Frankfurt School. The postmodernism of

Jacques Derrida, with its biting suspicion of any notion of a "subject" and the "meaning" that is allegedly correlated with it, has continued this deconstructive strategy. Jean-François Lyotard announced the "end of metanarratives," the great (hi)stories that have legitimated and driven the modern subject, be it that of the progress of science, or even that of the battle for *fraternité, égalité et liberté*. They are to be unmasked (along with their "subject") as the hypostases of particular schemata and regimes of power. Or, they are to be archaeologically dug out, unearthing the epistemological "wrinkle" that is "modern man."[46]

What characterizes all these approaches is a farewell to the subject, at least as it was understood during the golden age of modernity. Heidegger abandons it in favor of the history of being's "sendings." Marxist poststructuralists like Louis Althusser and systems theorists like Niklas Luhmann, turn toward self-referential systems. Foucault looks for regimes of power and knowledge. Linguistic philosophers focus on language games, eschewing such metaphysical abstractions as the subject, allegedly "behind" this language. Even that quintessential defender of modernity, Jürgen Habermas, has turned to the resources of American pragmatism in order to reconstruct philosophy on the basis of an intersubjective communicative rationality, turning away from philosophies of consciousness which, in his view, reached a decisive dead end in, among others, the philosophy of his teacher, Theodor Adorno.

Metz found himself sympathetic, perhaps grudgingly at first, to some of these critiques, particularly those leveled by the founders of the Frankfurt School, Max Horkheimer and Theodor Adorno. He took over their critique of the Enlightenment and of modernity under the rubric of the "dialectic of enlightenment" and, like them, became increasingly wary of any conceptualization of a "transcendental subject" that could be formulated and utilized above or behind the backs of the terrifying ruptures in history, paradigmatically represented by the Holocaust. He began to feel uneasy about the possible presence of such an abstract, ahistorical subject in Rahner's work. Yet, for all of this, Metz resolutely refused to join postmodernists in proclaiming an end to the subject. Metz remained convinced that at the heart of Christian faith, and at the heart of all that was most worthy of saving and protecting in Western civilization, was an understanding of persons as subjects, as beings endowed with the dignity and responsibility of becoming themselves, of recognizing and affirming themselves in and through the symbols, stories, and histories of their world. However much he recognized a *dialectic* of Enlightenment, he remained a passionate defender of the Enlightenment's essential *rightness*. Thus, however much he would move away from Rahner's approach, the turn to the subject is still central to understanding Metz's entire theological career, as can be seen from his definition of Christian faith in his mature work, *Faith in History and Society:*

> The faith of Christians is a praxis in history and society that is to be understood as a solidaristic hope in the God of Jesus as a God of the living and the dead who *calls all persons to be subjects in his presence.* Christians justify themselves in this essentially apocalyptic praxis (of imitation) in their historical struggle for their fellow human beings. *They stand up for all human beings in their attempt to become subjects in solidarity with each other.* In this praxis *they resist both the danger of a creeping evolutionary disintegration of the history of persons as subjects,* as well as the danger of the negation of the individual in view of a post-bourgeois image of the person.[47] (Emphasis added.)

For Metz it was never a matter of abandoning the notion of the subject and the normative understandings of reason and history that were based on it; rather, the task was to reformulate this notion in a way that saved it from dialectical self-destruction. It was his conviction, moreover (just as it had been Rahner's conviction before him), that this could not be done without a substantive appeal to the resources of Judaism and Christianity.

This task sets the intellectual agenda for Metz's theological work. It is the thread by which to follow the many twists and turns of Metz's thought, revealing their underlying continuity. It is in following this thread that we will also begin to see the gradual, yet more and more decisive emergence of the resources of a particular spirituality, providing the energy, the fundamental intuitions and aversions which guide his attempts to fulfill this more explicitly intellectual, theological agenda. If this is the intellectual task, what were the resources that Metz had on hand to carry it out? How would he continue to execute the turn to the subject in Christian theology without falling victim to its fatal aporias? To answer this question, and complete the task of providing an intellectual map of the terrain which Metz traversed, it is worth going back to the great progenitor of the turn to the subject in the German intellectual tradition: Immanuel Kant.

We have already seen that transcendental Thomism appropriated modernity's turn to the subject by means of a a "return to Kant" read through the lens of Thomas Aquinas's philosophy. This was the tradition into which Metz was initiated under Coreth and Rahner. But, there is more than one way to return to Kant, and it makes a great difference which path one chooses. Claude Welch points out four possible "routes" which theology was to travel after Kant.[48] First, by questioning the restrictions laid by Kant on speculative reason and the access granted through it to the experience of God, one strand of tradition would try to reopen conceptual access to God (e.g., Hegel, but also transcendental Thomists). Second, one could accept Kant's strictures, and continue by rejecting reason's right to establish any starting point at all for theology, so that theology would take its starting point in revelation alone (Barth). Third, one could follow Kant in locating the realm of religion in the moral realm (Ritschl). Fourth, one could expand the notion of reason to include an autonomous a priori area for religion (e.g., Schleiermacher's *Gefühl*).

Michel Despland has recently pointed out that there is another, more properly historical approach to religion, which is found in Kant's thought itself.[49] A careful consideration of this social-historical approach and its tensions with Kant's other ways of considering religion will help us to establish a conceptual map against which to chart the major changes in Metz's thought.

As is well known, Kant treated religion as constituted by the question "For what may I hope?" The standard approach is to see the parameters of this question determined by Kant's moral philosophy, in answer to the question "What ought I to do?" Thus, the second critique is the jumping-off point for understanding Kant's philosophy of religion, found in *Religion Within the Limits of Reason Alone*. This does not lead necessarily to a reduction of the religious to the ethical, or to a religion *of* reason as opposed to a religion *within the limits of* reason.[50] One can hope that one will do one's duty, and that in so doing one will attain to the *summum bonum*: happiness in proportion to one's virtue. In this context, I can rationally hope (a) that there is a God who guarantees that the *telos* of nature (upon which my happiness depends, but over which I have limited control) does in fact (often in contradiction to my experience now, e.g., that the wicked prosper and the virtuous suffer) cohere with this end, and (b) that I have the necessary time to attain the purity of moral will required. Thus the practical postulates of the existence of God and the immortality of the soul.

These hopes are reasonable because they are not heteronomous opinions imposed from the outside but reflect the legitimate interests of the rational subject himself or herself, insofar as he or she experiences both the dignity and responsibility of duty and the limited, finite character of human being, which militates against it. They are required for practical reason to make sense of its own nature, and act accordingly:

> The belief in freedom is implicit in moral consciousness insofar as it is moral. The belief in God and immortality is implicit in it insofar as it is *finite* as well as moral. It is implicit in it because the structure of finite morality has certain inner contradictions. The beliefs in God and immortality can resolve these contradictions only by reflecting them.[51]

Hope is here formulated primarily in atemporal, individualistic terms, as the joining of virtue and happiness. Furthermore, the attainment of the *summum bonum* is placed outside the world and its history. My hope for this world is that I might do my duty (and I cannot be sure even of this).[52]

I will follow Despland in calling this way of answering the third question (in primarily individualistic and atemporal terms) the ethico-religious tendency.[53] It has the advantage of offering a hope that I can reasonably entertain now. I can hope to be moral (in theological terms, I can hope to attain salvation) even now, in the midst of a corrupt age that, while being an age of *enlightenment*, is not yet an *enlightened age*.[54] Theologically interpreted, God becomes the "guarantor" of my identity as a subject. My own autonomy will not, in the end, be overcome by heteronomous tendencies, be they those of an unenlightened age or of my own pathological will.

There is however, as Despland argues, another approach to the question of religion. It is one that Kant worked out in his philosophy of history.[55] In his "Idea for a Universal History with a Cosmopolitan Intent" Kant speaks of the realization of reason not as an individual event, occurring in acts of knowing and willing, but as a state of affairs which pertains to the species as a whole.[56] This end is achieved in part by nature, which drives the human species toward it, willing or no. Because of our "unsocial sociability" we must live together, and yet we are always asserting our pathological, self-seeking wills.[57] This conflictual situation leads to the birth of reason, which might otherwise lie fallow.[58] Furthermore, humans' anti-social tendencies can force them into a compact, which may begin as a "pathologically enforced whole" but may become a "moral whole."[59] Even war, that most devastating of human predilections, has the virtue of forcing nations to achieve some sort of peace or face mutual annihilation.

Thus, nature has a sort of "plan" by which humans are led, or forced, from nature to culture, from culture to civil society, and finally to a league of nations.[60] Of course, Kant knew that a just society does not guarantee moral citizens. As he put it later, "the problem of organizing a nation is solvable even for a people composed of devils (if only they possess understanding)."[61] In his more sanguine moments Kant believed that the advances of history were irreversible, and that little by little history would create the conditions within which the frequency of acts in conformity to duty would increase. At other times he could contemplate the failure of history and its grand experiment in human freedom.[62]

The ideas here are, like many of those posited in the three critiques, strictly *regulative* rather than *constitutive* ones. They are adopted by reason in the interest of its own activity, and are "rational" only in this usage. Particularly important in this regard are Kant's considerations on teleological judgment in the third critique. There he asserted that nature (particularly organisms) would be unknowable apart from the concept of purpose. Hence, teleological judgment (which predicates purposiveness) is justified as a maxim of reflective judgment. Without a final purpose, in this view, nature would be unintelligible to us. Furthermore, since this final purpose includes that of human beings, it is not purely natural but moral, that is, *noumenal*.[63] Nature has an end which transcends nature. Nature may bring humans to the threshold of that end, but no further.[64] In a restatement of the moral proof for God's existence (here called a proof for the first time) Kant continues by asking whether the purposiveness of nature is complemented by a moral teleology. Significantly, the moral proof is now stated in more social, historical terms. The *summum bonum* is placed within history, as the happiness of *all* human beings in proportion to their virtue.[65] Otherwise put: rather than the realization of individual human subjectivity under its finite conditions, here we have the realization of the subjecthood of all, under the conditions of society and history. Kant follows the line of argumentation familiar from the second critique. It is legitimate and rational, out of the interests of practical reason, to posit the existence of a God who is the author of creation, including nature with *its* teleology, and history with its own moral telos, the latter under the governance of divine providence.[66]

Thus, Kant had what he believed to be a justified hope in progress. Nature has begun the process of the coming of age of humanity, but humans must complete it. We may hope that providence may bring this about in us, although we can form no concept of how this might come to pass. Put somewhat differently, all philosophical theodicies fail, just as all speculative proofs for God's existence fail. The former attempt to prove the reality and activity of divine providence in history, but this would be possible only for someone who "has obtained a knowledge of the supersensible (intelligible) world and has seen how this world lies at the basis of the world of experience."[67] This sort of insight is closed to human consciousness. Hence, the concept of providence (and the justified hope in its activity in a world which seems otherwise permeated by evil) is the result of reason, in its practical exercise, reflecting on the conditions of its own meaningfulness.[68] One may in this way have a justified faith and hope in the future, out of which one may—indeed must—act, even in the face of the seemingly overwhelming presence of evil in history.[69]

This way of framing the question gives rise to a different sort of answer, which Despland calls the ethico-juridical tendency in Kant.[70] What is the relation of this tendency and the ethico-religious? Even though the former is appended to the latter in the third critique, Kant never systematically interrelated them. It is not difficult to see why: a systematic interrelation would require an insight into the noumenal realm that is closed to human reason, as Kant insisted in his essay on theodicy. This points out the underlying strain in Kant's anthropology: human beings are constitutively involved in both the noumenal and phenomenal realms, but the former is not directly accessible to our reason. This fissure crosses not only my activity and self-reflection as an individual moral agent but also as a political agent in history. Kant consistently refused to bridge this gap in any except the most tentative of fashions.

One place where he tentatively connected these two sides of his system is *Religion Within the Limits of Reason Alone*, in which Christianity is conceived as a religion in which both tendencies are comprehended. To be sure, much of *Religion* moves within the parameters set up by the ethico-religious tendency. We may hope that we will in fact be able to do our duty, to have a disposition that is well-pleasing to God. Even though our wills are infected with radical evil, we can hope that God will make up what is lacking in us. We cannot in any way conceive of how this might come about because "conversion" as a radical change of disposition is a *change* (hence entangled in the phenomenal world) of a *noumenal* reality. We may, however, in the interest of reason and its activity, symbolize these noumenal events, although such symbols must be kept under strict control so that their use does not lapse into dogmatism. The topics covered in the *parerga*, however suspicious Kant is of them, serve as such symbols by which we might adequately present to ourselves these processes, which are in themselves unknowable.

But Kant also gives evidence that he considered Christianity in the light of his philosophy of history. However much he gives the standard account of Jesus as a great moral teacher and an archetype of that which is already present to reason as its self-given ideal, Kant also finds that in Jesus something *new* happened in history. Jesus not only represented the good principle but initiated its victory into history. Jesus' ability to live in conformity with the moral law can serve as encouragement, can "open the portals of freedom" to those who choose to imitate his disposition.[71] Furthermore, the "victory" of the good principle has a history and a social institution: the church.[72] Thus, an element of narrative or drama is introduced into the description of reason's actualization. Does this mean that reason is dependent upon a power outside of itself, that it must submit to heteronomy (albeit a beneficent one)? Such a conclusion would undermine the whole critical apparatus that Kant had labored over for decades and, hence, was not one he could easily accept. The best he could do was appeal to an analogy with education:

> Christianity's objective is to promote love of the concern for observing one's duty, and in addition it elicits this love, for its founder speaks not as a commander who requires obedience to his *will*, but as a friend of mankind who places in the hearts of his fellow men their own well-understood wills, i.e., the will in accord with which they would themselves freely act.[73]

The Divine Teacher does not compel reason to accept some foreign imperative but invites it to accept as a gift that very nature which is its own inmost essence. To be sure, like any good teacher, divine providence will rejoice when human reason comes of age and ecclesiastical faith approximates ever more closely the religion of reason. But we have not yet arrived at that time. We have not yet fully assimilated our own well-understood wills. For now it seems that just as the Genesis narrative is the only suitable "map" with which reason may understand its "fall" from nature, and just as the most adequate symbolization of providence and its workings on earth is found in the biblical narratives about Job,[74] so too, the person of Jesus and the narratives about him found in Scripture provide an adequate symbol which can represent and *effect* for us that transition from unreason to reason, which reason itself, crippled by the presence of radical evil, is unable to conceive or attain. Kant is here hinting, to put it most radically, at a view in which

> reason is dependent on the contingencies of history and the realities of institutionalization to establish itself and grow as reason. Morality is dependent on divine foundational activity, not just in order to realize itself under empirical conditions, but also in order to arrive at a correct concept of itself. God does not merely give to our wills the power they lack, but also reveals to our reason that which it seeks to understand.[75]

If Kant took these steps, he took them hesitatingly. In Book IV he describes how the church can, and too often does, fall victim to the pervasive temptation to abuse its foundational narratives, to attempt to apply them dogmatically instead of appropriating them for the purposes of practical reason alone. When forced to choose, Kant always returned to his emphasis on the autonomy of reason, as most fully expressed in the ethico-religious tendency, grounded in the second critique. We must base our faith on our morality, not the reverse.[76]

In summary, there is a tension in Kant's answer to the question, What may I hope? On the one hand I may hope that I will do my duty and that God will make up within me what is lacking, as long as I do all that lies in my grasp. On the other hand I may hope for the political progress of the race, continuing the trajectory begun by the promptings of nature. That is, I may hope for something for *us,* for you and for me. In *Religion* Kant opened up the possibility of bridging the gap between the ethico-religious and ethico-juridical by means of an intrahistorical redemption, initiated in the person of Jesus, continued in the church, leading to the crowning of political progress with moral progress. While he tentatively broached this solution, he did not wholeheartedly embrace it, in part because his anthropology, built up in the three critiques, did not allow him to do so.[77]

If this unresolved tension leads to a certain incompletion in Kant's system, it has the virtue of maintaining hope in a live tension, in which each of the two tendencies complements and relativizes the other. Hope is not allowed to be totally interiorized so that it loses its prophetic and political edge, yet neither does it become a totally secularized eschatology, a myth of progress in which history becomes a slaughter-bench for the victims of reason's cunning. Nevertheless, the difficulty in Kant's thought is that the two tendencies are for the most part only juxtaposed. One could take one tendency and ignore the other. The Ritschlians and *Kulturprotestantismus* emphasized the ethico-religious strain in such a way that any politically critical force of Christian hope was lost. The Hegelian attempt, as it developed through the Left Hegelians and Marxism, ended in collapsing the ethico-religious into the ethico-juridical, so that the hopes of the individual (most tragically, of the conquered and submerged victims of history's onward march) were sacrificed. The deeper problem is the lack of an understanding of the subject which can do more than juxtapose these two tendencies, or, differently expressed, could adequately understand reason's involvement in history. This became increasingly apparent as the nineteenth century went on. Beginning at least with Wilhelm Dilthey and his attempt to develop a critique of historical reason, German philosophers sought to remedy this problem.[78] Two generations later, Martin Heidegger addressed the same problem.

This rather lengthy discursus into the philosophy of religion of Immanuel Kant will have been worth the effort to the degree that it provides an intellectual contextualization of Metz's work. Throughout his career Metz accepts the particularly Kantian way of asserting that the goal of history is the coming-to-be of human subjectivity: reason's "coming to itself," coming to maturity (*Mündigkeit*, as Kant calls it). In this approach the "coming to itself" of reason is closely tied to the exercise of freedom as the self-positing of the subject in meaningful and meaning-giving practices. The end and fulfillment of human reason do not escape or negate the conditions of finitude, but, for a properly enlightened reason, these conditions will not appear as alien impositions upon the subject, but as transparent to its own interests, desires, and action. In more Hegelian terms, subjective reason will recognize its own form in the objective materials of its world.[79] The real will turn out to be the rational.

For Kant, God's presence to reason is essential for the realization of this goal—in the limited form of a postulate of practical reason or, more ambitiously, as God's activity is symbolized for reason in the narratives and doctrines of Christianity. Metz will argue this thesis throughout his career, although in different ways. Even more strongly than Kant, he will argue that in the event of Jesus Christ, and through the mediation of the Church, a principle has entered history which enables reason to come into its own, enables human subjects to receive "their own well-understood wills." Christianity is, in this reading, an authentic element (for Metz *the* authentic element) in the history and birth of the Enlightenment.[80]

A MAP OF METZ'S THEOLOGICAL JOURNEY

After recounting his shattering experience in World War II, Metz went on to describe the consequences of this memory for his theology: "A basic form of Christian hope is also determined by this memory. The question 'What dare I hope?' is transformed into the question 'What dare I hope for you and, in the end, also for me?'"[81] Elsewhere he elaborates on this social character:

> Jesus' visions of the Reign of God—of a comprehensive peace among men and women and nature in the presence of God, of a home and a father, of a kingdom of peace, of justice and of reconciliation, of tears wiped away and of the laughter of the children of God—cannot be hoped for with only oneself in view, in some kind of isolated transcendence inward, so to speak. In believing that others can rely on them, in communicating them to others and hoping them "for others," they belong to oneself as well. Only then.[82]

Metz's reference to the question of hope connects us with the Kantian approach(es) to religion outlined above. Metz is explicitly relating himself and his project to what we discussed above as the ethico-juridical trajectory for defining religion, arising out of Kant's philosophy of history. This shift began in the late sixties, as can be seen from a text from 1970. Metz is here discussing the current state of Christian theology in the light of his claim that it has become "too privatized":

> [T]he reception of Kant in systematic theology is quite characteristic [of the situation of modern theology]. It is true that Kant's formal transcendentalism was partially retrieved and discussed, but, not however, his doctrine of the primacy of practical reason, in which the social problematic of freedom explicitly came to the fore. . . . A debate with *this* Kant would mean that for theology not only, and not primarily, Kant's anthropology, but his philosophy of history, would be decisive."[83]

Soon afterward he argued that when Catholic theology took up again the conversation broken off in the late nineteenth century with philosophy it was with the Kant of the first critique, not of the second critique, and not with Kant's philosophy of history.[84] It is with the latter two strains of Kant's thought (and its descendants: namely, for Metz, the Marxist tradition) that Metz believes theology needs to enter into a critical conversation.[85]

When Metz speaks of that theological tradition which has primarily interacted with the Kant's *Critique of Pure Reason*, he means the transcendental theology of Karl Rahner, and, by association, his own early work. This gives us the starting point for Metz's theological journey: the first of the four options listed by Claude Welch for doing theology "after Kant." Taking up Kant's analyses in the first critique, one argues against his strictures on speculative reason with regard to knowing God, in the case of transcendental Thomism by including the intrinsic *dynamism* of reason in the transcendental analysis. This approach concludes that speculative reason *does* have access to God, and on the basis of this access Christian doctrines and practices can be retrieved and reformulated in a way that is both appropriate to Scripture and tradition and credible within the horizon of modernity. Metz's own contribution to this endeavor was to argue for the credibility of the Christian tradition within the horizon of modernity, primarily by contending that that horizon is *itself* already determined by the spirit of Christianity.[86]

Yet he was never fully comfortable with this approach, and this discomfort became rejection in the course of his conversations with Marxists, who represent an almost exclusive concern with the ethico-juridical tradition—the realization of reason in history and society. To be sure, as we shall see, even in his first phase Metz tried to make the transcendental approach more open to the concrete vagaries of history and to tie the actualization of the individual subject more closely to his or her relationship to other human subjects. In my reading, however, Metz abandoned this attempt sometime between 1963 and 1965. He began writing out of the conviction that Kant's dictum concerning the primacy of practical reason in matters of morality and religion had to be taken far more seriously than perhaps even Kant did himself. The theology Metz learned in the fifties would not allow his driving concerns to emerge clearly enough. In the terms of this study, it did not provide conceptual resources to articulate the "mysticism of mourning" or of "suffering unto God" which was now beginning to form more and more decisively his view of the world, of God's presence to that world, and of the mission of the Church in proclaiming and helping actualize that presence.[87]

For these reasons, in his second phase (approximately from 1963 to 1970) Metz abandoned the transcendental tradition and sought out other sources more closely connected with the approach to religion via practical reason, and in particular with the historical traditions which elaborated the ethico-juridical element in Kant. He began speaking of the "end of metaphysics," of its inability to consider the problem of the future and articulate the hope for the future (of all persons) which defines the religious. He begins to speak of praxis: the historical becoming of reason in history. God, present and active in and through Jesus Christ, is still constitutive of the becoming of subjects, but now this dependence is framed in terms of the history of freedom,[88] and the Church is the "institution of critical freedom" which guards and promotes that history.[89]

While this stage in Metz's journey is unified by its shift toward another side of Kant's thought, it is inherently unstable. This is because, as I argued above, there are really two approaches within Kant which begin from some understanding of practical reason and try to argue toward a conception of religion based on the justified hope of that reason. These two approaches (the ethico-religious and ethico-juridical) are juxtaposed in Kant, rather than being systematically interrelated within an anthropology (which, for its part, is restricted to the predominantly atemporal approach of the three critiques). Metz's intuition that it would have to be Kant's philosophy of history rather than Kant's anthropology that would fructify the needed shift shows that he was aware of these limitations. But, could his theology simply prescind from anthropology? The mere juxtaposition or vague conflation that seemed the almost inevitable consequences of using the Kantian legacy lead to the danger of confusion and (not entirely undeserved) misunderstanding.

The criticisms that were leveled against Metz's new political theology at the end of the sixties brought this home. He himself came to see that he had to be able to distinguish more clearly between the two ways of understanding practical reason, and the sorts of praxis associated with them. For example, speaking of his early work, Metz admits:

> As I began my work . . . this differentiation in the concept of praxis between ethical and social praxis was not worked out clearly enough. Consequently, I also took up the teachings of Kant and those of Marx too much at the same level. The statements made in this theology were consequently often purely moral, in the nature of an appeal or an exhortation. Hence they could not be protected against being inserted into widely different evaluatory contexts.[90]

Metz argues that Kant did not make this distinction, and that it only became clear with Marx, who formulated the interdependence of the moral praxis of the individual and the social praxis within which the former is embedded. This is not quite fair to Kant, as we saw. He *did* recognize a social and historical side to practical reason in his philosophy of history. It *is* true, however, that he only very tentatively connected it with his understanding of practical reason developed in the second critique, and that in the final analysis the ethico-religious strain predominated over the ethico-juridical.

Metz was sensitive to the accusation that he was collapsing individual-moral praxis into social praxis, or, in more theological terms, identifying the history of salvation with the history of freedom. Some asserted that his theology as political theology was merely a bad example of a theology of politics.[91] In response, he agreed that while moral and social praxis (corresponding to the ethico-religious and ethico-juridical tendencies, respectively) must be differentiated, and interrelated (as Marx had done), the former must not be collapsed into the latter. Here Metz sides with Kant *against* what he sees as the danger of Marxism:

> Christian praxis as social praxis—even in view of what I have just said about Kant [that Kant did not recognize the dependence of individual

moral praxis on social praxis]—remains *ethically* determined. For the demand that social conditions and constellations of moral action be considered does not intend simply the deciphering of moral praxis as social praxis and the relativization of the moral subject. . . . Out of this moral determination of social praxis of the Christian it follows that this praxis must not lead to the abstract or violent negation of the individual.[92]

The moral action of the individual, and the hopes involved therein, cannot be collapsed into the history of the species. In terms of my presentation of the Kantian legacy, Metz recognized that in his early attempts the two strands of Kant's understanding of practical reason and religion were not sufficiently distinguished and interrelated. How can one overcome the dangers of a mere juxtaposition of these two sides of human praxis? What is needed is an anthropology that can overcome the limitations of Kant's, that is, one that expresses the unity in difference of the individual-moral and the social-political sides of human being. Thus, immediately after his reflections on praxis, from which I took the previous two citations, Metz moves on to define political theology as political theology *of the subject*.

> If political theology as practical fundamental theology would avoid the danger of conceiving of its constitutive praxis divorced from the subject *it must elaborate itself as a theology of the subject.* This must be more closely illuminated and made more precise, since political theology is usually accused of obscuring "the subject" in favor of history and society, and because those theologies which political theology criticizes are, for their part, explicitly theologies of the subject (transcendental, existential, personalist, paradoxical-dialectical, or what have you).[93] (Emphasis added.)

Metz is still concerned with the "turn to the subject," but is now also conscious of the need to elaborate an understanding of the subject which would emphasize the social and political dimensions of Christian hope (Kant's ethico-juridical strand) without sacrificing the individual subject (Kant's ethico-religious strand). Laying out this anthropology is the crucial task of the last section of *Faith in History and Society*, "Categories," in which Metz presents his new understanding of the subject in terms of the categories (or, as I shall argue below, *existentialia*) of memory, solidarity, and narrative.

The most important lines of Metz's argument were in place at this point. It required further rounding out in terms of issues and concerns that had been with Metz's thought from the very beginning, and which are also a part of the Kantian approach to religion, particularly from the ethico-juridical strand, as I described it above: What is the relationship of God and human reason, by which the presence of the former is constitutive for the latter? Put somewhat differently, what is the relationship between Christianity and Enlightenment (topics covered earlier under the rubric of Metz's secularization thesis)? In what way is Christianity, while perhaps no longer "credible" within the horizon of modernity, nevertheless essential to modernity's creative continuation? Furthermore, one must not underestimate the impact on Metz's work of new experiences in the last decade of his work: most powerfully his trips to Latin America. Finally, as he had at this point developed the concepts to articulate it, Metz now became explicit about the kind of spirituality that was proper to the "mystical-political" correlation which is constitutive of Christianity. The spiritual force which had been moving his thought all along now emerged into full articulacy.

So we have three phases: in the first (1950–63) Metz operated (but increasingly "uncomfortably") within the framework of transcendental Thomism, with its primary reference to Kant's first critique. During his second phase (1963–70), unsatisfied with his attempts to bend transcendental Thomism to his own purposes, Metz moved to the "primacy of practical reason," that is, into a conversation with the tradition rooted in Kant's second critique and philosophy of history. But, this period was characterized by an unstable equilibrium, and Metz was forced to try to resolve this instability by developing a revised anthropology which could hold together the tensively juxtaposed elements of Kant's legacy, as it came down to him in the history of German thought. The major lines of this anthropology were laid down with the publication of *Glaube in Geschichte und Gesellschaft* in 1977, but Metz would continue to round out his approach, to carry through some of its consequences, to ground it more securely within the concerns and thinking of his past career, and to apply it within the constellation of his life as a contemporary German, Roman Catholic theologian.[94]

This preliminary survey has been executed with the intention of introducing us to this fascinating, at times frustrating, thinker. In addition, it has attempted to identify that conceptual strand best suited for tracing both continuities and discontinuities in Metz's thought: the concept of the subject and the turn to the subject in theology. Finally, it has alerted us to those issues where Metz's uneasiness is most focused, an uneasiness that kept him continually questing for conceptual resources and argumentative strategies adequate for them. His uneasiness focused on how adequately to understand human involvement in history and society, particularly in a history and society permeated with ambiguity and crucified by suffering. This uneasiness led him to some startling places and to draw on some novel resources—and most important (and most germane for this study) were the resources of apocalyptic spirituality. The purpose of the next three chapters is to trace out in greater detail his intellectual journey, paying particular attention to the central concern with the subject and the points of greatest uneasiness along the way. This will not only provide a more detailed warrant for the provisional characterization offered above but will put us in a position to explore the constitutive role of spirituality in Metz's development.

3

METZ AND THE
TRANSCENDENTAL METHOD

During the fifties, and about halfway through the next decade, Metz worked within the paradigm of transcendental Thomism and ended up being one of the most important of Karl Rahner's first students. It is essential not to underestimate the impact of this period on Metz's thought. A set of essential concepts and categories emerged that would continue to determine the shape and content of his thought. Furthermore, the transcendental method has a general form of argumentation, grounded in certain ontological and anthropological assumptions, which determines the *way* that Metz will argue and develop his thought, even after the break in the nineteen-sixties. In particular, it is during these years that Metz appropriated the turn to the subject, the insistence that theology should be realized and made relevant within the context of modernity on the basis of a carefully worked out understanding of the structure and activities of the human subject as a "hearer" of the word of revelation. As I argued above, it is this turn to the subject that provides the most adequate matrix against which to measure the continuities, as well as the shifts and interruptions, in Metz's four decades of intellectual work.

There are a host of issues which arise from a consideration of this period, including the background and validity of the transcendental method in general, the use made of Heidegger (both the "early" and the "later" Heidegger) by Christian theology, and the precise relationship between Metz's thought and Rahner's (an issue that extends beyond this period). Some of them have been adequately covered elsewhere.[1] The last issue, as I claimed above, has not yet been fully treated. It will obviously be touched on here, and the results of this chapter will serve as an important prelude for an adequate rendering of the relationship between Rahner and Metz, which will be broached in the final chapter.

The work of this chapter is primarily to outline the fundamentals of Metz's theological anthropology as it emerged in dialogue with Martin Heidegger and Karl Rahner. This includes identifying specific concerns of Metz: the "thought-form" of Christian theology, the relationship between Christianity and modernity, and the derivative relation of theology to philosophy. These are concerns which will never leave Metz. It is also both necessary and possible to identify those "stress-points" in Metz's appropriation of the transcendental method, those places where Metz tried to modify and stretch it (e.g., in his editorial reworking of *Hörer des Wortes*). These do not signal a full-fledged break with the transcendental approach but rather a discomfort within it which led to a decisive break only in the sixties. In working through these tasks I will establish the broader matrix within which I will interpret Metz's later work, a matrix that will prove indispensable for demonstrating both the change and the continuity in his thought. First I shall consider Metz's encounter with Heidegger's thought. In this section I shall also articulate Metz's understanding of the relationship between philosophy and theology, an understanding which continues virtually unchanged to the present day. Second, I shall look at Metz's collaboration with Karl Rahner: specifically, his editing of Rahner's two fundamental works on the metaphysics of knowledge and on theological anthropology. Third, I shall consider Metz's own contribution to the project of transcendental Thomism, as found in *Christliche Anthropozentrik* and in other related articles from the period from about 1957 to 1963. This will yield Metz's own approach to theological anthropology in terms of the concerns listed above. Then in the final section I shall summarize Metz's appropriation of transcendental method, both the essential structure that endures in his thought and his growing reservations about this method's ability to articulate human historicity and sociality. This will provide a jumping off point for the next chapter, which will detail the "interruption" of Metz's theological career.

METZ AND HEIDEGGER

Metz wrote his 1952 doctoral dissertation on Heidegger's "destruction" of metaphysics. A year later a condensed version of this work appeared in the journal *Scholastik:* "Heidegger und das Problem der Metaphysik."[2] Heidegger's attack on traditional metaphysics is well known.[3]

Insofar as traditional metaphysics carried on its investigation by investigating entities (*Seinden*), with conceptualities and logic appropriate to entities, it covered over the underlying being (*Sein*) of those entities, which is the ground on the basis of which alone these entities can be encountered by us as entities. As this covering over became more and more obdurate in the course of the history of Western philosophy, the underlying being of entities became more and more hidden, until metaphysics disintegrated into nihilism. This culminating point, according to Heidegger, was reached in Nietzsche. What is needed now is an overcoming of metaphysics and philosophy with their "willful manipulating of beings," so that that thinking which "lets being be" can come to the fore.[4]

Metz's response to this critique is typical of the transcendental Thomists.[5] This strategy argues the superiority of a metaphysics of knowledge, grounded in the *ens/esse* distinction of Thomas Aquinas, over the phenomenological ontology of Heidegger. Insofar as modern philosophy has failed to avail itself of this powerful conceptual apparatus, it has fallen back on understandings of human knowing, and the being which correlates with it, that are not adequate for the task at hand:

> Heidegger shares with Kant and Hegel the tacit presupposition that the truth of being is achieved *only* in the mode of *immediacy*. Since this strict immediacy is not available to the human ratio, Heidegger (along with Kant) will not allow that the intellective-abstractive concept could be the medium for the ontological identity of thinking and what is thought, between subject and object. . . . Because of this he seeks (along with Hegel) to "experience" positively the immediacy of being, beyond any conceptual-intentional mediation, in order to escape the Kantian reduction of the problem of truth to the level of an idealistically thought subjectivity of the transcendental subject. This attempt . . . does not overcome Kant's reduction, rather it radicalizes it.[6]

In point of fact, on this view, a careful transcendental analysis of human knowing shows more clearly and consistently that for humans the truth of being *is* known truly intellectually-conceptually, but known only mediately and analogically. Ontological truth cannot be achieved apart from ontic truth. Here the transcendental Thomists retrieve Thomas's epistemological dictum concerning the *conversio ad phantasma*. There is no knowing without a turning to the sensible image; nevertheless, through transcendental deduction the "coknown" in this knowing can be teased out—namely, that infinite horizon of being which is not exhausted by any entity or set of entities, and must be present to the knower if entities are to be known at all. A doctrine of the analogies of being, truth, and unity completes this system. Such a system provides an explanation of the character of the subjective pole of knowing (the human knower, *Dasein*) in relation to the objective pole of knowing (entities), in terms of the horizon of being which transcends and includes both poles. Furthermore, it does so without collapsing the subjective into the objective, or vice versa, and without obviating the distinction between the level of entities on the one hand (the ontic) which is determined by polarities (e.g., subject and object, the ideal and the real), and the transcendental level of being (the ontological) on the other.

Metz does not provide the concrete details of such a derivation, although he does refer the reader to the opening chapters of Rahner's *Hörer des Wortes,* in which Rahner summarizes his derivation of this position as presented in *Geist in Welt.*[7] Metz takes this derivation for granted. In any event, the similarities with the transcendental Thomist approach are clear. One criticizes modernity from Descartes on because its cognitive theory, and the metaphysics (or denial of metaphysics) that stems from it, are inadequate. The argument is that one can do better what modern philosophy has attempted to do in its turn to the subject by making use of the philosophical tools (properly transformed) of Thomism.[8]

Thus, Metz claims that the very ontological difference upon which Heidegger seeks to build his system cannot be sustained with the means that he utilizes (transcendental phenomenology). While seeking the ontological level of being as such, Heidegger never really escapes the level of Dasein. His phenomenological ontology is really a regional ontology of Dasein which may provide valuable insights into the being of Dasein, but cannot be generalized to being as such.[9] A monistic (rather than analogical) understanding of knowing leads to a monistic (rather than analogical) understanding of being, which ends up being an understanding of strictly *human* being. To be sure, Metz, with the other transcendental Thomists, agrees that the human, Dasein, is the place to begin in one's investigation of being. It is the fact that humans question being, that being is an issue for them, that it *means* for them, that makes them, among all entities, the privileged starting point. But, only a proper understanding of the dynamism of human knowing, operating within the analogical structure of being as a whole, can hope to provide a (necessarily mediated and analogical) understanding of being as such.

In a footnote Metz voices a concern that will become increasingly important to him in the following decade. He denies Heidegger's assertion that being as such is grounded in temporality, arguing that this claim is based upon an unwarranted application of the structure of being appropriate to human beings to being as such. But even within the human realm Metz is worried about how Heidegger's understanding of the temporality of Dasein relates to concrete history. Metz explains Heidegger's understanding of the temporality of Dasein, and then adds that "the more specific connections [between the ontological temporality of truth and being and ontic history] have remained up to this point unexplained, so that *a curious unhistoricity* [Ungeschichtlichkeit], *and artificiality* adheres to Heidegger's concept of history" (emphasis in the original).[10] Here emerges for the first time one of the leitmotifs of Metz's thought: to what degree does a theoretically derived concept of humans' involvement in history really direct them to the concrete events of history?

Metz never returned to a broad philosophical critique of the ontological underpinnings of Heidegger's system. He was, however, impressed enough with the potentialities of Heidegger's existential analytic, as a regional ontology of Dasein, to continue its critical appropriation. After he joined the first circle of students forming around Karl Rahner, Metz took up Heidegger's terminology much more explicitly than Rahner did, now from an explicitly theological standpoint.[11] This can be seen in one of the two theological encyclopedias which Rahner edited, the *Lexicon für Theologie und Kirche*, in which Metz contributed articles on *Gespräch* (dialogue), *Mitsein* (being-with), *Subjekt*, and *Befindlichkeit* (state-of-mind), in all of which he directly engaged the Heideggerian usage of these terms.[12]

A good summary of Metz's later stance toward Heidegger and existential philosophy, in which several key themes in Metz's thought emerge, can be found in an article he wrote on the relationship between philosophy and theology: "Theologische und Metaphysische Ordnung."[13] Metz begins from a theological perspective, assuming the reality of revelation and the validity of theology.[14] Given this, he asks how one can integrate metaphysics and theology, both of which give foundational interpretations of the one, integral person in his or her entirety, but from very different perspectives? Metaphysics is the conceptually illuminated self-understanding of the person achieved through a transcendental analysis of human being. Theology is the reflexively interpreted and secured self-understanding of the person, achieved by reflection on God's revelation, which comes to us in history.[15] The first is reflection on the *transcendental* (e.g., a priori) foundation of humans, the second is reflection on the *transcendent* (that is, transmundane or sacred) foundation of human being. Given these definitions (which, let it be noted, are both framed in the philosophical context of the turn to the subject), the question of the relationship between philosophy and theology hinges on finding a perspective from which both of these horizons of human self-interpretation become visible without collapsing one into the other.

For Metz the vantage point must be that of history. Indeed only because they are historical can human beings be such that they are susceptible to both orders at once. Conversely, because human beings are so constituted as to be the "point of intersection" between these two orders they are unique among created entities. This yields Metz's definition of Dasein:

> [Dasein] describes the specific Being of the human as the basis of a possible reconciliation of the two orders, the metaphysical and the theological. It is selected as the name for the specific interlinking of the transcendental and historical self-constitution (becoming-a-person [*Mensch-Werdung*]) of persons, which makes it possible that the human person is radically and unavoidably affected by a reality which comes to him historically (and is thus, in this sense, contingent).[16]

We note first that throughout this article Metz takes up and uses the Heideggerian title for human being: Dasein. His starting point, though, is not this entity's relation to Being, but rather its unique and paradoxical character according to which it is necessarily constituted in an ontological order which is accessible by transcendental deduction *but also has a history* which is constitutive for it, and cannot be avoided or absorbed into the former order. It is worth recalling our brief outline of Metz's career in terms of the Kantian problematic. There we saw that Kant tentatively broached the possibility of such a connection between the transcendental and historical constitution of human being in his philosophy of religion, but that his anthropology remained firmly rooted in the transcendental order. In light of that analysis it is evident that Metz is *starting out* with an anthropology that has (at least as a desideratum) a definition of human being such that it includes both the transcendental and the historical.

Given such an understanding of the human person, metaphysics can and should bring to light in a transcendental or a priori analysis the structural features of Dasein according to which it is necessarily open to and grounded in historical facticity. Metaphysics reveals that human being is always "in advance of itself." Whenever a person tries to ascertain in critical reflection the specific possibilities of his being, as soon as he tries to come to an understanding of himself that is truly his own (*eigentlich:* authentic), he will find that he has always taken up ground prior to any such action of self-reflection. This ground is the historical situation in which a person always finds herself, from which she can never extricate herself in order to find some realm of "pure" subjectivity, free of heteronomous influences.[17]

Of course, this sounds very Heideggerian. How does this analysis stand with regard to the Heideggerian existential anthropology? Of the three existentialia of Heidegger's approach, the one that grounds the involvement of Dasein in facticity is *Befindlichkeit*.[18] This existential of Dasein reveals that the world has already come to mean, is "lit up" or "cleared" (*gelichtet*) in a certain way, for Dasein prior to its own understanding projection of the meaning of its Being-in-the-world. One's existence can never become fully transparent to one's own choices, the result of one's own understanding and freedom. It has already been opened up in ways which can never be exhaustively determined, but which define and limit the ways in which the world has possibilities and is meaningful.

For Heidegger the consequence of this primordial existential structure of human being is that we can never fully make good on the exigency of having our being as our "ownmost," which exigency comes from our very Being as Dasein. We are continually "guilty." We can never fully take up our own existence as our own, except by a sort of limit-situation: the paradoxical stance of resolute "being-toward-death," in which we take up and project possibilities of our being while resolutely refusing to take up as absolute any particular possibility that is given. The only access to authentic existence lies in recognizing that our existence is groundless, that we are the "null basis of a nullity."[19]

This fact, that the most authentic possibility of Dasein is its possibility not to be at all, is what is to be appropriated and realized in its "being-toward-death."

For Metz this argument represents an invalid extension of the existential analytic outside of its proper realm. As we saw above, he agrees that "Dasein has already taken up a ground [Grund] to its existence even as it tries to secure [vergewissern] that ground in thought."[20] It cannot stand outside of its situation and rationally think through and decide upon the facticity of its situation; rather, that situation is already given to it, and is already internal to its free ratiocination and decision in such a way that it can never be disentangled from them so as to constitute some point of "pure subjectivity." But what this implies for Dasein is that it must turn acceptingly to history. Dasein must find some way of taking up the ground which is given to it (whether it will or no) as constitutive of it, rather than holding back from history as nothing but the domain of threatening heteronomy. For this necessary task metaphysics is of no help. It "can be existential philosophy, but not an authentic philosophy of existence."[21] It can demonstrate the fact that we are grounded in a history that is prior to and unavailable to our self-possession in reflection and decision. It can also illuminate what ground we have in fact, at this moment in history, taken up. It can show us the way that being and the world have come to mean for us, the horizon of meaning within which alone any possibility for the future can appear to us. But it cannot of itself provide the warrant to appropriate this horizon (even in the ironic mode of a "resolute being-toward-death" that Heidegger advocates) authentically as our own. The latter requires a turning to history as the transcendent (rather than transcendental) source of our being; theologically expressed, it requires turning to history as the place of a possible revelation. This turning is a religious act, and the science that follows upon that turning and interprets that revelation to us, if it comes, is theology. Thus, the metaphysical act of Dasein is one in which its ground is illuminated for it; the religious act is one in which Dasein actually takes up and accepts that ground. Metaphysics gives way to theology:

> It is therefore not only legitimate but unavoidable that as it strives for a reflective self-securing [Selbstvergewisserung] Dasein should start from an insight which is spontaneously entrusted to it, from a ground

to its Dasein that is immediately and inextricably realized within its own freely actualized existence, a ground which it confronts in a different mode from that of an intellectuality that is or could be exhaustively reflected upon.[22]

From this analysis Metz derives three tasks for the philosopher. The first has the character of a transcendental analysis and is carried on in relative autonomy with regard to theology. The other two are hermeneutical disciplines and stand more directly in the service of the theologian. The first, "the constitutive function of philosophy," is to demonstrate the existential involvement of Dasein in history. In this function philosophy shows *that* we are grounded in a world and history that are never fully available to our reflective and volitional self-disposition. The second, "cathartic function" of philosophy articulates the horizon of understanding in terms of which any event of existential import for human being must be interpreted. This task shows *what* ground we have, in fact, already taken up, *how* the world and history are lit up for us, mean for us, in a certain way prior to any act of understanding or volition. These two tasks open up the necessity and possibility of a religious act of faith in which we hear a word entrusted to us within history by a loving, self-manifesting God. Revelation and theology step in. But this word of revelation, if it is to be existentially meaningful to us, must come to expression in terms of the world and history within which any fact from the past or possibility for the future can mean for us at all. The "maieutic function" of philosophy assists theology in this task: to show that the individual doctrines and symbols of Christianity, properly construed, do disclose themselves as existentially significant for human being, and do express that one history of the revelation of our transcendent origin which is constitutive of and normative for Dasein.[23]

The danger and temptation of metaphysics is that it may refuse to give way. It may itself try to ground human existence out of its own resources, without reference to any transcendent reality. Metz identifies two great modern examples of this tendency. The first is Hegel's attempt to show that the history which is constitutive of Dasein is, in the final analysis, nothing other than the history of reason. Since the history of reason is at essence the history of human becoming, human reason *can* finally completely penetrate the concrete situatedness of our being in the world and in history and reduce them without remainder to their concepts. Philosophy swallows up theology.

The other modern strategy tries to absolutize the groundlessness of human existence as it is revealed by existential analysis, to make that groundlessness *itself* into the ground of human existence. No historical ground is to be sought or accepted, because the meaning of our existence is to have no ground. Metz's objection to this view is that it removes humans from history: "[This philosophy] at first understood itself (with Kierkegaard) as a protest against the gnosis of Dasein [in Hegel's system] and now has closed itself up in its (necessarily formal) analytic of Dasein, without setting humans free for a genuine historical encounter."[24]

These attempts to achieve a theoretical grounding of Dasein without turning to a concrete, contingent reality that is accessible to us only a posteriori in history, are forms of what Metz defines as "mythology." Philosophies which attempt this betray their essence:

> [Such a] philosophy, which understands itself most essentially as the most radical critic of any mythology, would become the most catastrophic form of mythological thinking, for finally mythology is rooted in the attempt by humans to produce out of their own means a substantive answer to that fundamental question of their *Dasein*, which cannot be made transparent to them but yet also cannot be avoided. Such mythology degrades all history into mere anthropophany, in which the human appears to itself eternally and without salvation.[25]

This comment illuminates the one that Metz had made earlier in his Heidegger dissertation about Heidegger's concept of historicity. There he voiced the suspicion that this concept is curiously *un*historical. Parsing this statement with his later comments on "mythological" philosophies, we see that his concern is that Heidegger's philosophy never releases human being into history to take up any one specific historical reality seriously as constitutive of its own existence. One might articulate the problem in this way: it is true that Heidegger's concept of historicity denies to us any ahistorical viewpoint from which we could render our existence fully transparent to ourselves. But the fact that our being (as historical) is neither rationally transparent to us nor fully available to our free and responsible self-becoming leads in Heidegger's thought to a *disengagement* from any one particular reality in history as fundamentally constitutive of who I am, as a reality to which I am irrevocably committed and responsible. My historicity does not commit me to history, but to my own becoming in history. What I necessarily affirm is not the reality of *a* history, with the substantive claims it makes upon me. Rather, I affirm my historicity, as an irreducible formal element of my projection of possibilities into the future.

To be sure, this historicity grounds and "needs" the concrete events of history, the way a factory production line needs raw materials if it is to create its products. But, does any one particular history matter more than another in my self-production? Historicity is given eternally, regardless of the particular ontic history for which it serves as the ontological ground. Could one event or tradition within history make normative claims on me, above and beyond constituting the inevitable facticity within which I happen to be embedded? If so, what existential of human being could make that normativity possible?

Such a stance is unacceptable for a Christian theologian who wishes to argue for the normative and constitutive significance of one particular history—that of the self-revelation of God, culminating in the life, death, and resurrection of Jesus the Christ. But recent debates over the "Heidegger case" have raised the suspicion of dangerous abstractness on political-philosophical grounds, particularly when the historicity of Dasein had been transposed in the later Heidegger into the history of Being. The "threats" of history become the threats to the openness of Being rather than the catastrophes of concrete, ontic history. They are countered not by responsible action, taking up within history the life-threatening dangers to humans, but rather by true, meditative thinking, which lets Being be.[26] Richard Bernstein voices the growing uneasiness with this view (if not outright condemnation of it) in this way:

> But this sort of thinking is what Habermas has called "abstraction via essentialization" where "the history of being is thus disconnected from political and historical events" whether they be extermination of Jews or the threat of nuclear annihilation. None of this is *essential.* "Under the leveling gaze of the philosopher of Being even the extermination of Jews seems merely an event equivalent to many others."[27]

This is not the place for a more exhaustive critique of Heidegger's position. What I have tried to show here is Metz's uneasiness with Heidegger's existential approach to articulating our involvement in history.

In terms of Metz's biography, and the scheme for his career that I suggested in chapter 2, one can put the issue this way: is Heidegger's philosophy adequate for understanding the catastrophic, disruptive meaning of history for the Germans of Metz's generation in general, and for his own personal history in particular? Soon after the war, many of Metz's generation (including Habermas) judged this philosophy inadequate, and in his struggles with Heideggerian historicity I believe that we can find, similarly, a growing uneasiness in Metz.

His response at this stage still stands within the transcendental approach. He concedes that Dasein "is indeed characterized ontologically by the fact that it takes up a stance toward itself."[28] The fact that humans take up a relationship to themselves, that their Being is an issue for them, is still important. But this understanding of the human, which characterizes the Heideggerian approach, is not the last word. The metaphysical order remains valid, and metaphysical or transcendental reflection remains important for bringing to light the "problematicality" of human existence, as well as for articulating the horizon of human understanding of self and being in terms of which any possible event of existential significance to human being must be interpreted. But if it is not to fall victim to a fatally abstract "theoretization" of human existence, metaphysics must overcome itself and be superseded by theology, which interprets and articulates the contingent but constitutive historical revelation of God. Only by lovingly, obediently taking up this one particular history, can Dasein complete and fulfill its own being. Reason has a history (is a history). But this is not a problem of reason that reason can solve. It is a problem which can only be embraced by a religious act, for which reason can prepare, and upon which it can subsequently reflect.

This does not require a *sacrificium intellectus*; quite the opposite. In the final section of this article Metz argues that metaphysics has been set free for its proper task—the conceptually illuminated understanding of the person through transcendental analysis—precisely because the social-historical situation within which it matured is marked by the Logos of Christianity. More specifically, since in the incarnation the divine does not absorb or overwhelm the human, neither in the intellectual sphere of Dasein's existence—insofar as it is true to the originary event of the incarnation of the Logos—will the word of revelation absorb or overwhelm the autonomy and necessity of our own self-reflection.[29] In this sense modernity and modern philosophy have not developed against the spirit of Christianity, properly understood, but out of and because of it. This does not mean that modernity is to be uncritically affirmed. It goes wrong when it fails to recognize its Christian heritage. It is precisely by accepting its mission to reflect with all rigor on the horizon of human self-understanding which has been opened up by revelation that metaphysics realizes its own relative autonomy. Then it can, to use Kant's words, receive its own well-understood will.

This historical argument about the nature and lineage of modern philosophy is a crucial part of Metz's thought during this period, for reasons that will become apparent when we consider his relationship to Karl Rahner. It is also the subject of a book-length treatment, *Christliche Anthropozentrik*, and will bear closer examination later. For the moment, let us summarize what Metz takes from Heidegger and what he criticizes. First, he accepts the general transcendental approach of Heidegger, grounded in a distinction between the ontological and ontic levels of analysis and a view of the human being as the privileged entity with which to begin ontology, because her being is an issue for her. Second, while he rejects Heidegger's more ambitious claim that being itself is temporal, he does agree that human being is not eternal and timeless, but has a history that is existentially determinative for it. However, while the formalisms of philosophical argument are to be sought among the Greeks, the epochal events which set them free and allowed them to attain their fullest development are not to be sought there, but in the history of Jewish and Christian revelation. This is an insight that will endure, as we shall see in subsequent chapters. In his subsequent reflections Metz will almost always frame his discussion of any philosophical or theological concept in terms of the difference between the given concept under the horizon of Greek thought and that of biblical thought. The latter horizon will always be the decisive one, because it originates in the decisive history of God's revelatory deeds and word.

Metz criticizes Heidegger for absolutizing the existential analytic. According to Metz, Heidegger can never escape the limits of human being; he finally remains trapped in a regional, indeed *ontic*, phenomenology of human being, which was precisely what he intended to escape.[30] Furthermore, his existential analysis of Dasein, for all of its emphasis on historicity, never really brings human being into a decisive encounter with a concrete history that is determinative for humans, to the very core of their being. This is because since it does not recognize its own limits, it will not cede ground to the science which reflects precisely upon the existentially determinative character for us of *one particular* history—the science of theology. Consequently, he does not overcome the dichotomies of Kant but radicalizes them. Heidegger's existential analysis, a particular version of the anthropological turn, is valid for Metz only if it does not close in on itself but serves as a prolegomenon, clearing the horizon of human being for that *religious* act in which Dasein is not only aware of its ground in history (a ground that is not fully at its own disposal, either cognitively or volitionally), but obediently and lovingly takes up that ground, commits itself to the history in which it finds itself.

We have seen that Metz is very early operating with a definition of the subject which straddles the transcendental and the historical, that he begins with the anthropology which Kant very hesitantly suggested toward the end of his career. Metz criticized Heidegger's attempt to "include" history within the existential constitution of Dasein. But has he, for his part, succeeded in doing anything more than juxtaposing these two elements? In the essay on philosophy and theology the primary justification for such an anthropology is a theological one: without such an anthropology theology and philosophy cannot be adequately interrelated. Obviously, a philosopher without theological commitments (like Heidegger), or a theologian without philosophical commitments (like Barth) would not find this argument particularly convincing.

He does press the argument, at least against Heidegger, that the concept of historicity is flawed. In a reproach that hearkens back to Kierkegaard's against Hegel, Metz accuses Heidegger of "theoretizing" human existence, of forgetting about the existing individual. He also suggests the historical argument that philosophy (as practiced in modernity) gained its autonomy as a result of concrete events within the history of Christianity, and that it denies this provenance only at its own peril.

All of this is only hinted at. How is Metz to move beyond a mere juxtaposition of the transcendental-atemporal and the historical-temporal, given the serious reservations he has voiced with regard to the only concept for bridging the two at his disposal at this point—that of historicity? This problem sets an agenda for this period of Metz's thought. He tried to develop a more positive anthropology, which would move beyond the limitations of Heidegger by making use of concepts and themes from Aquinas, in particular, embodiedness,[31] concupiscence, and integrity. The historical claims, only hinted at in Part III of the article we have considered here, are elaborated in the only extended argument of this period: *Christliche Anthropozentrik*. Before moving to these aspects of his thought, though, we must turn to the figure who was far more influential on Metz than Heidegger: Karl Rahner.

METZ'S COLLABORATION WITH KARL RAHNER

Having completed his work in philosophy, Metz joined the first circle of graduate students that gathered around Karl Rahner at Innsbruck in the mid-fifties. In the years that followed Metz became a close friend and collaborator of Rahner's. Metz has always praised Rahner's theology and attributes to its author all that is best in his own.[32] This relationship is without doubt the most important in Metz's intellectual biography, but, although I shall return to it in the final chapter, I will not attempt an exhaustive evaluation here. My purpose in this section is to outline Rahner's theological anthropology, as Metz appropriated it in the late fifties, and then to outline Metz's reservations with regard to this system, reservations that would eventually lead to a radical shift in Metz's own career when he left Innsbruck to take up his chair in dogmatic theology at Münster.

We have already met transcendental method as the route over which a number of Catholic theologians, working from neo-Thomism, made their way into modernity.[33] Karl Rahner is perhaps the most well known practitioner of this approach.[34] In his appropriation of modernity's turn to the subject he attempted a creative and critical *Auseinandersetzung* of Thomas Aquinas and the tradition of German Idealism, especially as found in Kant, Schelling, Hegel, and Heidegger. The essential structure of the transcendental method has two complementary moments: *reductio* and *deductio*. In the first, one begins from a constitutive realm of human action (e.g., the act of questioning or knowing) and determines the conditions under which alone that action could be possible. In the second moment these "conditions of possibility" serve as a new starting point from which one deduces a heuristic framework within which the realm of human action in question, as well as the realm of its objects (e.g., the objects of questioning and knowing) can be more richly interpreted.

Rahner defines his version of this method by asserting that "dogmatic theology must be theological anthropology and that such an 'anthropocentric' view is necessary and fruitful."[35] In his description of transcendental method we can detect the essential moments of *reductio* and *deductio*:

> If one wishes to pursue dogmatics as transcendental anthropology, it means that whenever one is confronted with an object of dogma, one inquires into the conditions necessary for it to be known by the theological subject, ascertaining that the *a priori* conditions are satisfied, and showing that they imply and express something about the object, the mode, method and limits of knowing it.[36]

A fundamental axiom of this approach, which it shares with modern philosophy from Kant to Heidegger, is the interrelatedness of knowing and being and the primacy of the former in gaining access to the latter. Only a careful inquiry into human knowing is able to ground metaphysical statements. For Rahner such an inquiry is also an indispensable part of making theistic claims intelligible and of interpreting the significance of revelation (thus grounding theology, as the science of methodological reflection on revelation). His first two books, *Geist in Welt* and *Hörer des Wortes* take up this task.[37] Before considering Metz's reservations concerning this approach, and the modifications that he made in editing them for republication, I shall present in summary fashion some of its important results.[38]

The task of *Geist in Welt* consists in "unfolding the moments of human knowing as a dialectical experience of relationship to the world and to the 'beyond' of the world, being."[39] The fundamental presupposition of this work is that being and knowing are primordially unified as self-presence (*Bei-sich-sein*).[40] Thomas's analogy of being is interpreted according to the degree of an entity's self-presence, with God occupying the place of the entity of absolute self-presence, which grounds the limited self-presence—hence the limited unity of knowing and being—in finite entities. In human being and knowing the original self-presence is unthematic and emerges only in and through the discrete, spatio-temporally dispersed acts of discursive intellection and volition.[41] But, conversely, it is the original self-presence that makes those acts of knowing and willing possible. A careful reflection on human knowing shows it to be a dialectical presence to self in and through presence to the other. Human presence to the other is first a presence in and through sensibility to objects of the material world. But if the other is to become an object for me, distinct from me, then I must return to myself from my immersion in the other achieved in sensibility. This return is the task of intellect. Intellect and sensibility together form a dynamic and dialectical unity-in-difference which is only possible because intellect is always already "beyond" any one object of knowledge. It is always already present to another "other" (but in this case *not* a thematizable object): the unlimited fullness of being as such. Thus, the horizon and term of human knowing, being as such, is always already present, unthematically and nonobjectively, to the human knower. And this we call God.[42] This unthematic presence to and transcendence toward God (the horizon of being) is what Rahner intends when he characterizes the human person as "spirit."

We are, however, spirit *in world*. Echoing Kant's famous dictum about blind intuitions and empty concepts, Rahner insists that presence to self and God is available to us only in and through our concrete, spatio-temporally dispersed acts of knowing and willing, along with the discursive words and images which are essential for these acts.[43] Echoing Heidegger's formulation of the dialectically related luminosity and hiddenness of being, Rahner asserts that the ground and horizon of being is present to us only as something about which we can (and must) inquire. It is revealed and coaffirmed, yet withdraws itself and remains mysterious, in all our acts of knowing and willing. As spirit in world, a dynamic unity-in-difference of spirit and matter, we must turn to the spatio-temporal world in order to realize our nature, in order to allow the encounter with the ground and horizon of our being.

In his second book, *Hörer des Wortes*, Rahner applies his method to revelation. The question is, what are the necessary a priori conditions that must obtain if human beings are existentially constituted as hearers of a possible, free word of revelation? He begins again from the question of being, but now he breaks the question down into three parts. First, he asserts that the question of being is about being (*Sein*), not about entities (*seinden*), again following Heidegger. In analyzing this question (*HdW2*, chaps. 3–5) he recapitulates much of the analysis of *Geist in Welt*. Being means self-presence: a unity of knowing and being. A careful analysis of human knowing shows that humans are characterized by an absolute openness to being as such, and so are spirit. They are already opened up toward a possible word of revelation, meaning the self-manifestation of this source and horizon of being, at the very center of their being as spirit.

Second, the question of being has to be asked (chaps. 6–8). We do not have at our disposal an intuition of being; our way to being (which, recall, is the way to self-realization) is through questioning. To be sure, being is luminous (*gelichtet*) to us as spirit, and we affirm it in every finite judgment and action, but our openness to this luminosity does not come from a direct "vision" of being but from an existential imperative that "the human being *be what he is:* one who always already affirms the openness to question (*Fragbarkeit*) and luminosity of being in the question and despite the problematicality (*Fraglichkeit*) of being for human being" (empasis added).[44] Will, the will to "be what I am," is an inner moment of knowledge. But my own being and acting are contingent. How can a *contingent* act provide access to and justify a *necessary* affirmation of being? Only if I accept and affirm my own existence as posited by an absolute will that is both free and loving. It must be a will because will is that faculty which makes what is merely possible (the contingent) into what is necessary. This will must posit freely or else the contingency of my being is not explained. It has the character of love because phenomenologically love is that stance toward the other which accepts and posits the other in its otherness. If follows from this transcendental analysis that the infinite horizon of being, which we name God, is present to us as *person*.[45] How can I become present to that will, penetrate it so that its act of positing becomes luminous for me as well, and consequently that the hidden necessity characterizing any free action becomes the ground for my own affirmation of being? Only by participating in and ratifying (*nachvollziehen*) its loving action—in this case its action of lovingly positing me and my world. I accept and affirm my own existence. I become a person.

This is the basis upon which Rahner can assert that there is more to be known about the ground and horizon of our being than what was found from the transcendental analysis of *Geist in Welt*. God is veiled to our rational (even transcendental) conceptualization, not just because my presence to God is in the form of a prethematic pre-grasp (*Vorgriff*), but because God is free and hence beyond the range of reason and concept (which ascertain and affirm what is necessarily the case). Insofar as

I am implicitly present to such a loving ground of my being I am still however open for a possible further word of revelation in the very heart of my existing. A *possible* word. It need not come, since this hidden ground is free.

Rahner concludes by considering the modality of such a word. He asserts that if it were to come it would have to be under the conditions of human knowing as already laid down in *Geist in Welt*, in terms of the ontological difference between being and entities. There it was argued that it is always the being of entities that we ask about. There is no knowing without a *conversio ad phantasma*. Hence, revelation would have to come in that mode, under the conditions of space and time. As spirit we only come to ourselves, achieve self-presence, in and through our involvement in history.[46] But this involvement is the way we work out our intense, straining listening for a word of revelation—in history—from that loving ground of our being which we necessarily affirm in every action. To be sure, no word may come, but this would still be a modality of revelation which would have existential significance for us.[47] We are thus necessarily *historical*, our being is marked by *historicity*.

To state anything further about this word—Has it in fact come to us in history? What is its content?—takes us out of the realm of philosophy of religion. The hearing of this word, and the conscious reflection upon it, once heard, take us into the realm of religion and theology proper.

The exact status of this argument is difficult to determine. Rahner would argue that *Geist in Welt* is purely philosophical. The argument in *Hörer des Wortes* is philosophical insofar as its form is philosophical (transcendental reduction and deduction); but it is a reflection on the possibility and intelligibility of the event of revelation. We know of this event only a posteriori, because it has already occurred in Jesus Christ. Rahner raises but does not investigate the question as to whether or not the analysis could have been performed if *no* specific revelation had come to humans in history, even though, as we have seen, he argues that the latter case could still be considered a "word" from God, but in the mode of silence.[48] We saw a similar ambiguity in Metz's work on philosophy and theology; indeed, in a footnote to Rahner's discussion of this question, Metz repeats his warning about philosophies that try to create from their own resources an answer to the question of human being.[49]

This brings us to Metz's editing of these foundational works. By far the more interesting is his work on the second. In *Geist in Welt* Metz translated the material from the *Summa Theologiae* into German, added footnotes, and changed the titles of some of the sections. He did add about five pages of text, but these changes for the most part are clarifications and additions in response to criticism of the book that had appeared over twenty years.[50] They do not represent any significant change from the mind of the author.[51]

In the foreword to *Hörer des Wortes,* Metz tells us of the changes he made in the revised edition of that work.[52] Since the original edition was the transcription of a series of lectures, much of Metz's work consisted in organizing the material so as to eliminate redundancies (e.g., opening and concluding summaries). Metz also added material to bring the book up-to-date with developments in Rahner's work during the two decades that separated the two editions. He worked into the text the concept of the supernatural existential, and the underlying approach to the nature-grace problem which Rahner elaborated in the fifties. Although the concept of obediential potency is present in *HdW1*, Metz develops more fully the approach to revelation that is implicit in that concept, as well as the implied relation between "transcendental revelation" and grace, and works them into the text. These changes are consistent with developments in Rahner's own thinking during the forties and fifties. Metz also seemed to be concerned that some of Rahner's language about being and God sounded too univocal and could create the misconception of a static concept of being, collapsing the ontological difference. So he introduced the term, *Seinshabe* (possession of being: found already in *HPM*). While interesting, these changes in my view do not significantly alter the approach of the original.

The most revealing category of emendation is announced in the foreword. When Metz describes the relevance of the book he does so in rather different terms from the expressed intent of the original lecture series. Rahner's original lectures took up the issue of the relationship between the philosophy of religion and theology. It charted a path through a two-dimensional space laid out by two axes: one defined by the debate between liberal theology (Schleiermacher) and neoorthodoxy (Barth), and the other by the debate between nineteenth-century Neo-Thomists and their rivals (Traditionalism, the Tübingen School,

Anton Günther, and others).[53] Twenty years later, Metz argues that the issues raised in the book are

> all the more pressing when the fundamental relation of persons to history is fading into the background due to the categorial predominance of an ideal of knowledge which is drawn from the natural and technological sciences, and the modern person finds it almost impossible to understand how his or her Dasein is grounded in history or is radically affected by history.[54]

This announces not only Metz's concern with history, which we saw in his dealings with Heidegger, but also the intellectual climate of the time. It may also indicate that Metz was beginning to read some of the Frankfurt School thinkers, who were always ferociously opposed to any form of ahistorical thinking, be it positivism *or* Neo-Thomism.[55]

If we follow this hint we find that throughout the book Metz consistently inserts clauses or expands existing references in order to stress the historical involvement of human being.[56] He also devotes a number of lengthy footnotes to elaborating on the interconnectedness of transcendentality and historicity, emphasizing again and again the historical involvement that is an exigency of human beings' mode of existing.[57] Certainly this is not foreign to the intent of Rahner's original text; a major part of the original sought to show that the place of a possible word of revelation from God had to be concrete human history.[58] One cannot avoid the suspicion, however, that Metz was not completely satisfied with Rahner's treatment on this point.

Metz's uneasiness becomes somewhat clearer if we consider another important reservation. This concerns the precise nature of the "other" to which human spirit must become present in order to become present to itself and (the obverse of self-presence) to the totality of being. Metz is concerned that the other is considered too much as a "thingly" other, rather than a personal other: *das Andere* instead of *der Andere*. This issue is raised in five crucial footnotes.[59] For instance, at the end of Section II, in which Rahner summarizes the argument from *Geist in Welt* that human being is spirit, Metz adds the following:

> Since the demonstration offered here of the subsistent transcendence and the transcending subsistence of the human spirit is oriented by the corresponding Thomistic approach, it is carried out exclusively as a

transcendental reflection on the possibility of an objective (*gegen-ständigen*) world of things. The attempt to carry out this demonstration from the perspective of a primordial experience of a *personal* with-world (*Mitwelt*) and the question of the inner connection between both ways of demonstration are not treated here.[60]

In *Geist in Welt* and in *Hörer des Wortes*, insofar as the latter is based on the former, Rahner starts from the knowledge of objects in general. Metz clearly thinks that what sort of things these objects are makes a difference. In some places he emends the text in order to emphasize that the "world" that is determinative for human spirit is not only, and not primarily, an environment (*Umwelt*) of things, but a with-world (*Mitwelt*) of persons. This becomes crucial in Rahner's derivation of human historicity. Rahner bases human historicity on the fact that human spirit only realizes itself in a receptive knowing, and thus is of its essence involved through sensibility in the material world. Matter, as the principle of individuation, is necessarily spatial and temporal because it is these qualities that enable matter to provide a principle for the repetition of the same.[61] In a note, however, Metz asserts that besides this approach, *materia* may also be considered as the "ground for the *un*repeatable uniqueness of a history of free persons."[62] Later, when Rahner summarizes the argument, Metz emends Rahner's discussion of persons' unavoidable involvement in "these things [e.g., external sensible objects]" to speak instead of "their with-world and environment (*Mit- und Umwelt*)."[63]

Metz is uncomfortable with the more traditional Thomistic argument because he wants to emphasize that historicity is grasped adequately only when it is grasped in its ground of the freedom of God's self-communication and in the embodiedness of humans as freely interacting persons.[64] Now, it is certainly true that this approach is also found in Rahner's work. In chapter 11, "Der Mensch als geschichtlicher Geist," Rahner argues that since matter as potency is always susceptible to further determination, and no one "moment" in the existence of a being fully exhausts its potentialities, temporality represents that characteristic of matter whereby it is "the inner stretching-out of an entity itself into the realized totality of its possibilities."[65] Rahner has human being in mind: he applies this understanding of materiality and temporality in order to assert that individual persons, as realizations of human nature, can realize themselves only within humanity as a whole, so that there is a specifically *human* form of historicity.[66] To this section Metz appends a note that

> this derivation of humanity as a personal with-world of persons could be offered more comprehensively. It is true that one would still have to begin with the person as a material existent, but it would then be possible to show that the "object" of [the person's] receptive knowing, if this object is to mediate a *substantive* (*inhaltliche*) self-presence, has to be not simply the other ["*das andere*"], but *the personal* [*der*] other.[67]

Metz's concern with the precise nature of "the other" that mediates human self-presence and his concern with historicity come together. Human experience of the other within a personal with-world is for Metz the only adequate context within which to develop an understanding of historicity.

In a later section (chapter 12), Rahner summarizes his derivation of human historicity. Once again Metz tries to push Rahner towards an emphasis on a knowing that is primordially a knowing of another person, not of another thing. While he points out that such a perspective has already been hinted at earlier in Rahner's assertion that will and love are inner moments of any act of knowing, he adds:[68]

> Nevertheless, the fundamental question still remains as to whether or not the approach developed here would not have to be *completely repeated* starting from and remaining continually within the perspective of the primordial and irreducible uniqueness of personal being-with [*Mitsein*] and the way things appear and are known within that way of being. The question is, of course, also at the same time directed at the Thomistic approach to the metaphysics of knowing in general.[69]

The "approach" refers to the derivation that begins with *Geist in Welt* and continues through *Hörer des Wortes*. Would the derivation of historicity be substantially different if such an overhaul of Rahner's transcendental method were carried out? Metz seems to think that the result would still have an "inner connection" with Rahner's approach here, but he does not justify this belief, and one wonders whether, if he had been pressed, he could have.[70]

This discussion has underscored the complexity of Metz's attitude toward the Rahnerian approach to anthropology and toward historicity; however, I believe that we can simplify it as follows. There are two approaches toward human being and historicity in Rahner's foundational work. One approach, which predominates in *Geist in Welt* and those sections of *Hörer des Wortes* which depend upon it, is based on human knowing of objects in general, hence on what Buber has named the "I-it" relationship. There is, however, a second approach in *Hörer des Wortes* which is based on the specifically interpersonal character of knowing, hence on the "I-thou" relationship. In the first, temporality is grounded in the nature of matter as the principle of individuation in space and time, and is thus rooted firmly in Thomas's philosophy and epistemology. The second, with emphases on history as the place of free becoming and on free, loving, interpersonal relationship, shows more affinity with the Idealism of Schelling and Hegel. Metz clearly prefers the second, and thinks that the first approach, and the realm of human experience it articulates, must be grounded in the second.

Andrew Tallon has argued that, in fact, the second approach is not precluded by the approach that Rahner takes up in *Geist in Welt*. Even more, he believes that there is evidence that one can find principles in Rahner's first work that will unfold into a full-fledged anthropology of interpersonal becoming.[71] While I am not fully persuaded that Rahner's early work and development are as seamless and harmonious as Tallon suggests, he does provide an important reminder of the developmental character of Rahner's work. This being true, then Metz's notes and emendations do (as Metz claimed in his preface) reflect Rahner's own mind and Rahner's increasing emphasis on person and community during the later decades of his career.[72]

Leaving aside the evaluation of the adequacy, consistency, and coherence of Rahner's thought, we have seen enough to conclude that Metz is worried about the concept of historicity in Rahner's thought, just as he was as a critic of it in Heidegger's philosophy. More specifically, Metz is worried about how well the concept of historicity can be developed from a transcendental approach, be it Heidegger's phenomenological ontology or Rahner's transcendental Thomism. His changes and additions to *Hörer des Wortes* show that he wanted a transcendental approach that *begins* with human involvement in history and society in a more primordial way than Rahner's rather intellectualist position at that time allowed.

A comparison of Rahner's approach, especially in *Hörer des Wortes*, and Metz's article on theology and philosophy illustrates again this underlying difference in argumentative strategy. In Metz's article we saw him begin by asserting that the essential historical engagement of a human being is the only way to make sense of his or her susceptibility to reflection from both a transcendental *and* a transcendent perspective. From there Metz argued *to* an understanding of that historical involvement as a history of the understanding of being, one point of this history being the moment at which metaphysical or transcendental reflection becomes possible. Rahner, on the other hand, begins from the *Seinsfrage* and the transcendental analysis of human knowing. From this, Rahner argues *to* a concept of human historicity. What is the relationship between these two approaches? Are they reverse sides of the same coin, or do they represent different approaches, at least tendentially, to fundamental ontology and anthropology?

The link lies in the historical argument about the history of the development of and relationships between revelation, theology, and metaphysics. Suppose metaphysics (which for Metz and Rahner always means transcendental analysis) becomes possible and autonomous only in and because of a particular history, and that it never transcends that history? Then one can, with Metz, start from an analysis of human involvement in history in general, and in one particular (Christian) history, and arrive at transcendental analysis as the culmination of this history's unfolding. *Or*, one can, with Rahner (particularly in *Hörer des Wortes*) begin with transcendental analysis and arrive at human involvement in history in general, and at that particular history which alone makes transcendental analysis possible. The above supposition about the link between metaphysics and history is suggested in "Theologische und Metaphysische Ordnung"; it is argued in more detail in *Christliche Anthropozentrik*. It is a crucial part of Metz's early understanding of his relationship to Rahner's transcendental approach.[73] If the argument cannot be sustained then Metz's approach and Rahner's would eventually have to come into opposition. If it can, then the only question is, Which avenue is more fruitful, given the situation of the theologian?

This fills out our picture of the agenda for Metz's independent work during the late fifties and early sixties. Metz needed to develop an anthropology that does more than merely juxtapose the historical and the transcendental. He needed to show how he could ground historicity more concretely in the specific histories of interactions between persons, certainly more so than Heidegger, and one suspects that he also had Rahner's approach in mind. Finally, he needed to come to terms with the

Thomistic roots of his own academic training, with its preference for the *ordo scientiae* over the *ordo historiae*. Metz's changes of Rahner's work show that he was not fully satisfied with Thomas's epistemology as a starting point for a fundamental theology, and that perhaps he even had reservations about the *Seinsfrage* in general as a starting point, unless it could be shown that such an approach had an "inner connection"[74] with the more social and historical approach that Metz clearly preferred. We now turn to how Metz worked out his own theological anthropology and tried to settle his methodological uneasiness within the transcendental approach. As I suggested above, this project was carried out as an attempt to construct a historical narrative that would ground the inner connection that Metz was attempting to establish between his own incipient approach and that of his teacher.

CHRISTIAN ANTHROPOCENTRICITY

Metz's independent work during the period from 1958 until about 1965 consisted of two types of material. He wrote a number of articles for theological dictionaries.[75] Several of these articles explored basic concepts in theological anthropology, often subsuming Heideggerian concepts within the conceptual apparatus of transcendental Thomism. In working through these concepts, however, Metz began to question the validity of using Thomas's thought in this way. To sort through these issues he wrote his theological dissertation, *Christliche Anthropozentrik*, which was completed in 1961 and published in 1962.[76] I will begin by surveying the former material, and then consider *Christliche Anthropozentrik*.

In Metz's view at this time, the most important contribution of Thomistic anthropology is its insistence on the intrinsic and essential embodiedness of the self-realization, and hence salvation, of the human person.[77] Embodiedness is, therefore, a central existential in Metz's anthropology. As an existential of human being, embodiedness subsumes the Heideggerian existential of *Befindlichkeit*.[78] To be embodied means that human spirit does not produce or possess itself absolutely; its self-realization is always enacted within the context of the prior situation in which it finds itself, and which it cannot ever exhaustively grasp intellectually or transcend. Metz further delimits this existential in a later article on another important Heideggerian existential, *Mitsein*.[79] Here

Metz asserts that the situation which is an irreducible element of one's being is primarily a social-historical reality: it is the world that is made up by one's involvement with other persons, working out their own embodied self-realization. Thus, in our bodiliness we are never merely the result of our own decisions but are formed in an equally primordial way by the past and present decisions of others.

While Metz makes a brief reference to an "ontologically clarified concept of *materia prima*" as grounding this understanding of the social character of human existence,[80] he clearly prefers to discuss it in terms of our embodiedness because he wants to distance himself from the roots of "matter" in Greek philosophy. In order to emphasize this distance even more clearly he makes a (for him) typical distinction between the understanding of bodiliness in the horizon of Greek thought as opposed to the biblical understanding. The former, argues Metz, operates in terms of a dualism of body and soul in which the body is not essential for the realization of the soul. The latter, on the other hand, is a holistic understanding in which "body" is a modal description of the entirety of human being. Bodiliness is not a subsequent act or manifestation of an already self-subsistent spirit or soul, but represents the existential situatedness of the person as a whole within a material, social, and historical world. Thus defined, bodiliness is equally primordial with the person's conceptual self-reflection and free decision, and stamps them in ways that can never fully be brought to light. This bodiliness can never be limited to one particular domain or element of human being, so as to isolate a purely subjective, absolutely self-transparent locus of human being.

Moving from phenomenology to theology proper, this existential of human being requires us to think of salvation as a reality for all of human being, spread out historically and socially. "I" cannot be saved apart from the environing social-historical world (*Mitwelt*) because there is no justifiable method whereby one could cleanly separate an "I" from the socially constituted situation (its embodiedness) that permeates every person's being-in-the-world. This assertion—that salvation must be for the other as much as it is for me, or even before it can be salvation for me at all—will become more radical as Metz's career progresses.

Metz lists four *existentialia* of human self-realization that arise from the more fundamental existential of bodiliness: passibility, perduring hiddenness, inner temporality, and perduring individuality.[81] First, passibility signifies the fact that the person is essentially and unavoidably involved in the world. The person's self-realization is inescapably subject to what is "outside" of the person. It does not follow from this that humans should hold back from their involvement in what is other, but that they should obediently take up the world as the situatedness of their freedom. Here again we see Metz's disagreement with Heidegger over the proper response to the fact that Dasein's being-in-the-world means that it is inescapably determined by heteronomous elements which can never become fully transparent and meaningful to it. The obedient taking up of my socially and historically embodied existence is the only authentic way to self-realization. Indeed, in Metz's reflection on "poverty of spirit," as preached and exemplified by Jesus, he defines it as precisely this sort of obedient acceptance of one's own finite, situated freedom. At this point in his career, poverty of spirit is Metz's alternative to Heidegger's "anticipatory resoluteness," as the human stance toward the world in which the meaning of being is authentically revealed.[82]

Second, my self-realization, because it is embodied and in this way partly other-determined, will always be to some extent hidden or veiled (*verhüllt*) from me. Once again, my own being and actions can never be dissected so as to find which elements are authentically my own and which are to be ascribed to heteronomous influences. In the end the distinction between autonomy and heteronomy is a relative one. This means, Metz concedes, that bodiliness makes our existence profoundly ambiguous and our self-realization threatened from its very core. Again, however, the proper response is not to withdraw from embodied existence. That would be impossible in any case. Rather, the challenge is to take up lovingly one's situated existence, precisely in its embodiedness.

Third, bodiliness implies an inner temporality (*Zeitlichkeit*) of human being. Bodiliness means that no one act of self-disposition (in knowledge and freedom) can complete the task of self-realization. One's being happens[83] in temporally dispersed acts. Consequently the task of self-realization requires that one accept and create oneself in this series of temporally diffused actions.

Fourth and finally, taken together these existentialia map out the task of human self-realization of the person as a unique, underivable individual:

> This bodily self-determination, happening (*geschehende*) in passibility, hiddenness and the spatial-temporal dispersedness of the

earthly hour, finally shows up to be the ground of the inalienable and underivable historical individuality of the human being, and thus as the content of the person's eternity, which, indeed, according to a Christian understanding, does not mature "behind" or "beyond" bodily *Dasein*, but rather *in* this bodily *Dasein* itself, and *as* its final validity.[84]

This existential task is threatened however by the very embodiedness which makes it possible. As we saw above, one's necessary involvement in the world means that one's self-understanding, desires, intuitions, attitudes, moods, and decisions are irreducibly stamped by those of other persons, together with whom my social-historical *Mitwelt* is constituted. This is Metz's interpretation of concupiscence.[85] We can never escape concupiscence, since the heteronomous elements of human being in the world can never be isolated and made fully transparent to us. It threatens us in our task of integrating the temporally stretched out moments of our existence as an authentic expression of our self-realization as one person, an achievement which Metz names "integrity."[86] In responding to the threat posed by concupiscence we may go—indeed, in each case have already gone—astray in several ways. We may become lost in the disparate and polyvalent elements of our embodiedness and never reach a definitive self-realization. We may surrender completely to the heteronomously determined elements of our embodiedness, thus denying the task of authentic *self*-determination. Finally, we may be tempted to dominate and control our world, and so achieve a pseudo-autonomy in which we try to make the world and our selves appear as if they were completely at our disposal and, consequently, make our persons appear as if they were realities *sui generis*.

As one would expect in a theological anthropology, Metz finds the authentic response to concupiscence in Jesus Christ. Jesus participated fully in this ambiguous existential of human existence, indeed *more* fully than we do:

> His integrity characterizes the distinctive power to take up without remainder this world, as it is existentially preformed in ways that are hostile to God and salvation, in its tendency to disempower and afflict us. Jesus embraces all of this, and in this world itself—thus in his powerlessness and poverty, in the kenosis of his own freedom—asserts his decision for God, indeed makes *the world itself* into the event and expression of the person's total self-surrender to God. This

is in strict contrast to our own concupiscent existence, in which our ability to take up and suffer through this situation has already in each case been broken, "compromised", . . . ([our] concupiscence is not a more intense, but rather a deficient power to suffer).[87]

Francis Fiorenza noted that this understanding of concupiscence differs from Rahner's, and the difference is illuminating.[88] For Rahner, too, freedom is the capacity to come to self-presence and self-realization in and through embodied existence. For both, no one action can fully incarnate my self-realization and self-presence. But, whereas for Metz concupiscence arises from the dialectical nature of our self-realization within an ambiguous *Mitwelt*, for Rahner the relevant dialectic is that of nature and person. "Nature," as the counterpart to the freedom that makes us persons, has a certain innate spontaneity and inertia which resists the integrating will of the person. It is this inner reality of human becoming that is the primary threat to self-realization, not the social constitution of the person in a *Mitwelt*. Metz's concern to place his anthropology in a more social and historical framework is evident in this early difference with Rahner.[89]

Metz's theological anthropology develops in a closer confrontation with Heidegger's existential anthropology than does Rahner's. I would argue that in subsuming Heideggerian concepts under existentialia derived from Thomistic principles of embodied existence, Metz initially believed that he had found a way to assert more strongly the historicity and sociality of human being. But as we saw above, Metz had abiding reservations about the adequacy of Thomas's epistemology and metaphysics for the task of defining historicity. In his only extended argument from this period Metz tried to clarify these reservations. *Christliche Anthropozentrik* also attempts to continue the task of putting the tradition of transcendental Thomism in dialogue with the history of modern (German) philosophy by pressing the claim that the latter is, in fact, grounded in the same thinker who is the founding figure for the former: Thomas Aquinas.

Christliche Anthropozentrik has four chapters. In the first chapter Metz articulates his own understanding of the way that reason is involved in history, and defines what he means by *Denkform* (thought-form). In the second chapter he derives the thought-form of Thomas Aquinas by contrasting it with the thought-form of Greek philosophy. In the third chapter he argues that this new thought-form, which is germinally albeit incompletely present in Aquinas, represents that thought-form which is uniquely adequate to the spirit of Christian revelation. Thomas is the first true theologian insofar as he explicates the content of Christian revelation against that horizon which alone is adequate to it (as opposed to the thought-form or horizon of Greek thought). In the last chapter Metz argues that the new thought-form in fact makes up the horizon of modern philosophy. Thomas, not Descartes, is the "father of modern philosophy." Modern philosophy has not developed against the spirit of Christianity but because of it and in conformity with it. Let us consider each chapter in more detail.

In his first chapter, using language that reminds one of Hegel or F. C. Baur, Metz argues that every thinker has to be understood in terms of his or her "inner standpoint . . . in order to recapitulate and affirm the multiplicity of concepts and statements as it arises from the concentrated simplicity [*gesammelten Einfalt*] of its principium."[90] This principio is of two sorts. The first, the material principle, describes the key concept which organizes the other concepts of the system. Not surprisingly, from what we have seen above, Metz asserts (but does not argue) that the material principle for Thomas's thought is embodiedness.[91]

More interesting is the other sort of principle: the formal principle or thought-form of a system. The thought-form does not refer to any particular concept but to the way that all of the concepts are thought, the spirit or understanding of being in general which determines which concepts are central to a thinker, and the way that he or she thinks them.[92] It is the horizon against which the concepts have meaning, and as such it cannot be fully thematized, since any thematization would itself rely on this horizon. This notion is clearly dependent on sources within German phenomenology and existentialism. *Seinsverständniss* is often used synonymously for *Denkform*. Further, Metz tells us that the thought-form yields the ontological rather than the ontic character of a thinker's system. Thus, the entire discussion reminds one of Heidegger's discussion of the *Seinsfrage* in the introductions to *Being and Time,* a work to which Metz makes reference.[93] Finally, Metz also describes an irreducible hermeneutical circle between the contents (what is thought) and the thought-form (how it is thought) of a system, a circle which is inescapable for reason because reason is irreducibly historical.[94]

With this understanding in mind Metz argues in his second chapter that Thomas's thought-form is at least germinally anthropocentric, as opposed to the thought-form of the Greeks, which is cosmocentric. Metz explains this to mean that for Thomas the exemplar or paradigm by which entities are evaluated is not the thing within a static cosmos but the person within a historical world.[95] Being and objectivity are not thought of in terms of static "thereness"[96] but in terms of self-presence in knowledge and will.[97] The world and time are not considered in terms of spatial categories but in terms of historical categories which draw upon our experience of the capacity and responsibility freely to embrace ourselves and in so doing participate in our creation and realization.[98]

Metz concedes that in many ways Aquinas's thought is still dominated by the cosmocentric, thing-oriented horizon of Greek thought.[99] This notwithstanding, Thomas's greatness lies in his willingness to stretch or to move beyond Greek categories when he uses them to try to articulate concepts drawn from Christian revelation. Thus, on Metz's reading, if we are to seek Aquinas's unique and epochal character we should *not* consider so much his strictly philosophical work in epistemology and metaphysics but rather his properly theological work, in which he allows the subject-matter (revelation) itself to determine the horizon of understanding.[100] This is Metz's own procedure. Unlike Rahner, who took as his starting point Aquinas's epistemology and metaphysics, Metz uses concepts from Thomas's *theological* anthropology: concupiscence, body and soul, grace, and so on.

In his third chapter Metz takes up the question of the origin of this new thought-form in Aquinas, using language once again reminiscent of German Idealism. He interprets Thomas's theology as marking an epochal turning point at which the spirit of Christian revelation "interprets itself" by producing the horizon of understanding (that is, the thought-form) which alone is appropriate for its conceptual mediation:

> Thomas becomes, in this view, a *primordially* Christian thinker, who does not simply happen (as an Aristotelean) to be concerned with Christian contents, but rather has entered into that "spirit" which announces itself in these contents. For the first time he thinks the objectivity of revelation with the horizon that revelation itself effects.[101]

Does this mean that in Thomas philosophy is subordinated to theology? Quite the opposite. In his last chapter Metz argues that the shift in categories that was initiated in Aquinas's thought is precisely the shift into the new anthropocentric horizon of modern philosophy in which philosophy was freed for its own proper task of reflecting on human subjectivity as it shows itself from out of itself (to use the language of existential phenomenology).[102] Descartes and Kant were only carrying through the shift to a new thought-form that was initiated because Thomas Aquinas was faithful to the thought-form immanent to the contents of Christian revelation. Not only is Thomas "the father of modern thought,"[103] but, "since in [modernity] the horizon of being which dawned in Thomas became operative, modernity is the philosophical implementation [*Durchführung*] of the spirit of Christianity."[104]

We have already seen that for Metz philosophy can never become fully autonomous, since it cannot fully produce or possess the situation out of which it philosophizes. This situation is determined by historical events that can be reflected on by means of a transcendental analysis after the fact but cannot be deduced transcendentally prior to or outside of those events. What guarantees the autonomy of philosophy is not the fact that philosophy gains power over or is able fully to transcend its situation, but the liberating character of that situation itself.[105] The determinative event for such a liberating situation is the incarnation.

Western thought, as it has come to a consistent self-interpretation out of the horizon of the spirit of Christianity, became increasingly set free to be itself because the central historical event of Christian revelation is the incarnation. In the incarnation the humanity of Christ is not subsumed or dissolved; rather, it is accepted and posited in its fullness. As the spirit of Christianity permeates the human *Mitwelt*, as it must if any one individual is to live in that spirit and so come to salvation, the entire human social-historical world too is accepted and posited in its fullness. Philosophy's coming of age in modernity is the intellectual dimension of this process:

> Thomas appears as that historical locus in which philosophical thought is affected by the "spirit" of Christianity, which shows its power and universal claims precisely by the fact that it illuminates the spirit of philosophy to itself and transformatively carries it forward into a new epoch. . . . A thousand years after the Divine Word became flesh, this incarnation asserted itself within the history of the human spirit and proved itself as the *total* acceptance and recapitulation of human *Dasein*.[106]

This is Metz's "secularization thesis," which shows a strongly positive attitude toward modernity and its adequacy as an interlocutor and milieu for Christian faith.[107] Metz does not affirm modernity uncritically. Indeed, possible errors become more serious in the anthropocentric horizon. However, this vulnerability to error is not solved but only exacerbated by hostile attacks against the spirit of modern philosophy, as they had been pressed by Neo-Scholasticism in the nineteenth century and the so-called "Christian philosophies" of the twentieth.[108] What is needed is a critical and constructive engagement with the history of modern philosophy, one that both allows the proper autonomy of philosophy but also criticizes philosophy when it tries to emancipate itself totally from its historical provenance.[109] This is the conclusion one would expect from a transcendental Thomist.

While suggestive, Metz's book is ultimately too sketchy to succeed. As I argued above, this historical argument, which ultimately posits the historical dependence of transcendental ontology, with its starting point in the *Seinsfrage,* is the key link between Rahner's more abstract, epistemologically and ontologically focused method and Metz's more historically focused method. But the argument needs more development if it is to play this role. While the interpretation of Aquinas is provocative, it reads too much into the Angelic Doctor. The book is in the same genre as Heidegger's book on Kant, indeed, as Rahner's book on Aquinas. The method of reading a thinker *nach vorne,* in terms of the subsequent history of effects of his or her thought, is a controversial one.[110] Metz was apparently aware of the incompleteness of his work. He planned longer works on embodiedness, concupiscence, and integrity, the key concepts for his own anthropology.[111] They never appeared. Metz only suggests, but never argues in detail, that modern secularized philosophy is in continuity with the course of Christian thought. When Hans Blumenberg mounted a massive counterattack on this sort of thesis a few years later, Metz did not respond.[112] By that time he had already abandoned the entire approach. Perhaps more worrisome is the framing of the book in a "history of ideas" approach. For all of his emphasis on concrete historical events which cannot be deduced intellectually before the fact, the language of the "spirit of Christianity" and the exclusive focus on ideas ignores the multitude of concrete historical events that would surely have to be considered in order to make an adequate case for the Christian provenance of modernity. Thus, we must judge Metz's attempts during these years as a suggestive but incomplete beginning.

CONCLUSIONS

Metz was only thirty-four when *Christliche Anthropozentrik* was published. While his work during the late fifties and early sixties shows a thorough grasp of the intricacies of transcendental method, it is hardly surprising that his original contributions to it were fragmentary and incomplete. As I mentioned above, he had in mind further works, in which presumably he would have addressed some of the lacunae in the early work. But he did not pursue any further the lines of development that he had just begun to outline. Almost from the moment he took up his chair in dogmatic theology in Münster in 1963 he moved off in a radically different direction. This "turn" will be the subject of the next chapter. Before moving on, though, it will be helpful to review the results of this lengthy chapter.

The important tasks given to Metz by Karl Rahner show that, at least in Rahner's opinion, Metz was thoroughly versed in the practice of transcendental Thomism. In his appropriation of this method certain key concerns emerge. After his initial critique of Heidegger he showed little further interest in the epistemological foundation of transcendental method. He was more interested in transcendental analysis of human freedom as it is experienced and worked out in the social-historical *Mitwelt*.[113] While he appreciated both the Heideggerian and Rahnerian approaches to human involvement in history, we have seen that he had significant reservations as to the suitability of the existential of historicity for expressing that involvement. He set himself to modifying the transcendental approach in order to arrive at an analysis of human being that both begins from concrete involvement in history (rather than the *Seinsfrage*), and ends with concrete involvement within society and history.

However much he felt the need to modify elements of the transcendental method that he learned from Rahner, he did not abandon it during these years. His modifications of Rahner's foundational works show that he believed transcendental Thomism to be open to the direction in which he wanted to move. Indeed, as I argued above, this direction was the one in which Rahner himself was moving: from the more strongly intellectualist position of *Geist in Welt* toward the approach of the second edition of *Hörer des Wortes*, in which the former position is at least complemented by an approach that draws as much on the domain of interpersonal relationships as it does on that of cognitive relationships between knower and object.

Rahner continued in this direction. Metz did not. Metz's initial steps toward a more socially oriented transcendental Thomism were abruptly interrupted. The steps he did take, in his encyclopedia articles and in *Christliche Anthropozentrik*, are suggestive but incomplete. Hence, it is impossible to state with certainty where he might have gone had he pursued that path further, and whether he would have been able to develop a theology that both cohered with the thought of his teachers and also satisfied his concerns about articulating the social and historical involvement of the human subject.

If Metz's early concerns with the way that theological anthropology expresses human involvement in history and society would eventually force him to abandon transcendental method, many of its basic tenets would continue to mark his thought up to the present day. First, one can recognize in Metz's later thought the method of *reductio* and *deductio*, whereby one starts from some constitutive domain of human activity and self-realization in order to derive certain structures of human being, which are then used to illuminate our present experience of ourselves, including our experience of salvation. Second and related to this, Metz continues to hold the conviction that there is a certain "depth-structure" to human reason, which he named "thought-form" or "understanding of being" in his early work. While he soon stops using terminology like this, as well as terms like "ontological" versus "ontic" levels of thought and being, I shall argue that the essential structure remains, especially in *Faith in History and Society*.[114]

Furthermore, Metz will never cease being a passionate defender of modernity and its turn to the subject. He will continue to argue that modern philosophy has not arisen in spite of the spirit of authentic Christian faith and thought, but because of it. Consequently, he will continue to assert the need for Christian theology to be open to dialogue with "secular" thought. But conversely, he will continue to protest vigorously against any philosophical system that attempts to construct (or deconstruct!) its notions of the human subject without taking into account the concrete history of the West, including its Christian origins, in which modernity and the turn to the subject were born.

His attitude toward philosophy will also be recognizably similar to that articulated in "Theologische und Metaphysische Ordnung." Although the *type* of philosophy he chooses as principal dialogue partner will change, his understanding of its constitutive and cathartic functions will not. He will select that philosophy which best illustrates the way that human reason is necessarily involved in history, and which best illuminates the current situation within which theology must frame its interpretation of the Christian message. As his evaluation of the *prospects* of modernity (not its intrinsic worth) change, so too does the philosophical partner he chooses, as well as his understanding of the third, maieutic task of philosophy. Philosophy will no longer be the midwife, bringing the language and concepts of revelation to speech *within* the horizons of the present understanding of being. Instead, philosophy must help theology to frame its articulation of revelation in a way that *disrupts* the contemporary "thought-form," not, to be sure, in order to eradicate it, but to fulfill it.

Finally, in Metz's early work it was a concept drawn from the history of Christian spirituality that proved central for his articulation of the authentic human response to the dilemma of human existence. Poverty of spirit defined for Metz the very core of the Christian vocation, which (as for Rahner) is the vocation of becoming human—*Gloria Dei homo vivens*. Yet, while on the one hand this ideal is in continuity with traditional understandings of poverty of spirit as indifference and absolute openness to the will of God, Metz frames it in a socio-historical context which precludes reading into it an *apathetic* indifference to the world, but rather entails an indifference that leads to more profound engagement in and with the world. This interpretation is quite close to the interpretation that Rahner gave to Ignatian indifference.[115] It is, however, also characterized by the greater attention to the dilemma posed by human sociality and historicity. The tragic, indeed horrific, consequences of this dilemma will become more and more pronounced, and the spiritual resources adequate to responding to it will be reformulated and augmented in the course of Metz's development.

Having established the concerns that were driving Metz's development, as well as the underlying framework of his thought, let us go on to the dramatic turn in his thought that transpired in the nineteen-sixties.

4

THE BIRTH AND DEVELOPMENT
OF POLITICAL THEOLOGY

NEW INTERLOCUTORS, NEW DIRECTIONS

Almost as soon as Metz took up his new post as professor of dogmatic theology in Münster his thought took a startling turn. In chapter 3 I argued that Metz had already been trying to push the transcendental theology he learned under Karl Rahner towards a more dialogical
theology, one in which the domain of human activity which forms the
starting point for the transcendental *reductio* is that of interpersonal
knowing rather than the knowledge of objects in general. Yet he soon
abandoned this approach. Why?

Part of the explanation must be sought in his involvement in a broader
spectrum of German cultural and intellectual life. Two important
points in the constellation of Metz's "force-field" began to exercise their
attraction-repulsion. First, he interacted more and more intensively
with intellectual traditions which continued (in some cases, by reacting
against) the German Enlightenment. These are the post-Hegelian critiques of Idealism: primarily in Marxism, but also the critiques of Kierkegaard and Nietzsche. Particularly important in this regard are Metz's
conversations with the philosophies of Ernst Bloch and the various
thinkers of the Frankfurt School: Max Horkheimer, Theodor Adorno,
Herbert Marcuse, and that more distant satellite, Walter Benjamin. All
of these thinkers, in diverse and idiosyncratic ways, had tried to forge
comprehensive (but not necessarily systematic) syntheses of the various
strands of post-Hegelian critique in German philosophy. Second, Metz
was gradually coming to grips with the catastrophe of National Socialism and the horrible "tremendum" of the Holocaust.[1] He came to
realize that this catastrophe implicated not only the German Enlighten-

ment but the Catholic theology in which he had been trained. Given his conviction, already formulated and defended in the first phase of his work, that the thought of the Enlightenment and the spirit of Christianity were inextricably intertwined, he came to conclude that if either were to be saved both had to be reformulated from the ground up.

What is more, Metz's Catholic environment was changing. The heady days of Vatican II were followed by the first rumblings of a conservative reaction. Metz set himself against this reaction. Perhaps partly as a result of his ongoing conversations with Marxists under the aegis of the *Paulusgesellschaft,* he had become convinced of the considerable element of truth in the Marxist critiques of Christendom, and in this light the conservative reaction to Vatican II appeared to him as a closing off of the promising openness to this critique exhibited at the council, as well as a premature strangling of those initiatives which could find new forms of ecclesial structure and praxis that would give a serious and creative response.[2] In addition, the Church of the Third World was making its presence increasingly felt. With the meeting of Latin American bishops at Medellín in the autumn of 1968, liberation theology emerged as a powerful new theological initiative, one with which Metz was in sympathy from the start.

The questioning of atemporal idealisms and metaphysics on the part of Marxist ideology-critiques; the profound ambiguity of any "business-as-usual" theology in the light of the challenges posed by the Holocaust; the challenge posed by the transformation of the Catholic Church from a monocultural Eurocentric church to a polycentric multicultural world-church: these are the "crises" which Metz has identified as the causes for his search for a "post-idealist, political theology."[3] Yet these crises have only been named and interrelated in the last fifteen years, because earlier Metz was still developing the conceptual apparatus with which to identify and articulate them. In the decade following his appointment at Münster, Metz dealt with these crises piecemeal. All the difficulties in interpreting Metz come fully into play during this time. The two key texts for his thought in the sixties and seventies are both collections of essays. There is often repetition, and without a clearly articulated framework beyond that of dealing with the aforementioned crises his work can easily appear as a pastiche of themes and concepts: suggestive, provocative, but finally lacking an integrative center.

Theology of the World is made up of essays that span the period from 1962 until 1968, during which Metz's thought was in flux.[4] The shift in his thought can be easily seen by comparing the earlier with the later essays that make up the book. He moved from an anthropocentric methodological focus, an incarnational theological focus, and a positive attitude toward the prospects of modernity at the book's beginning, to a focus on the philosophy of history as the matrix for expressing theological statements, a theological focus on eschatology, and a negative assessment of the direction modernity was going at its end. It is no wonder that readers have been frustrated by this work.[5] *Faith in History and Society* is also a collection of essays, written over the period stretching from 1968 to 1976. Its organizational plan is also unclear, although, as I suggested above and shall argue in more detail below, a new understanding of the subject provides the "depth-structure" which integrates the whole.[6] No new themes emerged after this book, although certain themes (particularly, the centrality of theodicy to theology and the spirituality of *Leiden an Gott*) were given more emphasis.

My purpose in this chapter is to assemble the themes and concepts which Metz developed as he struggled to deal with the crises he perceived facing theology. The reasons just adduced suggest that it is not helpful to proceed diachronically, analyzing particular books or essays. It is better to follow the trajectories of the new themes and concepts in Metz's thought, from their origins in the sixties and early seventies, through *Faith in History and Society,* and up to the present time. One way of mapping these trajectories is to find their origins in Metz's various interlocutors in the sixties and seventies. This will be my procedure here. I will look at Metz's encounter with revisionary Marxists, especially those named above, and his gradual remembering of the Holocaust. He drew important themes from these encounters and "refunctioned" them (to use Bloch's term) in order to fit his own emerging agenda. I will close with a summary of the crucial themes in Metz's mature political theology.

This is not an exhaustive survey of Metz's thought but one that treats those themes touching the concerns already identified in chapter 3, and themes that place Metz in the area of fundamental theology. What is the nature of human temporality and historicity? What is the nature of that *Mitsein* which permeates our existence to its very foundations? What is the relationship of Christianity and Christian theology to modernity and its "turn to the subject"? Given the answers to the first two questions, what is the appropriate methodology for bringing the resources of Christian faith to bear upon our current situation, understood in terms of the answer to the third question?

Hence, this chapter will be primarily expository. Its purpose is to let the various themes in Metz's mature thought show themselves in their own light. In the next chapter I will take up the constructive task of drawing out the understanding of the subject that underlies Metz's mature work and of teasing out the spirituality that informs and animates the whole. At that point I will in many ways be moving beyond Metz's own writings, attempting to read between the lines in order to draw out what is unsaid, presumed, and implied. What I hope to show in that chapter, however, is that the themes presented in this chapter achieve systematic coherence, are saved from being a pastiche of provocative observations, only in terms of the intellectual center made up by a new understanding of the subject and the apocalyptic spirituality of suffering unto God. Whether or not this construction violates the dictum that Metz took over from Adorno—"The whole is the untrue"—and systematizes too much, shall be left to the reader to decide.

ENCOUNTERS WITH MARXISM

Metz himself tells us that his encounter with Marxism provided the impetus for the first stage in the formation of his political theology.[7] I argued above that Metz's dialogue with Marxism resulted in his shift to what I (following Despland) named the ethico-juridical tradition in the heritage Kant laid down for German thought.[8] This strand, which came to fruition in Karl Marx and his many followers, and has been called the "second phase of the Enlightenment,"[9] insists that reason is not an atemporal transcendental given; rather it becomes in society and history. Its maturation depends upon the transformation of the social structures in which it is embedded. This second phase of the Enlightenment appealed to Metz since its starting point was the one he had advocated in his early work: human existence is embedded in historical and social interrelations and only comes to fulfillment in and through these interrelations. This is, indeed, for Metz the epochal discovery of Marxism: "the discovery of the world as history, as a historical project in which men and women become the subjects of their own history."[10]

At the end of chapter 3 I argued that in his own elaboration of transcendental Thomism and in his editing of Rahner's work, Metz had been trying to shift toward a more dialogical approach, one that preferred as its starting point the interpersonal "I-thou" mode of presence to the other. He attempted to rework the Thomistic category of embodiedness into an existential that would ground this modality of the subject's presence-to-self through presence-to-the-personal-other. Perhaps it was his encounters with Marxism in the mid-sixties that finally convinced him that these attempts were futile, that they would not lead to the understanding of the person in society and history for which he was striving. He concluded that the "anthropocentric turn" of modernity could be fully mediated to theology only if theology took up its continuation in the second phase of the Enlightenment:

> At the beginning of modernity the world appeared . . . as the (already historically formed) "material" for the free self-realization of humans before God. Of course with this the danger arose of seeing the subjectivity of the person in its free "mine-ness" (*Jemeinigkeit*) as something separated from the world and consequently of seeing the world as a purely manipulable world of objects. This danger drives a growing "de-worldification" of the existence of faith and the reification of the reality of the world. The usual appeal to the bodiliness (*Leiblichkeit*) of the existence of faith does not overcome this danger, since the understanding of the bodiliness of the human being—at least as commonly used—is itself determined by an individualistic "I-world" or "spirit-nature" schema. A decisive clarification [for this problem] was brought by that modification of the anthropologically turned modern understanding of the world which followed historically upon the ideology-critique of the nineteenth century. [In it] the experience of the world and the way of comporting oneself to it is realized in the horizon of interhuman *Mitsein,* and this not merely in the "private" sense of the I-thou relation but rather in the "political" sense of social interaction.[11]

I include this lengthy citation because it contains a continuation of Metz's critique of the abstract and worldless character of the existential approach, with its focus on authenticity and "mineness" (*Jemeinigkeit*). It also documents for the first time Metz's dissatisfaction with his earlier

attempts to overcome this problem by developing a personalist or dialogical anthropology grounded in the retrieval of Thomistic categories
(*Leiblichkeit*). Let us consider more closely the nature of his dissatisfaction.

In general Metz speaks of the challenge leveled by Marxism as
the challenge of doing theology "in the face of the end of its [Christi-
anity's] cognitive and social innocence."[12] Here he has in mind ideology
critique, both in general and as it was applied to religion by Marx under
the well-known rubric of "religion as the opium of the people."[13] Such
critiques attempt to show that substantial (if not all) realms of human
knowledge are guided by and support the interests of certain groups
within society, however much these realms may claim to be legitimated
by appeals to metaphysical universals, invariant cognitive structures, or
transcendent sources of revelation. This being so, this knowledge can be
evaluated only by a historical and contextual analysis of the situation
out of which those interests arose and in which the knowledge now
functions. A truth-claim may be rejected as false based on its failure to conform with "the way things are" (epistemic critique); it may be
rejected because of some systemic distortion in the way that it was produced and came to be accepted as "true" (genetic critique); or it may be
rejected because it functions in the present to support inequalities that
the majority of members in society would not accept if they were truly
aware of their own interests and of the distorted nature of the ideology
that hides their interests from them (functional critique). In the most
sophisticated theories all three types of critique are operative and interrelated.[14]

In the sixties Metz asserted that theology had not yet really met the
challenge posed by ideology critique. Many "modern" theologies try to
sidestep it by asserting that Christian faith and the salvation it proclaims
deal only with the individual, haunted by anxiety, threatened by the
uttermost possibility and end of his or her existence: death.[15] In his
reflections on concupiscence Metz had already called such an approach
into question, now he comes to speak explicitly of "deprivatizing"
Christian faith, which means bringing its resources to bear on the social
and political milieu that is an inalienable dimension of the individual.
As an *ad intra* critique this means disabusing the Church of its illusions
of political innocence and calling into question those of its praxes that
are related to that illusion. *Ad extra* it means bringing the resources of

Christian faith to bear on the social and political crises that face the society within which that faith lives and for which it is accountable.[16] Metz insists that this does not signal an abandonment of the individual person and his or her concerns. Rather, given the deeply interpersonal, indeed social and political dimensions of the individual subject, the concerns of the person can only be addressed in the wider context of the person's social and political *Mitwelt*.[17] These two critiques, *ad extra* and *ad intra,* define the tasks of political theology, as Metz first conceived it in the sixties.

While convinced of the significance of Marxism's ideology critique, Metz had little use for the orthodox Marxism represented by the Communist bloc. He quite rightly judged doctrinaire Marxism to be rigid and reductionistic. He certainly did not accept its reduction of religion to a reflex of social injustice and suffering, and he found particularly invidious its refusal to consider the positive, subject-forming role of guilt.[18]

He gravitated, rather, toward the revisionary left wing of Marxist theory. This was in large part because many of its representatives were interested in plumbing the depths of religious traditions in order to develop a richer analysis of the present situation and a more potent recommendation of the praxis needed to transform it. A closer analysis of these encounters is necessary: first Metz's rethinking of temporality and Christian theology because of his conversations with Ernst Bloch; second, the philosophy and theology of history he developed as a result of reading Max Horkheimer and Theodor Adorno, then finally his incorporation of the concepts of memory and narrative, particularly as he found them in the writings of Herbert Marcuse and Walter Benjamin.

Ernst Bloch: the primacy of the future and the principle of hope

Metz was thirty-four and had just taken up his position at Münster when he first met Ernst Bloch.[19] Thereupon followed a friendship marked by a long correspondence, many meetings, and frequent conversation and debate. Bloch is a crucial figure in Metz's development. Metz incorporated the Marxist focus on praxis, as well as its disdain for traditional philosophy and metaphysics, as these themes were idiosyncratically articulated by Bloch. Many of the most important themes in Metz's mature theology can be traced back to what he learned from

Bloch, however much Bloch was also a thinker "whom Christian theologians will have to learn from only by disagreeing with him."[20]

Bloch attempted to refunction themes from across the breadth of Western culture, including the heritage of Christianity, the philosophical traditions of German critical and speculative idealism, and the psychoanalytic work of Freud and his disciples.[21] The goal of this refunctioning was to rehabilitate the repressed category of the future and that dimension of human affectivity where it makes its presence felt: hope. He attempted to formulate an ontology of history in terms of the new and novel, the *novum*. Bloch came to believe that metaphysical categories appropriate only for what already is (*das Gewesene*) will inevitably break down in such an attempt; what is needed is a *docta spes* that articulates categories for that which has not yet been (*das Noch-nicht-gewesene*). Refunctioning religion is a crucial part of this project. In an interpretation that has much in common with Feuerbach's, Bloch argues that the authentic function of religion—one that has been and continues to be repressed by religious institutions and their theologies—is to be the bearer of human hope. Religion provides the symbols and narratives which articulate the "more" for which we long and strive in history—a "more" which is not to be found in a transcendent dimension *above* history, but *before* history, in front of us, awaiting our hope-inspired praxis for its irruption into our present. Among the heroes of Bloch's "underground Bible"[22] are the serpent, inciting Adam and Eve to leave the garden so that they could be like gods; Moses, who "turn[s] an idol of thunder and oppression into a source of leadership through time";[23] Job, the figure who will suffer no more under a capricious tyrant-god and calls this god to account;[24] and finally the Jesus who proclaimed our future to lie in himself as Son of Man:

> Jesus' words, "the Father and I are one," took on in this context their true sense of simple *usurpation*. The Son of Man not only broke through the myth of the Son of God, but also through that of the throne "at the right hand of the Father": now a Tribune of the people sits upon that throne, and so revokes it.[25]

Bloch continues tracing this revolutionary tradition through Marcion, through Joachim of Fiore and the Spiritual Franciscans, and then into the German mystical tradition: Meister Eckhart, Johannes Tauler, Angelus Silesius. Above all, it was Thomas Münzer who for the first time set free the revolutionary and utopian potential of this message, energizing the poor to rise up to overthrow and to transform their oppressive social world, so long justified ideologically by appeals to a transcendent Father-God.[26]

Bloch militates for a retrieval of the resources of religion, those resources which feed a hope in a beyond—but not a beyond that is above us, a *Deus absconditus* who rules us from his transcendent heavens; rather, a *Homo absconditus*, a kingdom of freedom which is our own as yet ungrasped and unrealized future. "What is necessary is to transcend without transcendence."[27] An authentic and appropriate materialist critique of Christianity will reject the transcendent hypostasis of God, which only legitimates heteronomy, but will retain the hope-sustaining space formally occupied by this God.

Metz was strongly attracted to this immense if problematic synthesis. It affirmed the thesis he had already defended: the inner connections between modernity—now conceived in terms of the second phase of the Enlightenment—and the biblical and Christian tradition. It began not from metaphysics or a transcendental analysis of the question of being, but rather from that dimension of human being in which we feel ourselves intensely and vulnerably involved in history: the longing and hope for a better future. Under the power of this attraction Metz changed his understanding of theology. In his contribution for a Bloch Festschrift he first used a new definition of theology. Basing himself on 1 Pt 3:15, he defines theology as giving justification for the hope that is us.[28] This shift in definition manifests the incorporation into Metz's thought of two important themes: (1) the primacy of the future and the end of metaphysics, and (2) the centrality of apocalyptic eschatology for Christian theology.

In *Christliche Anthropozentrik* Metz had already argued that the thought-form under which moderns perceive reality was anthropocentric rather than cosmocentric. There he claimed that in modernity static, spatial categories gradually gave way to dynamic, temporal categories; the world appears less and less as a pregiven, static stage for human actions, more and more as history, a humanly created, hominized world. This stress deepens during the sixties, but the way that the historical character of the world is grounded in Christianity changes for Metz, in part as a result of his encounter with Bloch. In Metz's early work it is through the incarnation that God accepts the world and founds its historical development towards autonomy; in his later work it is the eschatological, futural God who draws us forward and in this makes history possible.[29]

In this understanding of the character of our experience of the world as historical, theologies which depend upon transcendental schemata which present a God "above us" become increasingly problematic.[30] In order for theology to continue to operate out of an anthropocentric horizon it must take up an eschatological focus.

> The attempt to read and to understand all of theology as anthropology is an important achievement in contemporary theological work. Yet this "anthropologically turned" theology remains in danger of becoming worldless and historyless so long as it is not understood more primordially as eschatology. Namely, only in the eschatological horizon of hope does the world appear as history. Only in the understanding of the world as history can the significance of persons and their free action be justified within a theological understanding of the world. Only this central importance of human freedom makes possible a legitimate "Christian Anthropocentricity." (*Christliche Anthropozentrik*)[31]

Just as earlier we saw that Metz shifts from existential-transcendental theology to political theology, not to minimalize or neglect the concerns of the individual but more adequately to address them as they are really constituted in his or her *Mitwelt,* so too here with his new understanding of temporality and history. The early approach is abandoned in order to develop a more authentically anthropocentric theology, that is, one that takes its central hermeneutical categories from an anthropocentric, but now future-oriented, understanding of the world.

In the light of this new perspective Metz declared the "end of metaphysics." Taking a cue from Bloch, Metz declared the inadequacy for theology of any philosophy that is constructed out of categories and procedures which are oriented toward what existed in the past or what presently exists. Such philosophies, and the theologies which make use of them, cannot adequately treat the historical nature of human subjectivity, no matter how much they talk about "historicity."[32] At best the future can appear in such systems only as development toward a goal that is already contained in the origins of the present, not as the coming-into-being of something radically new.[33] Marx is cited as the thinker who first understood that the world cannot be adequately

grasped by contemplating what is, but only by reaching forward trans-
formatively in revolutionary praxis towards what is not yet.

> The eschatological City of God is *now* coming into existence, for
> our hopeful approach *builds* this city. We are workers building this
> future, and not just interpreters of this future. . . . The orthodoxy of a
> Christian's faith must constantly *make itself true* in the "orthopraxy"
> of his actions oriented toward the end times, because the promised
> truth is a truth which must be *made* (see Jn 3.21ff.).[34]

We shall see these emphases on praxis and the inadequacy of theory
deepen in his further encounters.

We have already seen that, reflecting on the social dimension of
human being, Metz called for the deprivatization of Christian doctrine.
Here we see that, reflecting on the primacy of the future in understanding temporality, he insisted that eschatology be the guiding *topos* for
Christian theology. These two themes in Metz's thought came together
in a growing realization that eschatology itself had to be deprivatized,
that its concerns had to include more than the death of the individual
and his or her private hopes for an afterlife. He became concerned that
the "demythologization" of Christian apocalyptic-eschatological symbols had "drawn their sting," had dissolved their power to elicit and
sustain a hope for a better world in the future.[35] Thus, he came to insist
more and more on retaining the apocalyptic content of eschatological
symbols, no matter how untimely they might seem, no matter how
ridiculous to "modern consciousness."

His reading of Bloch's *Atheism in Christianity* reinforced this conviction. Reflecting on Bloch's argument that demythologization is often, in
fact, domestication of subversive religious symbols, Metz wrote the following:

> One must ask the demythologizer not only about the "*Sitz im Leben*"
> of the myths but also about his own "*Sitz im Leben*"; one must always
> keep in mind where the critiques of myth are produced, and that
> "modern person" in whose name they allegedly occur: that is to say,
> the house slippers of the critic and the teaching podium of unceas-
> ing reflection, apathy's box seats, in short, the "comfortable study" of
> pure theory, which is well insulated against any "interruption," a
> place where everything is known . . . except that "mythical" language
> in which anxiety and suffering, hope and longing, have been con-
> densed.[36]

This issue is, *whose* hope is the theologian representing when he or she demythologizes eschatological symbols? What danger or crisis forms the horizon of interpretation? In advocating apocalypticism Metz is working from the assumption that the end-time of which it speaks—in language of danger and of hope—is not just that of the solitary subject, but of the social and historical world which cannot be separated from the subject. The "crisis" in the midst of which eschatology gives us hope "is not the experience of anticipation (*Vorlauf*) of one's own death; rather it is the disturbing question about the salvation of the other in death, that is of those who suffer unjustly."[37]

In the seventies he became more insistent on the necessity of framing eschatology as apocalyptic. Insofar as apocalyptic eschatology represents the confluence of Metz's reflections both on human sociality and on temporality, as these influence Christian faith and the ways that its message can and must be proclaimed, it is, as Metz himself avers, "the hem of my theological outline."[38] The masterpiece on this theme is his chapter on time in *Faith in History and Society,* which he dedicated to Bloch.[39] But since it was enriched by his encounter with Benjamin's thought, as well as his thinking back upon the Holocaust, I shall defer discussing it further until I have dealt with those topics. Now we turn to what Metz drew from his reading of thinkers of the early Frankfurt School.

The Dialectic of Enlightenment: Metz and the Frankfurt School

Having already seen Metz's critique of Heidegger, we will not be surprised by his critique of Bloch. Metz will always critique any philosophy that tries to "immanentize" human existence and what is problematic about it in such a way that the answer to human existence is immanent to it, generated from out of the human itself. This is his criticism of Bloch. "Utopias would prove to be the final cunning of evolution (*List der Evolution*) if there were only utopias and no God (before whom not even the past is fixed)."[40] Metz appreciated Bloch's demonstration of how the future-oriented present has emerged out of the Christian tradition but not his proposal that this tradition be secularized, leaving open the "space" formerly occupied by God, but ejecting its occupant. The relationship between modernity and Christianity could not be resolved so easily for Metz. Neither could the ancillary relation between reason and tradition. We have already seen that in his first phase Metz had insisted that Enlightenment reason detaches itself from its roots in the Christian tradition that nourished it only at the cost of losing the real but relative autonomy it had gained out of that tradition.

Metz found confirmation for this position in his reading of Max Horkheimer and Theodor Adorno, and it was to them that he turned for a philosophy of history and of human reason that was more nuanced than what Bloch afforded him. It is no coincidence that he cites them with increasing frequency in the late sixties. In the context of the chaos and violence that swept across Europe and the United States in 1967 and 1968, the increasing involvement of the United States in Vietnam, and the Soviet invasion of Czechoslovakia (which put an end to the promising rapprochement between theology and Marxism which went on under the auspices of the *Paulusgesellschaft*), modernity's prospects seemed dimmer than ever as that decade drew to a close. In this light Metz began speaking of the responsibility of Christianity not just to affirm the course of secularization but to save it from its own excesses. While they would not agree with the remedy Metz proposed, he found in the critical theorists of the Frankfurt School a potent diagnosis of those excesses and the threat they presented.

The history of the *Institut für Sozialforschung* is long and complex, and its members did not produce a uniform position.[41] But some generalizations, adequate for outlining Metz's appropriation of their thought, can be ventured.[42] Their understanding of reason and history belongs to a general family of theories with its roots in the work of Karl Marx and Max Weber, according to which something unprecedented has happened to human reason in modernity.[43] It has become determined by economic categories of control, consumption, and exchange. Hypostatized in this way, as "technical reason," it introduces a dialectical tendency into the drive for enlightenment. Technical reason has as its end only the domination of nature, and is in this sense "one-dimensional." But without any deeper dimension technical reason itself becomes an unquestioned force, a "second nature" that takes on a life of its own over and against individuals in society. Human beings, as a part of nature, become themselves the object of reason's domination of nature. The paradoxical result is that whereas the Enlightenment had as its goal an age in which human beings were emancipated from servitude to nature (and from those superstitions like religion which such servitude engendered), in fact it produced a new servitude to second nature:

a hypostatized and alienated technical reason. Enlightenment passes into mythology; emancipation from nature into new domination by second nature.

This historical analysis is founded on the methodological premise that the duality of subject and object can never be overcome. Horkheimer, and even more strongly Adorno, argued that all attempts to bridge this gap resulted in irrational decisionism (collapsing the object into the subject) or apathetic positivism (collapsing subject into object). Both tendencies have the same result: the disappearance of the subject as the autonomous agent of his or her history. Both are equally to be resisted. In this sense the Frankfurt School represents a return to Kant who, unlike his idealist succesors, held open the gap between subject and object. If Horkheimer accepts the Hegelian logical apparatus of dialectic, it is an *unabgeschlossene Dialektic,* that is, it never reaches an absolute, closed standpoint of the identity of subject and object. This proviso holds true of theory *and* of praxis. Thus, Horkheimer retreats from the Marxist claim (as in, for example, Lukács) that the subject-object dualism is to be transcended in praxis.[44]

This lands Adorno and Horkheimer in a dilemma. If there is neither a theoretical standpoint nor a "revolutionary subject" (e.g., the proletariat) that can rescue reason from its pathological condition, how can one justify one's critiques? Put in the terminology we have seen before, how can one justify one's *hopes* for reason? For what can one *reasonably* hope?[45]

While Metz from the beginning of his career had argued that secularization was an intellectual and social process that had authentic roots in Christianity and so should not be unequivocally resisted, he had never given it unconditional approbation. In the early sixties he spoke of the difference between hominization and humanization. The first refers to the process whereby the world comes to be seen as the result of ongoing self-formation of human beings. The latter refers to the goal of the historical becoming of freedom, whether defined as a kingdom of ends (Kant), the mature communist society (Marx), or a kingdom of freedom (Bloch). It is a society that is free of ideology in its negative form. Society's subjects are no longer deceived as to their genuine interests; knowledge no longer serves the interest of a few. The conditions of history and society are rational: that is, the subjects can recognize their own interests and activity in the structures of society.

For Metz hominization does not necessarily imply humanization:

> Do we not clearly experience that the technical hominization of the world that we have planned, the process of transforming its possibilities into realities, does not unequivocally create increased humanization (and does not the dangerous deceit of Marxism lie in this very attempt to parallel these two processes)?[46]

Indeed, we are in danger of becoming less and less the subjects and more the objects of the planning and manipulation of the future. Hominization leads to dehumanization.[47]

Toward the end of the decade Metz had already appropriated Weber's notion of instrumental reason (*Zweckrationalität*) and was describing the Church as a community of critique on the level of values and goals.[48] A few years later Metz had fully adopted the analyses of Horkheimer and Adorno. Consider, for example, this dense summary, which could have easily come from one of the Frankfurt School thinkers:

> Every attempt at a reconciliation between nature and humanity has at its heart a utopian and thus a historical-dialectical character. The human spirit (*Geist*), which elevates itself above nature, at the same time seeks to objectify its continuing dependence upon nature in the form of nature's domination. While this spirit as history is differentiated from nature to the extent that it points to that state in which it will be freed from the compulsions of nature, and reconciled to nature, at the same time spirit is no longer differentiated from nature to the extent that it, as technology, preserves and continues nature's compulsory forces, in a mounting exploitation and domination of nature. In this tensive field the species is organized as a part of nature that transcends itself, yet because of this is a part of nature that is in conflict with itself and continually wounds itself. Hence the process of becoming a human being (*Menschwerdung*) is always characterized by suffering, and there is no teleological-finalistic mediation of nature and human being.[49]

The reconciliation between nature and humanity is the goal of the humanization of the human world, the condition for the full realization and perfection of humans as subjects in history and society. It is also the goal of the second phase of the Enlightenment. Metz draws much from the dark vision of Adorno and Horkheimer. The Enlightenment is in

crisis, the becoming of subjects in society and history threatens to collapse back into new heteronomy. Writing in 1977, Metz diagnosed
both socialist and capitalist societies as deeply infected by the dialectic
of enlightenment.[50] In the West the responsibility and power to build
the polis has been handed over to technical planning-processes. In the
East an abstract hypostatization of "the people" or "the proletariat" is
proclaimed the subject of history, leading to suffering and oppression for
the living, breathing human subjects in those nations. Metz began—and
continues to this day—speaking of an increasing weariness that is becoming more and the more the response to the task of being subjects in
society and history, and an increasing willingness to adapt ourselves to
the demands of bureaucratized, technical societies, guided by instrumental reason. Using Kant's definition of the ideal of Enlightenment as
the public use of one's reason (*Mündigkeit*) Metz worries that modernity, or postmodernity, is in danger of collapsing into a second *Unmündigkeit*.[51] In the face of this crisis, according to Metz, only the resources
of religion can help:

> If we are to achieve a postbourgeois and post-individualist "rescue of
> the human subject," religion seems to me to be indispensable. With-
> out religion, I see the barbarism of a blind negation of the individual
> breaking out within a postbourgeois society. Without religion, the
> end of bourgeois society threatens to become the very "end of the
> human subject."[52]

Little in Metz's description of the modernity's dark prospects is original.
But, when we ask what it is about religion that makes it the necessary
condition for the "salvation of the subject" in history and society, we
have to turn to what is unique in Metz's understanding of the dialectic
of enlightenment. For Adorno and Horkheimer the dialectic of enlightenment seems to derive from an almost ontological defect in reason, one
that causes it to collapse inevitably into instrumental reason.[53] Metz, on
the other hand, draws on the specifically Christian *topoi* of sin, guilt,
and redemption.

Early in his encounters with Marxism Metz had objected to the
Marxist reduction of the phenomenon of guilt to a mere epiphenome-
non, the manifestation of immaturity and oppression in society.[54] Guilt,
he countered, insofar as it includes a willingness to accept responsibility
for the suffering that characterizes even our histories of emancipation, is
an essential component of becoming and being a subject.[55] The refusal to

take on this responsibility, the attempt to achieve an autonomy which is untouched by the suffering of others in our past and present, is what leads to dialectical tensions and disintegration in the ideals of the Enlightenment. Hence, the relevant dialectic for Metz is not the one between subject and object or reason and nature, but the dialectic between *emancipation*, which seeks the freedom of the subject from all forms of heteronomy, and *redemption*, which acknowledges the enduring responsibility of the subject for the suffering of others, a responsibility from which he or she cannot be released, however autonomous he or she is.[56]

In Metz's narrative, the decline of the Enlightenment begins when modernity tries to resolve the dialectic of redemption and emancipation by absorbing redemption into emancipation. Various Enlightenment theories attempted to come up with understandings of the subject (as rational and responsible) which would not be destabilized by the irrationality manifest in the suffering that arises precisely in and through the history of this subject's emancipation. Metz sees a parallel between these attempts and the attempts to come up with a concept of God which would not be destabilized, made unthinkable, by the horrific and meaningless suffering in history. Enlightenment atheists had rejected these latter attempts, but they did not realize the isomorphism between their own argumentative strategies and the theological arguments they were trying to subvert and replace. They insisted that human beings take on responsibility for history and its suffering rather than falling back on a concept of God who is alleged to be, on the one hand, the one all-good, omnipotent subject who creates and providently guides the cosmos, but who cannot, on the other hand, be assigned responsibility for the evil and suffering in the history for which he is the ultimate subject. "These theories replaced the *Deus Salvator* with *homo emancipator* as the universal subject of history."[57]

But suffering did not go away; indeed, as so many observers of the twentieth century have insisted, meaningless, irrational suffering and oppression were inflicted with at least as high a frequency, and certainly with greater efficiency, in the secularized nation-states born in modernity. Metz argues that various "exculpation devices" were then developed in modern theories of the subject in order to save *homo emancipator*, recently enthroned as the rational, responsible, and increasingly powerful subject of history, from being assigned responsibility for the increasingly irrational, meaningless, and devastating histories of suffering in modernity. Idealist theories develop a transcendental subject, a *Geist* which is coming to be in history. Suffering is the necessary by-product of the emancipatory becoming of this subject; the cunning of reason is not quite cunning enough to realize itself without sacrificing a few victims. Orthodox Marxist theories made the proletariat the authentic subject of history; resistance, irrationality, and responsibility for meaningless suffering and evil can be assigned to its opponents. It is the bourgeoisie that is responsible for the suffering that attends the revolutions which bring the proletariot to their destiny; they are the "enemy" who deserve whatever suffering is inflicted in turn on them. Finally, Metz argues that in the First World, with its highly sophisticated industrial and service economies, the subject of history has become abstract; it has become a hypostatized correlate to a deeply rooted but naive confidence in technology and progress. Those who suffer due to the ineluctable progress toward economic and political modernity are those who (tragically, perhaps, but there is nothing to be done for it) cannot or will not adapt themselves to the exigencies of living in the modern world.

In all of these theories of the subject of history, and the social praxes they legitimate, the key feature is the attempt to produce a subject which, in its emancipatory history toward full autonomy, is free from responsibility for the suffering attendant on that history. Some enemy or other is assigned responsibility for this irrationality, for these contradictions in history, so that the subject (of whatever sort) can be redeemed from contradiction, paradox, or irrationality. The problem is that these "subjects" become increasingly abstracted from concrete men and women, living, struggling, and yes often triumphing, but also suffering and dying in history. Various forms of the Hegelian *Geist* all have their slaughterbenches of history. The proletariat or the party progresses at the expense of the victims of the gulags. The dignity, autonomy, and responsibility of men and women are swallowed up in huge economic, political, and social institutions, whose relevant "experts" tell them what is required in order to keep the systems running smoothly and progressing toward a future which promises little more than the stabilization and continuation of what is now.

In short, whereas Horkheimer and Adorno speak of the never finished or closed dialectic of reason and nature, subject and object, Metz speaks of the dialectic of emancipation and redemption, one dimension of which is the relationship between responsible human action in history and responsibility for meaningless suffering. Horkheimer and Adorno traced the dialectic of enlightenment, with all its barbarous consequences, to the attempt to close or transcend the dialectic of reason and nature by means of idealism, positivism, or instrumental reason. Metz traces it to the attempt to formulate an understanding of the subject that needs no redemption, needs no release from the guilt that falls to it due to the meaningless suffering that occurs in its history. No coherent and humane concept of the subject can be achieved in this way:

> A history of emancipation without a history of redemption exposes the historical subject to new irrational pressures in the face of the concrete histories of suffering: either the pressure to suspend transcendentally his or her own historical responsibility, to live in continual enmity, or finally to negate him or herself as a subject. No determinate, concrete freedom is promoted by the refusal to accept guilt; rather only a laboriously concealed heteronomy. The autonomy and maturity (*Mündigkeit*) of a totalized emancipation is full of inner contradictions. . . . In the final analysis, living on only by means of repressed guilt or by projecting guilt on to some alibi-subject, this autonomy is precisely what Adorno so insightfully feared: banal. The expression of truncated freedom. The end of the history of freedom as the apotheosis of banality![58]

What is needed is not a more sophisticated theory of reason (not even Habermas's), but an understanding of the subject who is not only free to craft history and society in his or her own image but is also free to take responsibility for the guilt that attends this labor and the inner contradictions within the subject that this guilt reveals.

We have come very close to the central question that guides Metz's revised anthropology. The question of meaningless suffering and death in history is the question of our responsibility for this suffering, particularly as it has been inflicted on the crushed and subjugated victims of the history of reason's coming to autonomy. We will take this up in the next chapter. But to bring out its full depth we need to turn to another crucial figure in Metz's development, from whom he learned to speak of history as the history of suffering, and from whom he learned to emphasize the *anamnestic* and narrative structure of reason: Walter Benjamin.

Reason, Memory, and Dangerous Stories: Walter Benjamin

In considering critical theory we saw that its practitioners found themselves in a seemingly irresolvable dilemma. According to their analysis, reason under the conditions of modernity has become a one-dimensional, instrumental reason. Theoretical reason has become entranced by positivism. The sort of critical theory that Horkheimer and Adorno were striving to develop, which asserted that "the facts" are ideologically determined, and that empirical methods that seek nothing but an objective explanation of these facts are no less ideological, could not but appear to be utopian, romantic, or simply irrational to the traditional *Wissenschaften* as practiced in the academy.[59] Practical reason has fallen just as much under the spell of criteria of utility, of usefulness for satisfying certain needs and interests. But, as realms of society which were once relatively autonomous—art, the academy, private life—are brought under the management of instrumental reason, the true interests of society's members are increasingly hidden to them. Critical theorists vigorously protested the characterization of their thought as utopian, romantic, or reactionary, but then where do the rational grounds for critical theory and praxis exist which would remove this suspicion about their thought? Both of the mainstays of prior forms of critical theory, ideology critique and immanent critique, seem stymied.[60]

Faced with this dilemma, Adorno, Horkheimer, and Marcuse say that one can only search for traces, points of resistance from past and present, out of which one can hope for a future that cannot be derived from the totality of what is. Avant-garde art played an important role here, particularly for Adorno and, to a somewhat lesser extent, for Marcuse. But memory—remembrance, or anamnesis—also came to have an increasingly important part to play as a power which could resist modernity's attempt to remake the past in its own image, to rewrite it as a Whig history of progress in which the vanquished and forgotten are finally deprived even of their power to disturb our present self-satisfaction. As Marcuse puts it:

> Remembrance of the past may give rise to dangerous insights, and the established society seems to be apprehensive of the subversive contents of memory. Remembrance is a mode of dissociation from the given facts, a mode of "mediation" which breaks, for short moments, the omnipresent power of the given facts.[61]

In the late sixties Metz grasped this insight and wove it into the fabric of his thought. It completed the temporal structure of the anthropology that had been emerging over the previous decade. If the Christian's stance toward the future is one of *hope*, his or her stance to the past is defined as *memory*. It is primarily, paradigmatically, a memory of the passion, death, and resurrection of Jesus Christ. In this memory

> the dominion of God among us is revealed by this, that dominion of men over men has begun to be thrown down, that Jesus declared himself to be on the side of the invisible, the oppressed and exploited, and thus proclaimed the coming dominion of God as the liberating power of an unconditional love.[62]

The hope, for which Christians are called to give an account (1 Pt 3:14), is a specific hope. It is the hope on which past generations of believers lived, on which they staked their lives. It is a hope of those who are invisible, who have vanished, been conquered; it is a hope that the totality of their present—which denied them the dignity of being subjects of their own histories—is not all there is. It is this hope, grounded in the promises of a God "before whom not even the past is fixed," that Metz contrasts to Bloch's hope in a coming utopia.[63] Because their future is still outstanding, the memory of the promises made to those who have suffered and disappeared in the past projects a future that is more than a mere extrapolation of the present, because it cannot be encompassed by the history of success that culminates in what exists in the present. This gives these memories their disturbing, dangerous character. It also gives them their power to break through the systematically managed totality of present society, with its pregiven agenda of what a "reasonable" person ought to desire, hope for, and struggle for. Only these sorts of memories can save us from "the banality of what presently exists and the future which can be projected from it alone."[64] In short, only dangerous memories, of the type exemplified by the *memoria passionis, mortis et resurrectionis Jesu Christi* can break the dialectic of enlightenment.

The other key figure in Metz's appropriation of the concept of memory is Walter Benjamin.[65] Benjamin, who asserted that "there is no document of civilization which is not at the same time a document of barbarism,"[66] articulated and contributed to Metz's own growing understanding that history is at least as much a history of suffering

(*Leidensgeschichte*) as it is a history of progressive emancipation (*Freiheitsgeschichte*). The classic statement of Benjamin's critique of any simple, undialectical concept of progress, is his interpretation of Klee's painting *Angelus Novus*:

> Where we perceive a chain of events, he [the angel] sees one single catastrophe which keeps piling wreckage upon wreckage and hurls it in front of his feet. The angel would like to stay, awaken the dead, and make whole what has been smashed. But a storm is blowing from Paradise; it has got caught in his wings with such violence that the angel can no longer close them. This storm irresistibly propels him into the future to which his back is turned, while the pile of debris before him grows skyward. This storm is what we call progress.[67]

Benjamin brought together remembrance of the catastrophic past with an apocalyptic, messianic hope in the future:

> We know that the Jews were prohibited from investigating the future. The Torah and the prayers instructed them in remembrance.... This does not imply, however, that for the Jews the future turned into homogeneous, empty time. For every second of time was the strait gate through which the Messiah might enter.[68]

As Ottmar John has shown, Benjamin's critique of historicism, as well as his critique of fascism, takes form as a critique of the quasi-mythical representation of time which has come to dominate modernity: empty time, time as an homogeneous continuum of moments which have no goal, and finally no subject. This is the time that is the presupposition of the undialectical understanding of history as progress.[69] This sort of time has to be arrested; the thinking that it enables, indeed necessitates, has to be interrupted.[70]

This view of time is the perspective of those who have been crushed by progress; it is the perspective obtained from the midst of modernity's histories of suffering. It is also the perspective out of which one hopes for a future which is more than "more of the same." That is, it is the perspective which defines heuristically and proleptically the future of hope that Metz had taken as central to Christian faith.

Benjamin, then, formed the perfect complement to Bloch in Metz's reflections on the nature of time. He added a new depth-dimension to Metz's appeal for the authority of apocalyptic traditions in Christianity. The time which characterizes instrumental rationality is evolutionary time:

> The understanding of reality which guides the scientific-technological domination of nature, and out of which the cult of the makeable draws its reserves, is stamped by a representation of time as an empty continuum which extends evolutionarily into infinitude. Everything is mercilessly, gracelessly enclosed in this continuum. It expels any substantive expectation and thus engenders that fatalism that eats at the souls of modern men and women.[71]

Metz has nothing against the usage of the models of evolution or development in the natural sciences, or even in politics. Rather, he objects to an ideological usage, to the universalization of the model of evolution to encompass our experience of time and history in general.[72] Under the latter understanding of time nothing really new can happen in history; rather, the future can be only the extrapolation of the present. In Metz's view all the major contemporary political forces and ideologies have taken up this illegitimate representation of time. Left and right err alike to the degree that they see the future as arising only out of the continuation of present conditions and processes: whether it be revolutionary class struggle or the progressive amassment of techniques and commodities. The pseudo-religious mythic symbol of evolution leads to apathy and fatalism. Time is like the music on the radio that plays in between reports of catastrophe or atrocity. It plays on, "as if the passage of time had become audible, mercilessly rolling over everything, a passage that nothing can interrupt."[73] No one can expect anything new, only the eternal return of the same.[74]

This is the fear to which apocalyptic speaks. While apocalyptic may perhaps function to give consolation when one perceives imminent catastrophe, it can also speak to a deeper anxiety that arises from the feeling that *nothing* is imminent:

> Yet for modern persons there is an anxiety that has become more radical, not only an anxiety that everything could come to an end, rather—more deeply rooted—an anxiety that nothing at all comes to an end anymore, that everything is sucked into the wake of a faceless and graceless time, which finally rolls over everything like a grain of sand in the sea.[75]

Which attitude toward time, Metz asks, inspires and empowers radical action? A view in which time "is an empty eternity stretched out and dissolved by evolution in which anything and everything can happen except this one thing—that one particular moment should become 'the strait gate through which the Messiah might enter'?"[76] Or a time in which we hope for, indeed expect, the unexpected, unpredicted interruption of this endless continuum? Metz insists that it is the latter. Consequently, insofar as theology has demythologized Christianity's apocalyptic sting—a demythologization which is really only its remythologization under the horizon of the master-myth of evolutionary time—it has less and less to offer in the face of the ever increasing apathy of our time, in which we are increasingly becoming the voyeurs of our own dissolution as responsible subjects in history.[77]

In the final analysis, what Metz draws on from apocalypticism is not its penchant for manipulating prophetic passages so as to arrive at "the day and the hour." Rather, it is the assertion that we are living in extraordinary times, and that these extraordinary times, filled with danger and persecution, both justify and require an extraordinary response, one that cannot be legitimated, justified, or sustained under the ordinary dispensation of reality.[78] But part of the case that apocalypticism must make is that we *do* live in an extraordinary time, rife with catastrophe. What in one person might inspire the deep sense of longing and hope for an interruption of the course of things, might inspire in another a bored channel-switch on the remote control. This is where dangerous memories come in. As we saw above, for Benjamin remembrance is intimately tied with expectation. The memory of suffering, and the sense of the catastrophic that it inspires, are tied to a hope for a future that is different from and more than an extrapolation of our present. This memory of suffering, and the apocalyptic hope to which it brings us, nurtures that sense of the extraordinary character of our time which both sustains and justifies a radical response: a radical imitation of Christ. "Following Christ and looking forward to the second coming belong together like the two sides of a coin."[79]

How then to communicate this sense of danger? How to revive the atrophied faculty of memory, of remembrance (*Eingedenken*)?[80] The cognitive medium for dangerous memories is not the analytic report or the discursive argument. While necessary in their own place and time, neither is suited for the recovery of the past that has been forgotten (the past of history's victims), or for the temporally tensed, involved experience of danger with which apocalypticism is charged. It is narrative, it is the story, that does this. Metz draws again on Benjamin, as well as on Gershom Scholem and Martin Buber, each of whom in his own way tried to recover the lost art of storytelling.[81]

Several themes come together here. First, Metz's insistence that no pure theory can articulate and communicate the truth of Christianity finds expression in the primacy given to narrative over interpretation or argument.[82] The dependence of faith—indeed of human reason—on the narratives which come down through tradition is a continuation of Metz's early assertion that reason is dependent upon history in ways that cannot be made fully transparent to it by virtue of its own powers. Narrative is the only genre appropriate for communicating the way that the new—which cannot be theoretically defined or articulated in advance—breaks into history. Finally, narrative permits us to remember and make present to ourselves our history, without the dangers involved in theoretical conceptions of history, with their tendency to cover over history's catastrophes. The dangerous stories of past suffering invite us to hope for the salvation which Christian faith believes is coming even for those who have suffered unjustly and been crushed in the past. These stories "work," however, to the extent that we do enter into them, allow ourselves to be taken up by them and transformed by hearing or reading them.

In a sense Metz is again on familiar ground, taking up the hermeneutical strands of his Heideggerian background, as that was continued by Gadamer. Gadamer too argues that reason is irreducibly involved in traditions and narratives which bring what is different from our past (and yet not totally different, since they are from *our* past) into a transformative encounter with our present. Yet Metz combines Gadamer with Benjamin and Marcuse. The authentic function of narrative is not to build up identity; they do not only or primarily help us to interpret and reflexively secure our present experience. Rather, it is to break down, interrupt, and upset our present self-interpretation, to open us to an eschatological meaning of our present existence, that, if not encompassing the meaninglessness and suffering of the past, at least allows it to exist, to have its (counter)voice.[83] This meaning cannot be argumentatively justified, but hoped and labored for. In this hope, and the praxis it guides, the liberating power of the memories and narratives can emerge.

Metz compares narrative with sacrament: it is a *signum efficax*.[84] Using the examples of Hasidic stories, drawn from Buber and Scholem, as well as Benjamin's insistence that stories are not meant to convey information as much as they are meant to transform us through the interchange of experience, Metz conceives of narratives as signs or words that effect what they narrate. They work to the degree that they transform us, widen the horizon of our hope and the interests that guide our praxis. Theology's task is not to come up with a theory that can justify in advance the hope and faith communicated by the narrative, much less to replace them or relegate them to the status of helpful pedagogical aids to be used with simple believers. Rather, theology's task is "to protect the memory communicated narratively in the midst of our scientific world, to put it at stake and to guide this memory into new narratives, without which the experience of salvation remains dumb."[85]

Metz has come a long way indeed due to his encounters with Marxist theories. He took up a whole new battery of philosophical tools and concepts—hope, praxis, solidarity, memory, narrative, dialectic of enlightenment. Yet his intention throughout was to come to a more adequate understanding of human involvement in history and society in order better to mediate the truth and power of Christian faith to modernity. Before proceeding to a summary of Metz's mature understanding of Christian faith and theology, however, we must consider one final encounter in Metz's career. Many of the themes listed above intensified as a result of this encounter, and new ones entered his thought. We now turn to consider how Metz came to grips with Judaism in the light of Auschwitz.

ENCOUNTERS WITH JUDAISM AND THE EMERGENCE OF THE SPIRITUALITY OF "LEIDEN AN GOTT"

In 1972 Metz wrote the following in his journal:

In conversations with friends, not least with Bloch, it becomes ever clearer to me how much the Jewish traditions after Christ, the apocalyptic-messianic wisdom of Judaism, have been cut off and repressed in Christianity. The Old Testament must be read by Christians not only in the light of the story of Jesus, but in the shadow of that history of suffering which has befallen the Jews living in the midst of all too triumphant Christians.[86]

While in the late sixties Metz had begun speaking of the dark side of European history, his observations were general and abstract. Certainly, however, he could not have read Benjamin, Adorno, and Horkheimer without running up against the Holocaust. Benjamin took his life while fleeing the Nazis. From the late thirties on, the Holocaust was a central concern of the Frankfurt School, as the symptom par excellence of liberalism's dialectical self-transformation into barbarism. Only slowly, however, does the Holocaust become crucial for Metz's theology. Auschwitz is not mentioned in *Faith in History and Society*. Judaism is mentioned in the text three times, and although two of these references are to the history of Jewish persecution, this history is not directly associated with or given as an example of the history of suffering which Metz cites so frequently in this text. By Metz's own account, it was while working on a draft for the documents of a West German Episcopal Synod that this theme first emerged explicitly.[87]

But it is in the years 1978 and 1979 that both the history of the persecution and attempted annihilation of the Jews, and the histories of suffering in the Third World, particularly Latin America, enter Metz's writings with full force and give powerful concreteness to the concepts he had worked out over the prior decade.[88] Metz admits how slowly he came to grips with these catastrophes. It became particularly troubling to him that Auschwitz was never mentioned in Karl Rahner's theology.[89] I have been arguing that Metz's theological odyssey is best understood as an attempt to define a stance toward the world and history, articulated with new conceptual tools, for which the concrete catastrophes of history would be an irritating, interruptive presence internal to faith and for which theology would be constitutionally on the lookout. If I am right on this then at least part of the reason why it took so long for the Holocaust to become such an important event in Metz's theology is that it took time for him to develop the conceptual tools and to formulate a theology for which Auschwitz would show up as the central and devastating challenge to Christianity and to Christian theology. Having found the tools, Metz siezed upon the Holocaust as *the* test-case for his new post-idealistic, political theology. This led to three further results: first, the intensification of already appropriated themes; second, a reevaluation of the biblical roots of Christianity; third, the definition of authentic Christian spirituality as "suffering unto God."

First, then, dealing with the Holocaust engaged the full constellation of concepts and themes that Metz had been slowly assembling over a period of fifteen years. Auschwitz is the paradigmatic case of an inter-ruption in history, a meaningless surd which cannot be encompassed by any system of thought:

> For this theology [political theology], the "system" can no longer be the place of theological truth—not, at least, since the catastrophe of Auschwitz, which no one can ignore without cynicism or can allow to evanesce into an "objective" system of meaning.[90]

Only memory can make this catastrophe present to us without taming it and removing its sting. It can be brought within the horizon of Chris-tian faith and hope only by means of narratives which transform us as they irritate our present horizon of understanding and hope, as they call us to hope with and for those without hope. What more radical hope could there be than a hope for an inbreaking of God's redemptive grace, a grace which makes all things new, a grace which would enable even the massacred and disappeared to be subjects with us before God? Nurturing this hope through remembrance and narrative irritates our present limited horizon of hope; it also moves us toward more radical action. Again, if our present temporal situation is extraordinary, if it is characterized both by great danger and great hope—in short, if it is an *apocalyptic* situation—then an extraordinary response is required and justified: the response of a more radical praxis of imitation of Christ. Hence, we do not remember history's disasters in order to drown ourselves in guilt or paralyze ourselves with despair, but to move us to a critical and liberating response that is justified and required by the apocalyptic character of our situation. Jon Sobrino's admonition with regard to the crucified peoples of Latin America speaks Metz's own mind: "The sole object of all this talk [about crucified people] must be to bring them down from the cross."[91]

As he grappled with the Holocaust, Metz also found what would be for his thought *the* central question, a question that plays an analo-gous role to the question of being for Heidegger, or the question of meaningful existence for theologians like Tillich or Rahner. This is an issue that first arises in the seventies but rapidly becomes the center of gravity of his theology during the eighties: the issue of theodicy.[92] Metz's use of this technical term is quite idiosyncratic. The problem is the one traditionally considered under this theme: the contradictions involved in thinking and preaching an all-good, omnipotent God in the face of a creation (God's creation) filled with senseless suffering and evil. But in

Metz's view the correct theological response is *not* to produce arguments which overcome these contradictions. He insists that not only will any such theodicy fail by theoretical criteria but more seriously that the attempt to solve the problem on a theoretical level is misguided from the start. This is not the sort of question that theologians should think about, write about in a book with a nice tidy solution, and then move on to other matters. Theology cannot, should not, "solve" the question of theodicy at all:

> Its systematic task consists rather in this: continually to allow this question to arise, to make it clear that this question cannot be transferred to human jurisdiction, and to work out the concept of hope according to which *God* "justifies" Godself in the face of the histories of suffering of humankind. Christian theology conceives of the "yes" to God in the face of the theodicy-question as a "suffering unto God" (*an Gott leiden*), which is finally measured against that suffering of being abandoned by God, as it has become unforgettable in Jesus' cry from the cross.[93]

Here we see that, in Metz's usage, theology as theodicy has as one its primary tasks *deconstructing* the various "answers" that have been produced by theodicies, traditionally conceived. As we saw above in looking at Metz's theological rendering of the "dialectic of enlightenment," theology as theodicy will just as much unmask various secular attempts to explain away suffering in history or dissolve any sense of responsibility for it. This is the negative function of "theodicy."[94]

Its positive function lies in setting the agenda for theological reflection and also (insofar as we do not lose ourselves in spurious solutions) in pointing the intellectual work of theology beyond itself to the more fundamental work of prayer, of spirituality. The question with which one begins sets the agenda for his or her thinking. It determines heuristically how one will proceed and the canons for determining the adequacy of the answers one finds. What question best guides and impels the agenda of political theology? Theodicy: a question which, when honestly posed and confronted, makes it problematic, perhaps even obscene, to speak of history solely as the history of the self-realization or self-expression (without sin, which needs to be borne, which calls out for redemption) of any rational subject, be that subject God, be it *Geist*, be it the proletariat or be it democratic capitalism.[95] This irritating question can, in Metz's view, finally be "answered" only by looking to the apocalyptic future that is disclosed to us in God's promises. This draws us into the other themes that we have already seen: the apocalyptic future is disclosed to us when we identify with the victims of history through memory and narratives. It also brings us to spirituality. Theodicy does not finally issue in an argument that speaks *for* God, but presses those who ask it, in all its depth, into a stance of speaking *with* God: to prayer. Before we consider the form of prayer, of spirituality, to which the theodicy question finally brings us, we need to examine one more link in the chain, for Metz came most fully to express and argue the link between the theodicy question and a particular spirituality by reference to the Hebrew Scriptures.

The question ultimately has to be turned back on God. Metz was strongly influenced by Ernst Bloch's reading of Job as the figure who refused to accept his friends' theoretical theodicies.[96] Metz urges that we cry out, complain, call God to account. He criticizes Augustine for absolving the all-powerful creator God from responsibility by blaming evil in history solely on human sin.[97] As a consequence, the "hunger and thirst for justice," which defines the theodicy question as a question about God's responsibility for and response to injustice, is replaced by an anthropocentric question about individual human sin. As a "corrective" to this tendency to deflect the trajectory of the theodicy question, Metz calls for a retrieval of strands in biblical tradition that have either been ignored or excessively privatized: the prophets, the psalms of complaint and lamentation, Lamentations itself, and of course, Job. These strands of the tradition call God to account, grumble against God, but also expect more of God, expect more of history, and thus empower and require those who hear and enact them to *act* more out of those apocalyptic hopes and expectations.

In summary, Metz's encounter with Judaism led him to reevaluate the biblical roots of Christianity and, given his perduring thesis about the interdependence of Christianity and modernity, of modernity as well. Metz had always made a contrast between the Hellenistic thought-form and that of the Hebrew Bible. He becomes more specific in his mature thought, arguing that there is a particular heritage of thinking that the Hebrew Bible has to offer us, over against the heritage of the Greeks. Metz argues that whereas Greek thinking is characterized by ahistorical categories, the thinking of the Hebrew Bible is historical; its rationality is marked by anamnesis, by remembrance.[98] Metz insists that the latter are genuinely cognitive categories; the biblical response to the world is a thought-ful response, rather than merely a faith response which only comes fully to thought when complemented by Greek cognitive categories.

It is in biblical Israel that we find the correct way of posing and responding to the theodicy question. First, according to Metz, the biblical tradition carried out the negative task that theodicy indicates for theology: it continually raised the issue of suffering in history and refused to be consoled or silenced by conceptual solutions. This characterizes biblical Israel's "poverty of spirit":

> Israel's fidelty to God expressed itself in this form of poverty. Israel remained in the final analysis always a "landscape of cries"; its faith did not so much develop into answers for the suffering that they experienced, it expressed itself above all as a questioning that arose out of suffering, as an incessant questioning turning back upon God [*Rückfragen an Gott*].[99]

This poverty of spirit is the foundation for authentic biblical speech about God. Of course, poverty of spirit is also a classic trope in the history of Christian spirituality. Here, though, Metz connects it not with indifference to the goods of this world, but with a mystical stance toward God and world that Metz defines as *Leiden an Gott*: suffering unto God. This is the mystical disposition that is finally required by the cognitive disposition of turning one's questioning back toward God (*Rückfragen an Gott*). Let us explore this connection a bit further.

I claimed earlier that the questions one begins with are crucial determining features of the theology and spirituality that one ends up with. Questioning arises from cognitive dissonance, from a lack of reconciliation in one's experience. It then directs us in certain ways and toward certain places in order to seek answers. In other words, our questions arise out of, and guide at a fundamental level, how we respond to the world. Thus, it is important to know the source of the dissonance, where and how we are confronted with the data which disrupt our previous state of cognitive equilibrium, our sense that we have answered all the relevant questions. In positing the theodicy question as *the* theological question, Metz locates this source in suffering. It is particularly the senseless suffering of others that opens up a such a gap; it creates a painful dissonance in our experience of reality. If these questions cannot be "solved" theoretically, but rather turn us toward God, then the question which theology (as theodicy) can and should continually present to us leads us to a presence to God that goes beyond theology: it leads us to a spirituality. By appeal to the biblical resources named above, Metz suggests that "suffering unto God" is the fundamental and authentic Jewish and Christian way of being sensitive to the world; our suffering, but particularly the suffering of others which we experience or remember, should turn us toward God. But it should turn us toward God full of complaint, crying out, expecting a response. Job is the exemplar of this stance from the Hebrew Bible; Jesus is its incarnation in the New Testament:

> His cry from the cross is the cry of one who has been abandoned by God but who, for his part, has never abandoned God. This points us unavoidably to Jesus' God-mysticism. Jesus holds firm to divinity; in the abandonment of the cross he affirms a God who is quite different from the echoes of our wishes, however ardent; who is still more and different from the answers to our questions, however heartfelt and passionate—as in Job, as finally in Jesus himself. "And why do you pray to God if you know that no one can understand his answers?" the young Elie Wiesel asked the sexton of Sighet. And he responded, "So that he might give me the power to pose the right questions."[100]

To pose the right questions. This is the crux of things for Metz. In the sixties he had spoken of the eschatological proviso: the future of God is more than, and hence relativizes, any particular human future.[101] In the seventies and eighties Metz's worry was that Christianity had been domesticated into a "bourgeois religion." Its questions, and hence its answers, had been set by instrumental reason. They were excessively individualistic questions and assigned religion the function of managing, soothing, and pacifying those concerns that could not be dealt with or successfully silenced by highly advanced capitalist systems.[102] It is the spirituality of suffering unto God—which exposes us to the full force of suffering in history but does so in the light of the good news of a God who has promised to hear and respond compassionately to the cries of those who suffer—that bursts our theological systems and ignites our questions anew, but now directed most primordially toward God, in the language of prayer.

Metz insists on a "negative theology" of hope: no image of God can be constructed based on what we hope for now, no matter how ardent or legitimate that hope may be. God as *Deus semper major* escapes any individual context of hope, questioning, or desiring. This does not mean that we hope for less, or stop hoping, but rather that we hope for more, that we allow a universal horizon of hope, which includes even the unredeemed suffering of the past, continually to interrupt and transform our hopes, and the "God" defined by those hopes. One could very legitimately put in Metz's theology the words uttered by Meister Eckhart: "God deliver me from God."

The power and virtue of the Hebrew Bible, and of Mark's Jesus, lie precisely in the unwillingness to allow one's hopes, one's hunger and thirst for justice, to be prematurely cut short by any sort of argumentative strategy. It is this unwillingness to be consoled by anything short of God's apocalyptic interruption of history that energizes an authentic hope and praxis for the sake of all persons in history. It mourns more in order to and because it hopes more, expects more, and determines its actions according to this "more." This *excessus* cannot be argued to because it is part of the mystery of God and the mystery of human suffering, mysteries which are intertwined in the person, actions, and fate of Jesus of Nazareth, mysteries which can be fully grasped only in discipleship. The spirituality of *Leiden an Gott,* which Metz articulated as he grappled with the horror of Auschwitz, is the indispensable initiation into that discipleship which awakens us to the pertinent data, directs the questioning, and indicates the shape of an adequate response. It is the heart, in all senses of the word, of Metz's political theology.

A SUMMARY OF METZ'S MATURE THEOLOGY

I shall bring this chapter to a close by summarizing Metz's mature understanding of theology and the key themes and concepts that must be taken into account by any systematic attempt to articulate his thought. There is no better place to start than from the summary definition of Christian faith that Metz himself gives in *Faith in History and Society*:

The faith of Christians is a praxis in history and society which is understood as solidaristic hope in the God of Jesus as the God of the living and the dead, who calls all to be subjects in God's presence. In this thoroughly apocalyptically expectant praxis (of discipleship) Christians prove themselves in historical struggle for men and women: they commit themselves to a reality in which all persons become subjects in solidarity, and in this praxis they resist the danger of a creeping evolutionary dissolution of the history of men and women as subjects, as well as the danger of a negation of the individual in view of a new, as it were, post-bourgeois image of the person.[103]

Faith is a praxis: a way of relating to and acting within history and society. This praxis is understood as a solidaristic hope (*solidarische Hoffnung*). It is also apocalyptically expectant discipleship or imitation of Christ (*Nachfolge*). Here the future-oriented, apocalyptic temporality of Metz's theology finds expression. Christian praxis is guided not only by what can be reasonably hoped for, expected, or projected at present. The hope that guides it is a solidaristic hope: that is, it is a hope with others; it encompasses the hopes of all those who have been called by God to be subjects in God's presence, including the dead, including the dead of Auschwitz, Ayacucho, the Middle Passage, or Wounded Knee.

This hope, and the expectation that the radically new—that which is not reducible to our reasonable expectations—can and will break into history, calls forth, justifies, and is nourished by the praxis of imitation of Christ. In particular this means bringing Jesus' love and partiality for the marginalized into the political and social structures in and through which we create and recreate ourselves. It means overcoming the apathy and cynicism in which the suffering, injustice, and oppression, about which we are so well informed today, inspires only the helpless shrug or the world-weary wisdom that knows so much about "the way things are" and hopes for so little. This praxis is not justified or legitimated in advance by any pure theory, but only in terms of the new state of affairs it wishes to effect. As Horkheimer said, "the proof of the pudding is in the eating," to which Bloch adds, "this eating gives us something to do: we have to cook the pudding first."

While it cannot be justified purely argumentatively, this faith can be nourished. It can be sustained, often irritatingly, among believers. A space for this universal solidaristic hope in the God of the living and the dead is held open by dangerous memories, passed on in narrative. The master narrative for Christians is the dangerous story of Jesus' passion, death, and resurrection. This narrative opens us to the manifold, tragic recapitulations of that story, and allows us to remember those who have suffered and been vanquished in history. Remember with hope. They too are called by God to be subjects in God's presence. This hope is allowed us only to the degree that we identify with the disappeared of history, hope with and for them, and act out of that hope.

Finally, this faith is nourished by the spirituality which we have seen emerging at the heart, *as* the heart, of Metz's theology. What sort of stance will initiate us more deeply into the *imitatio Christi* that Metz advocates? What will wake us up, not just from our dogmatic slumber, as Kant would have it, but (to borrow a phrase from Jon Sobrino) from the sleep of inhumanity?[104] Without this wakefulness, without a particular, and often painful sensitivity or attentiveness to the suffering in our world which is so easy to overlook, particularly in our highly managed mediacracies in the First World, the theological arguments and praxes of Metz's political theology cannot get off the ground, because the data they grapple with do not show up as significant. It is not academic system or theological argument that will do this, but spirituality. We have seen that Metz names the spirituality that does this a mysticism of "suffering unto God." It will be the subject of the final chapters of this book, but it is important to place it here in our first provisional summary of key themes in Metz's thought.

Only such faith, hope, and love, articulated in anamnesis and narrative, nourished by the spirituality of "suffering unto God," allow us to be genuinely present to our social and historical *Mitwelt*, including its catastrophes. They allow us to bear the fact that the great structures and documents of culture, in which we recognize our dignity and value as subjects, are also, as Benjamin insisted, documents of barbarism for so many. In them we resist the urge to make clean, black-and-white divisions in history, placing the blame on "the other," whoever that might be. We also resist the tendency to ascribe the processes and events of history to a faceless force of evolution or historical dialectics. However much these short-term strategies allow us to preserve an illusion of innocence, perhaps creating the psychological and social space to get on with things, in the long run they harbor a great danger: that one day the dialectic of enlightenment might close in on itself irretrievably. Having refused to recognize ourselves in the dark underside of history, we gradually lose a sense of our presence even in the grandeur and triumphs of history. We would then no longer be the subjects who create and express ourselves in our society and history but rather the objects of social and historical processes which, although created by humans, are no longer humane but run according to standards of efficiency, standardization, and maximization of profit. Such systems would run on, with no other goal than their own reproduction, in a time with nothing new, no interruptions, no "new heaven and new earth." And no human subjects either.

This is the Christian faith. What of theology? What are its tasks? While Metz has insisted on the primacy of praxis in solidarity with the hopes of others, while he maintains that the Christian community is a community of narrative and memory before it is a community of interpretation or argument, he does not deny that argument has its place. Although Metz deeply distrusts any "division of labor" between theological disciplines, I believe that we can use his early work as a guide in order to distinguish three functions.[105]

The first function is "to protect the narrating memory of salvation in our scientific world."[106] Theology must defend the categories of memory and narrative as authentically cognitive categories, in a world dominated by technical rationality. This is not far from the first function of philosophy that Metz had cited in the early sixties: the constitutive function. Recall that Metz had formulated as one of the tasks of philosophy that of showing that human reason is dependent upon concrete historical events in order to become present to itself and to understand its transcendental constitution. Similarly here, fundamental theology has the task of defending the narrative and anamnestic character of reason against positivism or historicism, both of which undercut the authoritative character of memory and narrative.

A second function of theology is to critique and elaborate the content of narrative, including its institutionalized form as dogma. Metz sees Karl Rahner's work as a virtuoso performance of the elaboration of faith. In Metz's reading, Rahner's theology shows how the doctrines of the Catholic Church can be retrieved and narrated as the mystical life-story of an everyday Christian, living out his or her life in the presence of God.[107] Yet, Metz includes in this task a hermeneutic of suspicion with regard to Christianity's narratives and dogmas. Perhaps not everything can be retrieved. If dogmas, or the narratives of faith, have lost their dangerous character, if they have been co-opted and tamed by forces of oppression, then they need to be critiqued. This includes criticizing those instances of demythologization in which the content of Christian narratives and dogmas are excessively privatized, thus drawing their apocalyptic sting and dissolving their dangerous and thereby liberating character within the public sphere. Metz suggests that an essential tool for such a task would be a practical-critical theory of memory and narrativity in the social practices and processes in which knowledge is handed on, and that such a theory would need to be worked out in collaboration with social sciences (at least those that were willing to accept the challenge from the side of theology that they take seriously the irreducible element of narrative and memory in the processes of society), but Metz offers few hints as to what such a theory would look like.[108]

Finally, a third and related function for the theologian is the maieutic task of eliciting new narratives, of helping Christians understand their own life-stories in the light of the memory of the passion, death, and resurrection of Jesus, and in this way to pass on this dangerous memory narratively.[109] In none of these functions can argumentative theology replace the narratives with a theory or new set of propositions for the faithful to believe. It is strictly *actus secundus,* yet an essential one.

The primary focus of Metz's work is not the work of retrieving and critiquing dogma and narrative from the past; neither is Metz a facilitator for a base Christian community, however much he admires them. I would suggest that Metz has primarily occupied himself with the first task, that of defending the cognitive nature of memory and narrative in the understandings of reason and the subject in contemporary society and the academy. This brings us to his use of the term "subject," which appears three times in the definition of Christian faith given above. As I argued in chapter 2, while shifting away from an anthropological focus in the sixties Metz was in fact assembling a new set of themes and concepts which would allow him to operate out of a new fundamental understanding of the subject, an understanding that first emerges in *Faith in History and Society* and thereafter permeates his work up to this very day. This is the conceptual locus of Metz's theology.

The themes and concepts which such an anthropology would have to integrate are now clear: praxis grounded in a solidaristic hope; the anamnestic and narrative character of reason. Furthermore, this anthropology would need to illuminate why theodicy has come to play such a pivotal role for Metz as *the* question that determines the nature, method, and goals of theological reflection. It would also need to explain Metz's emphasis on apocalyptic eschatology as the mode of temporality that characterizes Christian existence and theological discourse. Finally, it would need to explain Metz's interpretation of suffering unto God as not only the authentic Christian mystical stance in modernity but the stance which can save the ideals of the Enlightenment from its own destructive dialectic. These themes, presented piece-meal in this chapter, are indeed provocative on their own. But can they be integrated so as to show how they mutually imply one another, to show that they constitute more than an eclectically derived collection of essentially independent insights? Are they more than a set of ad hoc modifications, which still depend for their coherence on an underlying transcendental anthropology, namely, Rahner's?

I have already hinted that these themes can be integrated, that they make up a systematic theological anthropology in their own right. The next task is to justify these hints, and to show that the animating spirit and focal point for Metz's elaboration of this new anthropology is the spirituality which we have already seen here, the mysticism of *Leiden an Gott*.

5

METZ'S THEOLOGY:
IN DEFENSE OF THE HUMAN

In chapter 3 we saw how deeply Metz was involved with Heidegger's existential analytic on the one hand, and transcendental theology's attempt to refunction it for deploying the resources of Christian faith on the other. Dissatisfied with that approach, he struck out in radically new directions, developing new approaches to Christian theology and new themes within it, as we saw in chapter 4. It is time now to make good on the twofold claim that was provisionally advanced in chapter 2. On the one hand, during the seventies Metz's thought crystallized around the conceptual locus of a new understanding of the subject, one that integrates these new themes. The result is a fundamental theological anthropology that stands both in continuity with and difference from that of his early theological work; also one that is more than a "corrective" to Rahnerian or Heideggerian understandings of what it means to be human. It is a genuine and provocative alternative in its own right. On the other hand, if a new understanding of the subject is the organizing conceptual center of Metz's mature thought, it is a certain spirituality that forms its animating spirit.

This chapter covers the same ground that we surveyed in the previous chapter, but with a systematic intent. Here we will see how the various themes in Metz's mature thought cohere and form a system in which the different parts are dialectically and indispensably interrelated into a whole which has satisfied Metz's concerns with the theological and philosophical thought he learned in his first decade of academic work. The systematic intent will be served by examining his thought in comparison with the anthropologies of Martin Heidegger and Karl Rahner. There are four reasons for this approach. First, the underlying structure of hermeneutic phenomenology (Heidegger) or transcendental anthropology (Rahner) best organizes Metz's thought—

a presupposition which will be justified by the end result of this chapter. Second, such an approach will show the similarities and differences between these thinkers; indeed, it will show the continuities and differences between the "early" and the "later" Metz. Thus it will enable us to establish more precisely the way in which Metz's anthropology is a genuinely new alternative. Finally, it will not only enable us to see the role that a particular spirituality plays in Metz's thought in particular, but also to see how this particular spirituality decisively separates Metz's theology, not only from Heidegger's philosophy, but from the thought of Karl Rahner as well.

The structure of the chapter follows from this approach. I will begin with a survey of what I take to be the purpose and essential features of a fundamental, hermeneutic anthropology (section 1). As with any hermeneutics, the one offered here will have a necessarily circular structure. The originating hermeneutic situation has to be described with as much precision as possible (section 2), and then the underlying structures or existentialia of human being which are disclosed within that situation (section 3). Then a certain limit-situation is chosen, a point which negatively conditions the hermeneutic situation (one's own death for Heidegger and Rahner, the death of the other for Metz), in order to describe that mode of human life which discloses the meaning of human being. This, finally, allows a deeper understanding of the situation with which one began one's interpretation, and provides a jumping-off point for the larger project of which the anthropology is only the beginning: interpreting the meaning of being for Heidegger; interpreting the meaning of our existence in the presence of God for Rahner and Metz.

PURPOSE AND STRUCTURE OF A FUNDAMENTAL THEOLOGICAL ANTHROPOLOGY

None of the three thinkers with whom I am concerned here is interested in working out a comprehensive anthropology. Each undertakes his anthropology with another purpose in view. In *Being and Time* Heidegger undertakes an existential analytic of the human as Dasein in preparation for the broader task of interpreting the meaning of being as such. The human as Dasein is thus chosen because it is that privileged entity for which the meaning of being is at issue, and which in its day-to-day concernful dealings with its world always exists with (or, perhaps closer to Heidegger's sense, "within") a certain unthematic (and not fully thematizable) understanding of what it means to be. For Rahner the purpose of working out a transcendental anthropology is to establish the heuristic framework within which the contents of faith can be made meaningful to the believer. The human is the privileged starting point because he or she is created and held in existence by God as a potential "hearer of the word"; the fundamental structures of human being are thus already proportionate to God's revelatory address. Conversely, the genuine meaning and importance of God's word cannot be attained by perceiving it as a set of propositions that comes to persons from the outside and is thus subsequent to their constitution as human subjects. Rather, the most radical significance of God's word is only understood when its utterance and reception is grasped as constitutive of the human subject, immanent to its becoming. The human as the subject understanding, and the word of God as the object given for understanding, do not make an exception to, but rather the most radical instance of that principle of co-determination of subject and object, or being and knowing, which is fundamental to transcendental ontology.

In each case, then, there is a conviction that human beings are constituted by a relationship to something that transcends the level of their day-to-day dealings with the world, yet is only accessible to us in and through these dealings, while rendering them meaningful. For Heidegger this relationship is Dasein's relationship to being; for Rahner and Metz it is the person's relationship to God. The exploration of this relationship, and the explication of its fundamental features, are intended by the adjectives "existential," "ontological," and (in Rahner) "transcendental." The features of our day-to-day dealings with the world, as well as those human endeavors which explore those dealings, are intended by the adjectives "existentiell," "ontic," and (in Rahner) "categorical." The ontological endeavor cannot proceed directly; rather it must occur as an intepretation of our ontic dealings with the world and the ways that these both disclose and cover over the more fundamental ontological relationship.

The common features of their fundamental anthropologies, then, can be encompassed by defining the endeavor as an interpretation of the ontic dimension of human being in terms of the deeper and more specifically constitutive ontological dimension of human being, an interpretation which not only allows that deeper dimension to emerge, but also a more nuanced understanding of the ontic level itself. The divergence between different applications (which are significant) will follow from the particular pre-grasp of the ontic situation with which one begins, and the nature of the ontological relationship (to God or to being) in terms of which one interprets it. That is, this is an interpretive, *hermeneutic* enterprise, and so operates in terms of the hermeneutic circle (or, to put it in the terminology of transcendental Thomism, within the backwards and forwards dynamism of *reductio* and *deductio*). I will have more to say about this in a moment, but first it is necessary to highlight the apologetic and critical purpose of fundamental anthropology.

All three of our thinkers, but especially Heidegger and Metz, carry through fundamental anthropology with an apologetic intent. That is, they recognize that they can only realize their anthropologies—and the wider project for which anthropology is the propadeutic—by clearing away or deconstructing a false understanding of the human person, one which completely covers over and renders inaccessible the deeper, constitutive dimension of human being which they seek to disclose. For Heidegger, for instance, human fallenness (*Verfallenheit*) can be a form of absorption in our dealings with the world in which we are forgetful of the background intelligibility of being, which for its part can never be articulated in terms of any set of finite entities and our dealings with them. This fallenness is disastrously reflected in that thinking which tacitly assumes that ontic categories exhaustively encompass human being, so much so that the ontological question of being simply is no longer raised at all. This tacit, inauthentic understanding of being needs to be deconstructed. Analogously in Metz, the modern atheistic situation is not characterized so much by the explicit denial of God's existence as by the sense of the irrelevance of God. The question of God is simply no longer raised in our historical and social dealings with the world. Just as for Heidegger an inauthentic understanding of human being-in-the world has to be cleared away before the question of being can be meaningfully raised, so too for Metz with regard to the question of God. Metz does not engage in anything like Heidegger's "destruction" of Western metaphysics. His characterizations of individual positions are sketchy and often unfair. In brief, for Metz the understandings of human being that must be called into question are intended under the rubrics of positivism and idealism, insofar as in both, "memory" and "narrative" do not constitute genuine cognitive categories but only subsequent embellishments of some unmediated pure idea or theory of human being already worked out elsewhere.

For these fundamental anthropologies then, it is not enough to start from the ontic situation of our day-to-day dealings with the world and simply take over from it an understanding of the deeper, ontologically fundamental ground of human being. The ontic situation of human being has to be viewed with suspicion and a particular stance sought which discloses without distortion the ontological constitution of human being. This particular stance, and the being of human being that it discloses, is denoted by means of the adjective "authentic." An authentic understanding of human being is wrested from our everyday ontic dealings and understandings of being. How? By identifying a limit-situation within the various ontic possibilities of human existence, a situation which negatively conditions human being in such a way that if one follows it through to its deepest meaning (or *lack* of meaning), then the various disguised or distorted understandings of human being can be stripped away, and the authentic one allowed to shine through. For Heidegger and Rahner, as we shall see, this limit-situation is one's own death. For Metz it is the death of the other—which is for him the root source of the theodicy question.

Both Rahner and Metz insist that the apologetic or critical function of fundamental theology cannot be realized without engaging the core of Christian faith. There is no atemporal stance outside of the situation of Christians' involvement with their world which the theologian can take up in order to analyze and pronounce upon that involvement.[1] The theologian must identify with the believer's historical situation, including its doubts, engaging the believer's world precisely where it is most problematic, where its meaningful grounding in the believer's relationship to God is most in danger of being covered over and rendered irrelevant. This is in part why Metz insists that the central category for hermeneutics must be that of *danger*.[2] Metz and Rahner differ over their understanding of the precise nature of this danger, but both are interested in marshaling the resources of Christian faith to meet it, and in doing so by means of a critical and constructive interpretation of what it means to be a human subject in the light of the subject's constitutive relationship to God.

Hence, for the two theologians fundamental theology (indeed, the whole of theology) can in no way replace the lived faith of believers, i.e., their meaningful dealings with their world in the light of their relationship to the God of Jesus Christ. We have seen this explicitly in

Metz. The purpose of developing an understanding of the subject is for him primarily critical and apologetic: to defend from reductionistic anthropologies (and those praxes which are related to them) the understanding of the subject which alone makes committed Christian belief and praxis meaningful objects of hope. Further tasks of the theologian—evaluating the ways that the contents of faith (whether conceived primarily under the category of doctrine, as in Rahner, or of narrative in Metz) have been and should be appropriated by believers in a specific situation, and that of maieutically eliciting further, novel appropriations of that faith by believers—are not taken up by Metz although he admits their importance. In *Faith in History and Society*, his is a practical *fundamental* theology.

Since, then, Metz's and Heidegger's (and, I would argue, Rahner's as well) fundamental anthropologies are hermeneutic, it is necessary to begin by outlining how the initial hermeneutic situation is conceived, as well as the provisional ontological or existential structures disclosed in an analysis of that situation. Then, since fundamental anthropology has a critical or apologetic element, it is necessary briefly to survey the understanding of "fallenness" (to give it Heidegger's name) which characterizes inauthentic human being, as well as the limit-situation which allows us to wrest an authentic understanding of human being from out of its endangered, inauthentic mode of existence. This allows a return to the existential structures already disclosed in order to describe their existentiell, everyday realization, in which that fundamental ontological relationship (to being, or God) is disclosed and, finally, in terms of which a deeper understanding of the meaning of human being can be made manifest. We turn then first to the initial characterization of the hermeneutic situation.

THE STARTING POINT FOR A "POLITICAL HERMENEUTICS OF DANGER"

What is decisive is not to get out of the circle [of understanding] but to come into it in the right way.[3]

We must endeavor . . . to leap into the "circle," primordially and wholly, so that even at the start of the analysis of Dasein we make sure that we have a full view of Dasein's circular Being.[4]

Although at the point at which he wrote *Being and Time* Heidegger is not prepared to concede, as his later postmodernist readers are, that understanding is interpretation or metaphor all the way down, he does reject any atemporal starting point, such as Husserl's transcendental ego, upon which to found one's interpretation of being. It is impossible to extricate oneself fully from the situation that one is attempting to understand. What one must strive for is a starting point that is broad enough so as not to exclude prematurely some region of human being from one's interpretation, and a method which does not cover over the presuppositions with which one began, but rather requires one to return to them and deepen one's insight into them. This necessarily circular character of human understanding is described by Heidegger in terms of the hermeneutic situation, or the existential "fore-structure" of human understanding.[5]

According to Heidegger this structure has three elements.[6] First, there is a certain background to one's interpretation, a field of view which embraces and lays open in advance the phenomenon to be interpreted. This he calls the "fore-having" (*Vorhabe*). Second, the interpreter has a "fore-sight" (*Vorsicht*): a certain vantage point or perspective from which to view, organize, prioritize, and systematize the phenomenon as it is given in the fore-having. Finally, the interpreter has some preliminary concept, partly explicit, partly tacit, of what he or she expects to find: the "fore-conception" (*Vorgriff*). The hermeneutic situation cannot be exhaustively justified or proven in advance but only as the interpretation is carried through, as it yields both an understanding of the phenomenon and an enriching modification of the original elements of the hermeneutic situation.

The phenomenon to be interpreted here is the human subject; it is to be investigated with regard to the deeper ontological relationship that characterizes it. This requires the most comprehensive field of events and aspects within which the human subject actualizes that relationship. For Heidegger this means the totality of human involvements with beings, the full scope of human everday life, with that unthematic understanding of being that it both reveals and covers over. This is the fore-having. The perspective from which Heidegger chooses to start is Dasein as the being whose being is at stake for itself, the being which has always already taken a stand with regard to the meaning of its being. As Heidegger puts it, Dasein is the entity whose being is, in each case, its own.[7] Finally, Heidegger's fore-conception is that "care," which will prove to be the fundamental existential constitution of human being, can only be made sense of in terms of temporality.

Rahner too is interested in an interpretation of what it means to be human. While his early work (especially *Spirit in the World*) is dominated by an intellectualist position which restricts the fore-having to the domains of human inquiry into and knowledge of other beings, in his mature work Rahner broadened the field for interpretation to encompass "the awareness of the faith of the Church as it exists in the concrete today."[8] This is not restricted to the content of Scripture or to documents and pronouncements of the official magisterium. It is composed of the interplay of all the diverse elements of thought and action in which Christians live out their lives "in all [their] radical openness to the absolute mystery called 'God' and in [their] unequivocal attachment in history to Jesus of Nazareth."[9] Like Heidegger's, Rahner's interpretation takes its guiding perspective from the fact that human being is problematic to itself, that our existence is a question for which the concrete working out of our life-careers is an attempt at an answer. The clearest difference, of course, lies in the fore-conception. Heidegger begins with the conception that the final meaning of human being will have something to do with temporality, ending with the more strongly formulated assertion that the meaning of human being is grounded in the ultimately groundless ek-stasis of Dasein in(to) temporality. Rahner, on the other hand, begins with and follows through on the fore-conception that human being only "makes sense" in terms of its relationship to God.

What about Metz? How can the originary hermeneutic situation for his interpretation be described? The answer lies in a precise understanding of what Metz means when he calls his fundamental theology a "practical hermeneutics,"[10] or later a "political hermeneutics of danger."[11] To derive this let us turn to chapter 4 of *Faith in History and Society*: "Concept of a Political Theology as a Practical Fundamental Theology."

Opening this chapter, Metz tells us that "'praxis' and 'subject' are the guiding concepts of this practical fundamental theology."[12] The closest thing to a definition of the subject (which would serve as a "fore-sight" for Metz, as Heidegger's cryptic definition of Dasein did above) is this:

"Subject," is indeed no arbitrary definition which can be interchanged with another. The subject is the person who is intimately

involved with his or her experiences and stories [or histories—
Geschichten], and is continually identifying him- or herself by means
of them.[13]

The subject is the self-interpreting being. This definition is consistent
with Metz's "discovery" from the sixties that the human world is not
a static pre-given cosmos which defines for him or her what it is to be
human; rather, the human world is the historical project of men and
women, in which they recognize less and less the vestigia of some
divine being or metaphysical order, and more and more the traces of
their own historical becoming. This understanding of the subject goes
back at least as far as Hegel, for whom the culmination of history, the
point at which reason has come to maturity, is that point at which subjective reason (the creative principle behind the projection or creation
of human culture) recognizes objective reason (the order disclosed in
the institutions and structures of human society as well as in nature) as
its own project, its own self-interpretation.

In this understanding of "subject," then, Metz accepts the general category of hermeneutics, and the interpretive task it enjoins, as
the genus of his practical fundamental theology. Yet the concept of the
subject is complemented by the "primacy of praxis." It is this complement that determines Metz's hermeneutics as a political hermeneutics of danger. As with "subject," however, Metz does not give us a
straightforward definition of praxis, although he does speak of the
various ways that his usage of the term is determined. He tells us first
of all, that praxis cannot lead to an "abstract negation of the individual."[14] It seems reasonable to assume here that he is worried about
variants of Marxism which reduce the individual to nothing more than
a reflex of the collective. Like the critical theorists who were so important for his reception of Marxism, Metz will admit that the particular
constellation of bourgeois individual versus civil and political society is
false, but he will not go on to concede that any notion of individual
versus collective is unwarranted.[15]

Second, he tells us that authentic Christian social praxis reflects
not just the interests and needs of those who are presently alive and
judged competent to express and act upon those interests. Rather, it
must be determined in part by the voiceless, both the victims of the
past and those who presently have no voice in the public sphere, perhaps because they will not give up those elements of their tradition
which are deemed "irrational" by current standards.[16] Finally, Metz

tells us that praxis has a *pathic* structure. It includes areas of human acting which are not "productive" in the usual sense of the word: mourning, or empathy with past unredeemed suffering; celebration of those moments of fulfillment in life which cannot be calculated as "successes" or incremental stages toward success;[17] above all, Christian prayer.[18]

If we recall that Metz's interest in the Marxian concept of praxis draws on Marx's celebrated thesis that the task of philosophy is not to interpret the world but to transform it, it seems most likely that when Metz stresses praxis he wants to stress that meaning is not passively received but is created by human activity. Furthermore, that activity is not just the incarnation of or extrapolation from our present understanding or interpretation of the meaning of being a human. That is because our present existence, riven by sin, cannot sustain a coherent interpretation. In short, our present is characterized by danger.

In a passage that is significant for Metz's understanding of "danger" as the premier category for hermeneutics, he criticizes a too-easy appropriation of the term "meaning" into Christian theology:

> The all-too-easy dealings with the category of "meaning" (especially the "meaning of history") in theology has to be critically interrogated. . . . If it is true that theology too cannot do without this category, it must never be forgotten that it cannot thereby be a matter of an unendangered meaning, which one can then draw out of one's ironclad treasure chamber or one's ontology, when it really must be introduced and "described" by the intelligible power of Christian action itself. The theological treatment of the question of meaning must not mislead us into a quasi-objectification of "meaning," into simply ignoring the problem of the salvation of meaning or of the historical threats to the reserves of meaning, thereby forgetting—through a lack of apocalyptic consciousness—that the one toward whom the Christian expectation of meaning is directed does not just return as the one who fulfills the Kingdom of God, but also as the one who overcomes Antichrist.[19]

There are two sorts of "danger" to meaning and to the reliance on the category of meaning in theology. First there is the fact that for Metz, speaking bluntly, things do not now make sense. The presence of absurdity and evil in our midst makes any comprehensive attempt to make sense of things absurd or even obscene. The Holocaust is the paradigmatic case in point here. Due to this abysmal tremendum no complete meaning of being can be found within or projected from the present situation. But, an apocalyptic redemption of meaning *can* be *hoped* for. Meaning is an eschatological concept for Metz.[20]

Conversely, the subject who is the correlate of meaning, is not merely given, so that this subject could be identified and examined theoretically in advance, the meaning it should ascribe to existence worked out, and then the specific individuals who instantiate the abstract concept offered the resulting interpretation of the significance for them of Christian faith. Those theologies are inadequate, then, that only look for a more persuasive interpretation of the Christian message without addressing the deeper problem as to whether or not there is anyone who cares, whether there is a subject to hear it anymore. Human beings only *become* the subjects of their own history through struggle. One detects here in Metz the presence of the Marxist claim that a given social-political system enfranchises certain groups in society as the subject and disenfranchises others. The weight of destitution can crush the power of creative self-interpretation. The capacity of groups to identify themselves in and through their own experiences and histories can be endangered when their traditions are stripped from them (Metz refers to the fate of African slaves brought to the Americas).[21] The historically attested failure of these "dangers" ever completely to suppress the subject-forming self-interpretation of peoples makes them less frightening and dangerous to Metz than the possibility that human beings would simply cease to raise the question of meaning, would abdicate this right and responsibility to become and remain subjects of their own history. This is a sort of limit case of the decay of the human capacity to be the subjects of their own history, a drying up of the reserves of meaning, as he puts it in the quote given above. It is to this that Metz later refers when, in speaking of the advanced technological societies of the First World, he points to the possible "successor" of the bourgeois subject:

> The public advertisement for a successor to the human subject, a successor who has no memory of past suffering and is no longer tortured by catastrophes, has already begun. *Time,* for example, has recently placed a picture of this successor on one of its covers: the robot, a smoothly functioning machine, an intelligence without remembrance, without pathos, without morals.[22]

Anyone familiar with Heidegger's description of the fallenness in which the "self" of Dasein is "the they" (*das Man*), will recognize this description. This inauthentic mode of existence is one in which the person has become so absorbed in the day-to-day dealings with beings that the question of being no longer arises, the tacit understanding of what it means to be remains completely covered over. It is not even really a matter any more of the individual accepting "what *they* say," since this implies a chosen assent. In this nightmare "limit case," the moment of questioning, rejecting, or accepting never even arises. The person lives in the world of the "they" unquestioningly. In later writings Heidegger too will speak of the danger that the "clearing" in which being gives itself, and which Dasein primordially is, might close. The question of being might be definitively covered over. Heidegger too sees technological society, whose understanding of being is characterized by "enframing" (*Gestell*), as a premier source of this danger.[23]

The differences between Metz's and Heidegger's understandings of danger are, of course, striking, and of the greatest significance. The later Heidegger can contemplate this nihilistic closing of the space for the question of being as yet another dispensation or sending (*Geschick*) in the play of being, over which human beings have no control. For Metz it is a result of human sinfulness.[24] Furthermore, this sinfulness is manifested in political structures. The salvation of the subject and of meaning must therefore take up the task of transforming and creating new political structures in which persons can shelter and nourish both their desire and their capacity to recognize themselves as the agents of their own historical and social self-becoming.[25]

So, Metz's hermeneutics is a political hermeneutics of danger. It is *political*; that is, the subject and the meaning which its existence intends are formed in concrete social structures, a result of human communal action. It is a hermeneutics of *danger*. Every political, historical incarnation of the subject, and the meaning whereby persons in community try to understand what it means to be, is riven by aporias, by the meaningless surd of evil. Meaning, indeed, finally the subject, is an eschatological concept. Trying to conceive of an interpretation of the subject which would be complete, which could be given apart from the endangered character of being a subject in history, is necessarily abstract—dangerously abstract.

The *Vorhabe* for Metz, then, will be the specific dealings with the world. Like Heidegger and the later Rahner, Metz does not choose only cognition in which to ground a fundamental interpretation of the subject; we are more than disembodied intellects, and attempts to determine what it means for us to be must make use of more than the ideas that we think. Particularly important for Metz are the narratives in which persons recognize their identity. He praises Rahner's anti-elitist emphasis and names Rahner's theology a "mystical biography of an undramatic life," that is, one that concerns itself with the day-to-day dealings in and out of which Christians try to understand their identity.[26] Metz's particular perspective, his *Vorsicht*, emphasizes that human beings only become and remain subjects in the midst of struggle and danger, that they do so as they struggle to transform the world and themselves in such a way that they can come to recognize their own self-becoming in their experiences and stories. Finally, like Rahner, Metz's initial *Vorgriff* is that human being only makes sense in terms of its relationship to God; but his insistence on *danger* as the premier category of hermeneutics, his stress on the eschatological, indeed apocalyptic character of our being as subjects, will lead him to his own version of the Heideggerian thesis that the meaning of being is connected with temporality—by which he will mean something quite different from both Heidegger and Rahner.

Once again we see that Metz requires a starting point for the understanding of what it means to be human that is firmly embedded in history and society. To be sure, both Heidegger and Rahner will argue that human being is both historical and social.[27] But, we have already seen Metz's dissatisfaction with their approaches. The meanings which we construe and construct, in which we come to recognize ourselves, are fragmented. Our being-in-the-world as subjects is equally threatened and fragmentary. Any interpretation of the meaning of human being cannot be gained at the cost of covering over this fragmented, endangered character of our historical experience. Furthermore, it is not just my own being, the transparency and meaningfulness of my social environment and practices, that is at stake. It is *our* being, it is the coherence and meaningfulness of what the human community in its broadest sense undergoes and enacts that is at issue. The freedom and rationality of human being as self-interpreting and self-creative must from the very start and continually thereafter be referred to the community of all persons "who are called to be subjects in God's presence." Given this situation, how must we understand the most fundamental features of human being?

METZ'S CATEGORIES OF BEING A SUBJECT

The last section of *Faith in History and Society* is subtitled "Categories." In his brief introduction to this section Metz describes the nature of these categories.[28] The three categories (memory, narrative, solidarity) are chosen as basic categories instead of "subject," "praxis," "society," and "history," because the latter are present "axiologically" in Metz's approach. While Metz does not explain what he means by this, in the light of the interpretation offered here it would mean that the latter are already operative in the way that Metz has characterized the originating hermeneutic situation, out of which he derives the categories. Metz tells us that these categories stand in an inner connection, that only together do they form the basic categories. This is not unlike Heidegger's existentials of state-of-mind, understanding, discourse, and fallenness. They are equiprimordial, coextensive, and codetermining elements of the "being-in" of Dasein, which is the most basic way of describing the way that we are in the world. Metz tells us further that a number of other categorial determinants of a practical fundamental theology (love, interaction, work, reason, speech, etc.) can and should be uncovered along with and based upon these three. But, as we noted above, Metz is not interested in an exhaustive anthropology, but rather intends only to uncover the basic categories in terms of which the broader project—determining humans' constitutive depth-relation to God—can be worked out.

There is a further aspect of Metz's general treatment of the categories which supports the hypothesis that they function in his fundamental theological anthropology the way that Heidegger's existentials function in his existential analytic. One can identify two modalities of each category. For instance, after a general treatment of the category of memory, Metz asserts that the type which actualizes the authentic meaning of human being is the modality of *dangerous* memory. The same holds true for narrative: first general treatment of the character of narrative is given, then a focus on *dangerous* stories as that type which will move human beings to critical-transformative praxis. Finally, he treats solidarity in general, and also the mode of solidarity with all, even and especially with the dead as that which grounds the becoming-subjects of all persons. This way of describing the categories suggests Heidegger's treatment of the existentialia as they are disclosed in the everyday life of Dasein, which is revealed to be "inauthentic," in the sense that it does not open up Dasein to itself as the self-interpreting source of its meaningful practices. But, he then offers in Division II those existentiell modes of the existentials which disclose Dasein's authentic existence: the state-of-mind of anxiety, understanding as anticipation of death, discourse as reticence. As described above, the key lies in finding some possibility in the human's existence and consciousness in terms of which what it means to be is most perspicaciously disclosed.

This structure suggests the following method of describing the fundamental elements of the subject in Metz's theology. First we briefly consider the three categories. Then we focus on that possibility in terms of which the authentic meaning of human being is both disclosed and actualized. Then we consider the existentiell modification of the three categories in which this possibility is reckoned with, rather than being covered over by various inauthentic strategies. In the course of this analysis it will become clear why authentic narrative and memory must have a dangerous, disturbing, disrupting character, and why solidarity must be in principle universal. It will become clear why for Metz the question of theodicy is *the* question for theology. Finally, we will be able to describe why it is that a certain spirituality, or mysticism, as Metz describes it, is at the center of his theology.

The first of the three categories which Metz treats is that of memory. I argued above that Metz first encountered this category in his reading of Marcuse, Adorno, and Benjamin. He quickly adopted it as the central concept with which to insist that reason only becomes free in its self-constitution in and through its history: "In the term 'memory' the mediating structure between reason and history is articulated."[29] He argues that it is a constitutive category in the histories of both philosophy and theology. In the former he traces it from Plato's doctrine of anamnesis, through Aquinas's notion of an a priori light of reason and Descartes's notion of innate ideas. In the latter he points out that in the biblical tradition the process of salvation in which the person is constituted and maintained as a subject enters into history at concrete points (e.g., the exodus; the life, death, and resurrection of Jesus of Nazareth). This process cannot be analytically derived but is only present to us anamnestically.

As is so often the case in Metz, the problem has always been correctly to mediate these two traditions, the one grounded in the history of salvation recounted in Scripture, the other grounded in Greek thinking. Hegel is the paradigmatic modern attempt, from which Metz traces two traditions, both of which have styled themselves as critiques (in the Kantian sense) of historical reason: hermeneutic philosophy (including Heidegger and Gadamer) and critical theory (including Marcuse, Adorno, Benjamin, and Habermas).[30] Starting with the former suggests that Metz's category of memory stands in the place of the Heideggerian existential of state-of-mind; it reflects the way that my present is in part determined by my past. The world is opened up to me in a certain way prior to my own reflection and decision. I can never escape this character of my existence, even in the laudable interest of critiquing the distorted and oppressive elements of the past. Metz is in agreement with Gadamer's critique of the Enlightenment prejudice against prejudice. Yet he also concedes the problem of those hermeneutic traditions which in emphasizing the presence of the past to reason end up with a submissive attitude toward the past, as when in Heidegger the category of history, under the influence of his understanding memory, mutates into that of fate (*Geschick*).[31] It is the second tradition, that of critical theory, that revealed the critical reserves in memory. Yet it too ran into problems. Because of critical theory's emphasis on ideology-critique, the constitutive power of the past for the present can in the last analysis only be mediated to reason by means of some psychological or sociological theory of development, which no longer draws on the power of the specific events that are remembered themselves. This is Metz's critique of Habermas.[32] Thus, while both traditions recognize the past as somehow constitutive for the present, in Metz's view neither is able to offer a concept of memory in which persons recognize in their history, in the specific events they remember out of it, their own struggle to become subjects—and in this recognition are empowered and compelled to continue the struggle.

The second category, narrative, functions in Metz's fundamental anthropology the way that discourse (*Rede*) does in Heidegger's. Discourse in Heidegger's thought is an existential that is prior to language or assertions; rather it makes them possible. Discourse refers to the way that our being-in-the-world is already meaningfully articulated in a certain way prior to our interpretation of it. We are immersed in this already-articulated world in and through our concerned involvement with it. This already-articulated character only becomes (partly) explicit, its "in order to" structure clarified and expressed, under certain special cases: when equipment is ill-fitted for our project, or under the highly specialized conditions of science. This primordial "articulated-ness" of the world is the existential condition for the possibility of all explicit assertion and language, and thus, of thought. It is never fully manifested to us because it is in the background, and as such could only be brought to complete conscious articulation by virtue of another background discourse. Hence, thinking always depends on discourse and not the reverse. Thought can never transcend discourse so as to work out a purely theoretical, propositional account of our meaningful involvement in the world. It is on the basis of this existential structure of Dasein that Heidegger wages his deconstructive critique of metaphysics.

Metz's category of narrative also grounds his rejection of metaphysics as the fundamental discipline for theology. Theologies must always be open to "interruption" by the narratives of Christians. Just as genuine thinking in Heidegger must always immerse itself in language (the "house of being"), so too in Metz must theology draw upon the reserves offered to it by narrative. It is in these narratives that the experiences of Christians are passed on, without the danger of reduction that accompanies the purely propositional character of doctrine. What is truly new, what cannot be encompassed by systems which only operate empirically out of what is or has been, can be suggested and evoked in narrative. We saw in chapter 4 that narrative is uniquely suited to revivify memory, that it is a way of stimulating empathy, of creating a community with the one who is telling the story, opening up the possibility of sharing his or her experiences. While argument or interpretation are necessary (as is "thinking" for Heidegger) they are grounded in a community of narrative and not the reverse. Metz does concede the danger that narratives can be taken over and used ideologically. They can be used to create an alternative world, a "rosy past" or a Whig history which insulates us from the dangers which threaten us in the present.[33] Like memory, narrative can atrophy or be abused.

Metz states that solidarity, his final category, is determinative for a "fundamental theology as political theology of the subject, which is guided by the idea of the becoming-subjects of all persons before God."[34] It is the category whereby the other two become practical categories:

> In solidarity memory and narrative win their specific mystical-political praxis. If memory and narrative are not practical categories

without solidarity, just as little can solidarity bring forth the human-
izing form of Christianity without the other two. Only together can
memory, narrative and solidarity be the categories of a practical fundamental theology.[35]

It is important here to remember that in his definition of Christian faith
"solidarity" entered in connection with hope. Faith is "a praxis in history and society which is understood as *solidaristic hope*"[36] (emphasis added). Solidarity, then, refers to the social character of our hope
and action. We always act with, hope with, other persons. Again, recall
that when Metz uses the Kantian question "For what may I hope?" to
delineate the religious, he emends the question: "What dare I hope for
you and, in the end, also for me?"[37] Thus, solidarity reflects the hopeful, future-directed character of human being. It also expresses our
sociality, the fact that our being is always a being-with (to use Heidegger's term).

Comparison with the Heideggerian existential of understanding is
illuminating. In his usage of this term Heidegger wants to emphasize
that our involvement in the world is always and only meaningful in
terms of some future possibility. If state-of-mind reveals our facticity,
reveals the fact that we are "thrown" into the world in ways which we
can never become exhaustively aware of, then understanding discloses
that we are always already "ahead of ourselves," projecting into some
future possible way of being in the world. In choosing solidarity as a
fundamental category of human being, Metz wants to insist that this
possibility is always a possibility for some "us." In connecting it with
hope he is arguing that this possibility is not just one that we project
forward out of our present but that it could be one that comes to us un-
expectedly, interrupting or redeeming our sense of what it means to be
in this present situation.

Solidarity is therefore a constitutive way that human beings are in
the world together. We saw earlier how Metz picked up Bloch's critique of Heidegger. For Bloch and Metz the implicit "us" with whom
Heidegger's thinking is in solidarity is the world-weary intellectual. On
the other hand, Metz's concern with Marxism is that its circle of solidarity is too small, that it includes only the party or one particular class, to the exclusion (and possible elimination) of those outside.
Dialogical or personalist approaches conceive of solidarity with the
"thou." Many modern theories have accepted the form of solidarity

that is implicit to bourgeois capitalism: a solidarity based on exchange, a relationship of interchange between two agents, presumed to be already equal, each acting on his or her enlightened self-interest.[38] None of these forms of particular solidarity can reveal the deepest meaning of human being. In each the recognition of the other as a subject is made dependent upon some preestablished understanding of the subject of the historical becoming of humans in history, a subject for which the circle of solidarity is in each case too narrow.

At this point we have seen the three categories of Metz's fundamental interpretation of what it means to be a subject: our being is meaningful in terms of the past which we remember, it is meaningful in terms of the community in and with which we hope and labor for a future, and all of this is primarily present to us in an open, never fully thematizable mode of being that can only be adequately captured narratively (however much theory and argument is then necessary to bring out the implications of narrative and relate them to other dimensions of our knowing and acting). Each of these is, however, endangered in various ways by atrophy, suppression, or distortion. Memory can wither into little more than cybernetic chronicle, detached historicism, or a Whig history of my own individual present. Narrative can assuage our fears, edify us in our tiny reservations of culture and the arts, or entertain us in our fortified havens in a heartless world, in each case contributing to the avoidance of that labor in history and society for the dignity of all persons as subjects in and through which the depths of what it means for us to be is revealed and realized. Solidarity can become the narrow "us" of the lifestyle enclave, of the party, of our particular class, race, or creed, within which we barricade ourselves against the fearful, often hated "them." How is the authentic modality of these three fundamental categories to be disclosed so that they both articulate and evoke a praxis which struggles for that future possibility in which all persons become and remain subjects in God's presence?

AUTHENTIC BEING IN HISTORY: *LEIDEN AN GOTT*

Now we are at the heart of the matter. To this point, a provisional interpretation of human being has been offered which draws upon our everyday dealings within a shared world, in terms of which we implicitly and explicitly understand what it means to be human. It is one which is grounded in insight into the uniquely human power of self-constitution by means of the construal and creation of meaning in and through our involvement in a shared world. A temporal structure has already been disclosed; that is, the meaningfulness of our existence has been disclosed in part by the way that the past is constitutive for our present and by the way that we are already "ahead of ourselves" in terms of future possibility. Finally, the meaning of our existence has been shown to have an irreducibly linguistic structure; it is mediated to us narratively.

Yet none of these existential structures is without ambiguity. They can each be realized in such a way that both the ability and the responsibility that is attendant upon being a subject is evaded. Heidegger articulates this possibility in terms of fallenness, in which the "self" of Dasein is "the they": the state-of-mind in which the world is revealed is idle curiosity, the forward-projecting understanding is characterized by ambiguity, and the discourse in which the world is primordially revealed (as hidden) to us is idle talk.[39] Rahner too considers the possibility that human beings, threatened by guilt, will flee the task of authentic self-realization in knowledge and love.[40] We have already encountered Metz's version of this deficient mode of human being when we considered his own refiguring of the dialectic of enlightenment.[41]

Thus, for Metz (and for Heidegger and Rahner as well), being a subject is not given in advance, but characterizes a particular modality of human existence in which the fundamental structures of human being are actualized in such a way that the ability and responsibility to become and remain the subjects of our own histories, experiences, and actions, is made transparent to us. Yet if being a subject is an interpretive wager, if in a very real way it is always outstanding, always "in front of us," to be worked out in our choice and actualization of the possibilities for which we hope and labor, then how can we gain a perspective on the being of the subject which could serve as a point from which to critique the deficient ways in which we realize our being? If one had a straightforward metaphysics of the person, a more or less atemporal master plan of what it is to be a subject, then one would have such a critical vantage point. As we have seen, Metz agrees with Heidegger, Bloch, Adorno, and Horkheimer in rejecting this approach.[42] What then?

As I have already suggested, the response chosen by Heidegger in Division II of *Being and Time*, one which Metz follows in his own way, is a sort of *via negativa*. One identifies a possibility of human being which negatively conditions the whole interpretive-creative project and uses that as a way of identifying and critiquing the ways in which Dasein's existentiell realization of its existential structure is deficient. For Heidegger this negative possibility is the possibility not-to-be that is disclosed in death.[43] Death negatively conditions the self-interpretive practices in and through which I understand what it means to be be-cause it characterizes their outer limit. The final and definitive possi-bility not-to-be encompasses and sets a limit to all the ways-to-be, all the particular projects, possibilities, and expectations in and through which my present is meaningful. It is a perduring, inescapable possi-bility that negatively conditions all my attempts to understand myself in terms of my future. More importantly it is a possibility that can-not be interpreted in terms of the "they" self, since "they" do not die. I do.[44] This possibility thus opens up the instability of the world in which Dasein exists, including its various strategies, techniques and discourses for making sense. Insofar as I am destined to die, being-toward-death[45] is an existential of my being, it is a permanent mode of the way I am. I exist in such a way that there is an outer limit of "not-ness" that negatively conditions all my attempts to attain identity as a subject by taking over various strategies (practical, theoretical, aes-thetic, ethical, religious, or what have you) from "the they." This de-stabilizing way in which the world is manifested to me is characterized by the state-of-mind of anxiety.[46]

There are many ways of dealing with death in which its radical and destabilizing significance is covered over. Its importance for Hei-degger, however, lies in the fact that it is a universal possibility which stands before all of us, and it is one that cannot be made sense of by the "they." It serves as a way of separating the "they" which is the self of inauthentic Dasein from the "I" of authentic Dasein. Whatever stance Dasein takes toward its existence, whatever way in which the exis-tentials are realized, if it is to manifest the radically groundless self-interpretive, self-creative existence that Dasein is, then it cannot do so in such a way that it covers over the "notness" that is disclosed in the existential of *Sein-zum-Tode*. Heidegger defines this stance as one of anticipatory resoluteness, "authentic Being towards the possibility which we have characterized as Dasein's utter impossibility."[47] It describes a particular way in which the three existentialia are real-ized existentially-ontically: state-of-mind as anxiety; understanding as being-guilty; discourse as reticence.[48]

Like Heidegger, Rahner finds "being-guilty" to be the permanent existential of the person's existence which radically threatens and destabilizes the person's attempt to construe or create his or her identity, to attain eternal validity in and through free decisions.[49] The person's being as a free subject is being-in-history, already conditioned by the decisions of others in such a way that the person can never gain control over this conditionedness in reflection or decision.[50] Furthermore, like Heidegger, Rahner interprets death as the outer limit of the attempt to achieve coherence and validity in one's life.[51] What is the existentiell stance in which the responsibility and ability of the person as free to work out in his or her life an "answer" to the question of what it means to be (the question that the person is) is exercised in a way that does not deny, cover over, or flee the radical ambiguity of that existence which is manifested in guilt and in death? Unlike in Heidegger, it is a being toward God as absolute mystery. Not surprisingly, for Rahner the Christian theologian this stance is most deeply exemplified and presented to us as a real, existentiell possibility in Jesus Christ:

> In the unity of this triplicity of faith, hope, and love, Jesus surrendered himself in his death unconditionally to the absolute mystery that he called his Father, into whose hands he committed his existence, when in the night of his death and God-forsakenness he was deprived of everything that is otherwise regarded as the content of a human existence: life, honor, acceptance in earthly and religious fellowship, and so on. In the concreteness of his death it becomes only too clear that everything fell away from him, even the perceptible security of the closeness of God's love, and in this trackless dark there prevailed silently only the mystery that in itself and in its freedom has no name and to which he nevertheless calmly surrendered himself as to eternal love and not to the hell of futility. In that sense his death is the same as ours. . . . In the last resort what happens in death is the same for all: we are deprived of everything, even of ourselves; we all fall, each of us alone, into the dark abyss where there are no further ways.[52]

This is a mode of being which does not just come into play at the actual moment of death, but is a part of our following of Jesus, whose entire life is to be interpreted as that of "the crucified one." The temporal end-point of our lives is nothing but the culmination and most radical disclosure of what has been transpiring in our lives from the very beginning; hence Christian spirituality as a following of the crucified, "taking up one's cross," is an existentiell possibility that is the authentic response to the call to be a subject (what Heidegger calls the "call of conscience") that is possible and necessary throughout one's life.[53]

Having seen how Heidegger and Rahner take up the issue of how to distinguish authentic from inauthentic being of the person, we turn now to Metz. What limit-situation does he educe in order to distinguish authentic from inauthentic ways of being, or better, for Metz, ways of striving to become and remain a subject? We have already come across it. It is the presence of meaningless suffering and death *of the other*, the histories of suffering which characterize the history in which we exist and become subjects (as being-in-history) at least as much as the histories of growth and attainment of freedom. Like Rahner and Heidegger, Metz focuses on guilt as the manifestation of that negative possibility which sets a limit to and endangers our attempts to become and remain the subjects of our own history. But it is not the call of the authentic self, as in Heidegger, but the call of the suppressed or repressed other:

> What dimension does this becoming-guilty-before-the-other have? Does not an unconditioned claim upon us, which cannot be relativized by anything, announce itself when we accept the experience of such guilt? A claim that does not pass away or fall silent even when the other, before whom we have become guilty, no longer exists? What does one experience who, upon waking in the morning, considers his existence [*Dasein*] and in this must concede that at the fringes of his life stand nothing but ruins, ruins of men and women who have been destroyed by his egoism? What does one experience who in the face of such experiences does not immediately engage in desperate reflex-actions to try to relativize them? Does not such a one fall into an abyss, which measures the extent of his despair or his longing for forgiveness? To whom can his cries turn if they are to be more than vague moaning? Do we not know all too well that they can turn to no one if they do not call in the direction of the one whom we name "God"?[54]

The meaningless death of the other is a universal existential of human being in history. Here again we recall the importance for Metz's mature thought of Benjamin's dictum that "there is no document of civilization which is not at the same time a document of barbarism." History as a project of human becoming is radically ambiguous in that it is inextricably intermixed with irrationality, with the oppression and destruction of some for the sake of those who are socially enthroned as the subject. Thus just as one's own death for Rahner and Heidegger, the death of the victim for Metz radically destabilizes our attempts to find or create meaning in our present.

Furthermore, this negative existential is one that can be and has been evaded. These evasive strategies, or exculpation devices, are the stuff of Metz's interpretation of the dialectic of enlightenment, as we saw in chapter 4.[55] They cover up what it means to be human, as do the corresponding strategies in Heidegger's and Rahner's thought. So we have a reality which negatively conditions any attempt to make sense of our existence in history. The existentiell stance toward the world in which we do this must not be constructed with one's back turned to the negativities of history revealed by the suffering of the other, the paradigmatic case of which for Metz as German Catholic theologian is the fate of the Jews in his own history and society:

> There is no truth for me which I could defend with my back turned to Auschwitz.
>
> There is no sense for me which I could save with my back turned to Auschwitz.
>
> And there is no God for me to whom I could pray with my back turned to Auschwitz.
>
> When that became clear to me, I tried to stop doing theology with my back turned to the invisible, or forcefully made-invisible, sufferings in the world;
>
> with my back toward the Holocaust;
>
> with my back turned to the speechless sufferings of the poor and oppressed in the world.
>
> This probably was the starting point toward the construction of a so-called political theology.[56]

It is crucial to note that the issue of the death of the other is not merely a matter for moral theology, or for political ethics, although to be sure it is an issue there. It is not a matter of approaching the catastrophes of history with an understanding of what it means to be Christian which has already been secured in other ways. Again, a comparison with Heidegger is illuminating. Heidegger is not (for the purposes of his existential analytic) interested in the various existentiell strategies we have for "dealing with" the issue of death, strategies which we use to bolster identities we have already formed by taking over various meaning-making strategies from the "they." He wants to use one's own death as a lever to "pry open" from the very roots our understanding of what it means to be. A similar case is true for Metz. In his practical fundamental theology he wants to use the meaningless death of the other, for which we share responsibility because of the very involvement in history and society by means of which we understand what it means to be, as a lever to penetrate to the roots of an understanding of our existence in history and society.

We are now in a position to return to theodicy and understand why it is *the* question in Metz's fundamental practical theology of the subject. It is the question that frames most pointedly the problem that suffering raises for any attempt to understand history as the creative self-expression of *any* subject, be that subject an omnipotent loving God, or rational human persons in community. It thus contains the question of what it means to be human in society and history, and is in this way analogous to the *Seinsfrage* in Heidegger and Rahner. But it also contains the correct vantage point from which to grasp most radically the ambiguity, indeed the endangered character of that being, insofar as it places squarely before us the problem of meaningless, irrational suffering of others, a suffering which is not incidental to, but at the heart of the very history in and through which we are attempting to make sense of our lives. As such it is a political question. It is not concerned first with my individual death but with the deaths of others, and the ways in which I am implicated in those deaths in and through the social and political histories which are constitutive for the meaning of my present existence. In short, the theodicy question, as Metz formulates it, is one that places our inquiry into what it means to be a Christian squarely at the point of intersection of being involved in a social and historical world which is threatened by radical meaninglessness but yet on the other hand wishes to speak a word of good news about God, whose promises hold out a hope that transcends the endangered character of our social-historical existence. This is the starting point for a revised anthropology for which Metz had been searching.

It is worth emphasizing again that the theodicy question is not one that is to be rationally "solved," any more than the *Seinsfrage* for Heidegger or Rahner. Rather, it both articulates and evokes a stance toward our involvement in the world and in history which is open to that involvement's ambiguous, endangered character. Just as the *Seins-frage* for Heidegger and Rahner irritates us, keeps us from closing our-selves off in some finite realm of beings in our attempts to understand what it means to be human, so in Metz's thought does the theodicy question irritate us. It keeps us from falling into the various exculpa-tion strategies which entrap us in the dialectic of enlightenment, open-ing up instead the possibility of a different existentiell stance toward our involvement in the world and history:

> "The question," Martin Heidegger once remarked, "is the piety of thinking." I would add, turning our questioning back on God (*Rück-fragen an Gott*) is the piety of theology. Theology as I have tried to understand and convey it, cannot "solve" the theodicy-question. Rather, its task lies in this, to formulate the question as one directed back at God, and to work out the concept of a temporally charged expectation that, if anything, *God* will "justify" Godself in his own time, in the face of the history of suffering.[57]

What then is the existentiell stance in Metz's thought that would correspond to anticipatory resoluteness in Heidegger, or to trusting surrender into the absolute mystery of God for Rahner? Like Rahner, Metz finds the authentic existentiell response to the question of what it means to be, and the question of unjust, meaningless suffering that makes the first question so pointed, in a basic stance toward God. For him, though, it is *Leiden an Gott*. As we saw above, this is a stance toward God which is full of complaint, lament, but also of passionate expectation and hope that God will respond.[58] For Metz this means a following of the crucified; but unlike Rahner, his is no longer the Jesus of Lk 23:46, "Father into your hands I commend my spirit." Rather, it is the impassioned cry of Mk 15:34, "My God, my God, why have you abandoned me?"[59] As we saw above, *Leiden an Gott* is closely connected with biblical Israel's poverty of spirit, which Metz defines as the inability (poverty) to be consoled by the sorts of evasive strate-gies in the face of meaningless suffering which cover over the frag-mented, endangered character of human being.

Suffering unto God and poverty of spirit turn us hopefully, expec-tantly toward God. It allows us, indeed compels us, to become and remain subjects, even in the face of our own guilty complicity in the destruction of others:

Such "poverty of spirit" is the defining mark of the biblical history of the becoming of subjects and the discovery of the unconditionally solidaristic freedom of the subject in it. To the dignity of this freedom belongs also the ability to become guilty, and thus in guilty failure to continue to be a subject; that is, not to succumb to any mythical, psychological, or aesthetic spells which dissolve guilt.[60]

We should now be able to describe the existentiell mode in which the three existentialia of memory, narrative, and solidarity are realized within this stance of suffering unto God. First memory. From the above insistence that an authentic existentiell stance will have to remain present to the disappeared, the victims of history, it is the memory of their history (which is, recall, the underside of *our* history) that will give memory its critical-liberating power.

> In this form of receptivity, history, as the remembered history of suffering, wins the form of "dangerous tradition," which cannot be silenced or "sublated" [*"aufgehoben"*] either in a purely submissive stance toward the past—as occurs in many hermeneutical theories of reason—or in an attitude toward the past that approaches it only in terms of ideology-critique—as occurs in many critical theories of reason. History's mediation to reason is in each case of a practical nature; it occurs in "dangerous stories" in which the interest of freedom is narratively introduced, identified and presented.[61]

This is the form of memory that disrupts the hegemony of what is, that interrupts our tendency to identify the past which is constitutive for our present as a Whig history leading up to our successful present. For Christians the paradigmatic memory is the *memoria passionis et resurrectionis Jesu Christi,* a memory which as we narrate and commemorate it sacramentally, continually opens us up to other crucified persons and peoples (to use Ignacio Ellacuría's phrase) in our past and present. But, always with a critical and practical intent. Metz is in complete agreement with Jon Sobrino's statement: "The sole object of all this talk [about crucified peoples] must be to bring them down from the cross."[62]

One final note on memory. Metz often uses the word *Eingedenken,* which is a German neologism. In this regard it should be noted that the German adverb *eingedenk* means "in remembrance of," as it is used in the Catholic order of Mass: "Do this in remembrance of me." This is indicative of Metz's liturgical contextualization of memory. Indeed, he will go so far as to say that while for a long time the power of memory was forgotten in philosophical and dogmatic theology, it was remembered in the Church's liturgy. Therefore, a Christian's embrace of "dangerous memories" is nourished both by Scripture and by liturgy. These are important clues as to what the practices of the spirituality of *Leiden an Gott* would look like.

The mode of narrative which corresponds to dangerous memories is that of dangerous stories. As we saw above, narrative involves the one who hears with the experiences narrated. It is a sacramental reality, one which produces a community with the other who is telling the story and with the subjects of the narrative itself. It is a community within a history which is still ongoing, which cannot be encompassed theoretically. The narrative structure in which the possibility of solidarity is created is one which admits of interruption, of "plot twists" which are unexpected. Dangerous narratives, those which recount the history of suffering, present our involvement in history in such a way that the negativities of history, those points which tend to be occluded by false attempts to interpret comprehensively and theoretically the meaning of our being in history and society, are not covered over. When we understand and accept the power of these stories they change us, involve us in the struggle to bring crucified peoples off the cross now, and also invite us to hope for the end of the story, a hope that even the crucified peoples of the past will be redeemed by God.

This brings us to hope and solidarity. Dangerous memories and narratives invite us to a universal solidarity with all persons, especially the forgotten victims. They invite us to share the hopes even of these, rather than narrowing the horizon of what we hope for, of what we believe possible or reasonable. As a *universal* solidarity it has a comprehensive character, extending to the conquered and forgotten. Solidarity with them turns us, full of complaint, but also hopefully, toward God. It is God who justifies Godself in the face of their suffering, and in whom we seek redemption from the complicitous guilt that threatens our own existence. Since we are not then seduced into the various exculpation strategies which come from fleeing our guilt, we are open to the suffering of the present, to *preferential* solidarity with the crucified peoples of the present. In this instance solidarity calls us to an imitation of Christ, to an unconditional recognition, love, and commitment for the sake of the other, particularly the other who is needy, who has no other claim on us for recognition than his or her being created and called to be a subject in God's presence.

Universal and preferential solidarity complement one another. Universal solidarity without preferential solidarity has no practical power; it never enters into the fray, really making the hopes of the crucified peoples of history *our* hopes and leading us to act accordingly in the present. Preferential solidarity without universal solidarity becomes cynical or hateful demonization of the other, which then easily gives rise to new histories of domination, oppression, and suffering. In a "mystical-political dual-structure, solidarity arises as a category of *the salvation of the subject* where it is threatened by forgetfulness, by oppression, by death; it arises as a category of commitment and engagement so that all persons might become and remain subjects."[63]

The three existentials are interrelated. Dangerous memories and narratives arouse and nurture solidarity. The hopes and expectations out of which we act (solidarity) are continually challenged and broadened by our remembrance of the unredeemed hopes of the victims of the past. We include their hopes in our own. On the other hand, without hopeful solidarity the catastrophes and negativities that become present to us in dangerous memory and narrative lead to maudlin despair, or guilt-ridden paralysis. Taken together these three determine the existentiell stance in which we do not cover over the horrors of history but allow them to remain present to us even though they radically threaten the ways in which we try meaningfully to act and understand in our present experience. We turn toward God, not in a trusting surrender, but in a complaining, expectant interrogation of God. This is a stance, finally, in which we are ourselves transformed since it challenges us to enlarge the horizon of our hopes and actions to include the crucified peoples, both past and present, without whom we ourselves cannot fully become and remain subjects. It is a spirituality, rooted in biblical narratives, nourished in individual and liturgical prayer, certainly giving rise to thought, but only fully actualized in action on behalf of others.

SUMMARY: THE ENDANGERED SUBJECT AND APOCALYPTIC TEMPORALITY

To take history seriously means understanding that nothing, not the highest, not the best, exists without danger, that everything is surrounded by danger, and that the meaning of history is always in danger wherever it is sought or thought of as something unendan-

gered. . . . Christian faith, if I understand it correctly, is just the capacity *to affirm and live an endangered identity*. Precisely in this are
faith and history bound to one another.[64] (emphasis added)

Dangerous memory; dangerous stories; universal-preferential, mystical-political solidarity: these make up the temporally tensed, expectant
following of Christ that is nourished by the spirituality of *Leiden an
Gott*. Only in and through this following is the full meaning of our existence disclosed as one oriented toward the Kingdom of God, a state
in which all persons are subjects in God's presence. But the Kingdom
of God is both "already" and "not yet." It is already present in the
solidarity which is nurtured by the memory of those who have died, a
solidarity in which their hopes continue to voice within us, coloring
our own hopes and transforming our action. But it is not yet here:
again the insistence on the category of danger.

Christian faith is the capacity to affirm and live an endangered identity. It offers hope to those who are crushed by dehumanizing poverty,
war, institutional racism, sexism, and classism. To those who are not
the direct victims of history's negativities, to the degree that they have
not been stripped of their identities by them, it offers the capacity to
continue to affirm and to live, in the face of guilt: the guilt of complicity
that comes by means of the ambiguous societies and histories in and
through which we gain our identities, or even the guilt of surviving.
But it is a capacity that requires of us conversion, a continual turning
toward those endangered points in our world and our history which
most clearly disclose the incompleteness, the frightening vulnerability,
and the endangered fragility of our identities as subjects. It is one that
forbids us to take refuge in a too-easy cynicism or despair; it prohibits
the various exculpation devices which seek to assure us of the legitimacy and sufficiency of whatever degree of emancipation in history
and society we can achieve on our own efforts. Instead, it enables and
requires us to admit that in this regard we are always *simul justus et
peccator*, and yet to continue to live and act hopefully, precisely in that
ambiguous, endangered existence which defines our being as subjects
who are, just as much as the Kingdom of God, "already" but "not yet."

Finally, being a subject involves temporality. Metz has his own way
of asserting what Heidegger implied in the title *Being and Time*. What
it means to be a human subject is finally inextricably interwoven with
a particular type of temporal involvement. Looking back, Metz argues

that theology forgot this in its search for atemporal metaphysical ways of grounding its understanding of Christian existence:

> Symptomatic for me . . . of this forgetfulness concerning time in theology is the way in which Martin Heidegger has been theologically received: not as the one who began to question the premises of a time-less metaphysics (even if, perhaps, in the wrong direction), but rather as the existential analyst of Dasein.[65]

Or again:

> Not in the Presocratics but rather in the eschatological landscape of theodicy of the Bible is the epochal question about "Being and Time" and the temporalization of metaphysics to be sought. . . . But even though . . . all theological statements about being are endowed with a temporal mark, in theology hardly anything is as little cultivated as an authentic, uncovered understanding of time.[66]

This brings us to the last of the themes that we identified as central to Metz's mature theology: the emphasis on apocalyptic. We saw that from the start Metz was concerned with Heidegger's understanding of Dasein's temporality. Later he was concerned about the underlying ontological presuppositions which guided the "demythologization" of apocalyptic symbols. It is this "depth-understanding" of time that Metz is concerned with. If one has accepted the "evolutionistically tinged" myth of homogeneous empty time, stretching out endlessly behind and before, then the remembrance of past suffering becomes unbearable, and hope for a future radical transformation ridiculous. Like Walter Benjamin's angel, one would be blown backward by the storm of progress, unable to close one's wings and tarry, even for a moment. The radical imitation of Christ, nurtured by memory and inspired by solidarity, becomes ridiculous, imprudent, unreasonable.

This "evolutionary time" is the temporality that paralyzes the affirmation and living of an endangered identity that is at the heart of Christian faith. Apocalyptic temporality, on the other hand, expresses a time that has a boundary, and not the boundary of an ever-receding horizon, bounded by nothingness. Rather, it is bounded by a loving, just God, who comes toward us to meet us, to whom time belongs, who interrupts the course of things, before whom we can all be changed, in a moment, in the twinkling of an eye (1 Cor 15:51f.). In this form of temporality, in which there is both danger but also hope, we are not made "into the voyeurs or terrorists of our own decline."[67] We tarry for just a moment, for just a moment, which is no longer one part of a continuum of time that rushes on "without grace," but one which is "the strait gate through which the Messiah might enter into history."

The various elements of Metz's theology thus fit together as the building blocks for a revised transcendental anthropology. The question with which one begins is the question of whether or how our involvement in history and society can be meaningful, given the terrible tremenda of history: the theodicy question. The response is not a theoretical solution but a type of existentiell stance within history, a *Leiden an Gott*, which is particularly present to the meaningless death of the other, which expresses itself in dangerous, interruptive memory of past suffering, and the mystical-political solidarity and praxis that is nurtured by that memory and expressed through dangerous stories. This *spirituality* discloses what it means to be a subject in history because it does not cover over history's negativities, and because it discloses the deeper ontological grounding of our endangered identity in a relationship to the God of Abraham and Sarah, of Job, and of Jesus of Nazareth. It is this God toward whom our hope and trust is directed, in complaint and lamentation as much as in praise and celebration. This fragile, endangered identity as subjects, in solidarity with all men and women, is finally one that lives in an apocalyptic temporality, a time infused with tensed expectation, in which we hope and act in relationship to the God who can make all things new.

This then is the fundamental theological anthropology which provides the focus around which the different themes, images, and concepts of Metz's theology are organized. In argumentative form and in the emphases on the immanence of the past and the importance of the still outstanding future to our attempts to perceive, think, and act meaningfully in the present, it is in continuity with the hermeneutic and transcendental approaches that he mastered in his early work. However, it has been altered by his encounters with revisionary Marxists, the changing conditions of the Roman Catholic Church, and, above all, by Metz's attempt to find a theology which can adequately bring to expression those dangerous memories which so mark his own and his nation's recent past—memories of savage war and numbing apathy, a memory of holocaust. Insofar as these memories, and memories like them, cry out to all of us in this troubled age, Metz's alternative is one that deserves to be taken very seriously.

I have attempted to show how important the existentiell stance of *Leiden an Gott* is for Metz's theology. This "mysticism," as he calls it, represents the authentic response to the gift and challenge of existence that come to us from God. It concretizes a realization of the most fundamental structures of human being (memory, narrative, solidarity) in such a way that our individual being opens up to the needs of others, and in such a way that we are able to risk, and to bear, the painful task of taking up (as we must) our histories, histories shot through with ambiguity and guilt. Ultimately, it is the stance in terms of which the diverse themes and arguments of Metz's mature theology cohere and show themselves as a genuine and integrated way of being human.

If this mysticism of *Leiden an Gott* is more than Metz's own creation, what are its historical roots, and where did Metz come across it? Finally, if we are ready to call it a spirituality, with genuine roots in the history of Christian (and Jewish) spirituality, then what can we learn from Metz's struggle to articulate it, a struggle which entailed such a substantial revision of his earlier theological approach? This brings us back to questions raised in the first chapter. To them we now return, armed with the detailed case-study of Metz's mystical-political-theological development.

6

THE MYSTICAL-POLITICAL STRUCTURE OF CHRISTIAN SPIRITUALITY AND THEOLOGY

> Karl Rahner knew better than anyone that all discourse about God has an authentic linguistic base only insofar as it is rooted in a discourse with God; he knew, in other words, that the theoretically inalienable and indispensable linguistic realm of theology is the language of prayer.
>
> Johann Baptist Metz

We have followed Metz through the course of his theological development, concluding with his mature system. The spirituality of *Leiden an Gott*, which is the heart of Metz's mature interpretation of the venerable spiritual disposition of "poverty of spirit," has emerged as the crucial element of any authentic following of Christ, of being a subject along with other subjects, in the presence of God.[1] This existentiell stance is not only the authentically Christian way of "being-in-the-world," it defines the location from which Metz's theological anthropology appears in its full breadth and coherence. In this stance the fundamental human existentials of memory and narrative are realized as *dangerous* memories and narratives. Solidaristic hope is realized as a universal solidarity with all, including the defeated and disappeared of our histories, which energizes a particular solidarity with those similarly threatened today. Since this stance is located in a form of presence to God, it maps out a genuinely *theological* anthropology: human beings can only fully accept the gift and challenge of their personhood in a form of relationship to God. Finally, this relationship to God is not only one that is *elicited* by the experience of suffering and evil in history, but one that *sustains* hopeful endurance and resistance within and despite that experience.² It marks Metz's as a political, praxis-oriented anthropology.

It is no accident that Metz first began to speak of *Leiden an Gott* at the same time that he brought together the conceptual resources that he had been gathering for over a decade into a "system," in *Faith in History and Society*.³ It has been the argument of this book that Metz's theological restlessness, muted in the fifties, strikingly evident in the sixties, was driven by a desire to find the words to speak *about* God in a way that corresponded to a deeply rooted (in his own childhood memories) way of speaking (or being starkly silent) *before and to* God. In chapter 3 we saw that at first he tried to modify the concepts and argumentative strategies of Rahner's theology in order to meet his underlying discomfort with the system as a whole. In chapter 4 we saw how in the sixties he ranged broadly, gradually assembling a new set of concepts, metaphors, and scriptural loci, which he finally deployed as a new, political theology in the seventies. Simultaneously he began articulating and advocating the existentiell stance that he names a mysticism of suffering unto God (*Leiden an Gott*). Yet, for all the novelty of Metz's new political theology, it has striking and important continuities with his early work and, indeed, with Rahner's theology. This was shown in chapter 5 by constructing the fundamental, theological anthropology implicit to Metz's political theology *in parallel* with both the existential anthropology of Heidegger and with its theological reconfiguration in Rahner.

I have claimed not just that this disposition of suffering unto God is an important part of Metz's mature theology; even more, I have claimed that it is *the* animating center of Metz's theological *itinerarium*, that its presence in Metz's theology is paradigmatic of the way that a spirituality will press a theologian to stretch the intellectual tools he or she has been given for understanding, communicating, and inviting others into, that particular spirituality. This claim is warranted first by the fact, mentioned above, that the conceptual ripening of Metz's political theology came simultaneously with his articulation of a specific mystical stance, and that, furthermore, none of his writings since have failed to mention, and mention prominently, this "mysticism." But there is another way to support this claim, and that is by returning to the point I made in the introduction: that ultimately the most important difference between the theological journeys of Karl Rahner and his student, Johann Baptist Metz, is that their theologies are animated by different spiritualities. This is the key that unlocks the puzzle of their relationship. In order to complete my argument for the relationship of theology and spirituality (and of politics as well) in Metz's thought, as well as to set the stage for some more general concluding remarks on that relationship, I will return now to substantiate this claim.

RAHNER AND METZ REVISITED: THE MYSTICAL-POLITICAL DIMENSIONS OF THEIR THEOLOGIES

The usual way of approaching the differences between Karl Rahner and Johann Baptist Metz is to play on the adjectives generally associated with their theologies: "transcendental" and "political." There are many summaries of Metz's critique of Rahner on this score, which I will not repeat in detail here.[4] Briefly, on this view Metz abandoned Rahner's theological method because he believed it inadequate for articulating or meeting theology's political responsibility; his primary criticism has been that it was overly privatized and, all of its talk of historicity notwithstanding, never *really* entered into history, with all of its ambiguity and evil, all its suffering, its crushing and seemingly irredeemable defeats. As I argued in my introduction, this approach, while true as far as it goes and initially helpful, is ultimately unsatisfactory. One can agree with Metz, in which case one would have to argue that Rahner has not responded to the new social and political situation of the post–Vatican II world. This is a judgment which cannot be sustained, and one which it is difficult to ascribe to Metz, insofar as he (the political theologian) continues to hold up Rahner as *still* the paradigm for theological work today.

One could disagree with Metz, and argue that he did not or would not understand Rahner's system. But this disregards the esteem in which Rahner continued to hold his pupil. After all, Rahner said that "Metz's critique of my theology (which he calls transcendental theology) is the only criticism which I take very seriously."[5] One could argue that Metz merely developed implicit aspects of Rahner's system, which has the corollary assertion that Metz's own theology depends upon Rahner's for its foundation. This seems to have been Rahner's own view. He concedes that every concrete initiation of Christians into the experience of the mystery of God (every "mystagogy") "must obviously from the very beginning consider the societal situation and the Christian praxis to which it addresses itself,"[6] and allows the possibility that he has not done this sufficiently. However, he goes on to assert that, on the one hand, this is a matter of "filling out" his own theory; and that, on the other hand, a political theology "is, if it truly wishes to concern itself with God, not possible without reflection on those essential characteristics of man which a transcendental theology discloses. Therefore, I believe that my theology and that of Metz are not necessarily contradictory."[7]

As attractive as this view is, finally it too fails to satisfy. As I showed in chapter 3, Metz *began* his career by attempting to "fill out" Rahner's theology in the way Rahner suggests. He abandoned that attempt after the mid-sixties. Furthermore, in chapter 5 I showed that Metz's work really does have a "reflection on those essential characteristics that a transcendental theology discloses," albeit one that is different from Rahner's. Metz was not filling out a basically Rahnerian transcendental theology; he was seeking to revise the project from the ground up. Drawing on Thomas Kuhn's famous (or infamous) notion, Metz sees in his efforts a fundamental "paradigm shift" away from transcendental theology.[8] Finally, there was at least one issue over which their disagreements were simply too strong to be contained by a "complementarity" thesis: the status of apocalyptic images (more on this later). These problems with the "complementarity" or "corrective" thesis press us to look again at their differences.

An important clue for finding *both* what closely unites them *and* what differentiates them emerges when we examine the contexts within which they most clearly express their attitudes (of respect *and* reservation) toward one another. Metz most strongly praises Rahner's theology because it brings together Christians' everyday experience of God and the doctrines of Christian faith:

> Rahner's work is, in my opinion, quite simply this: a theologically substantive report on life in contemporary Christianity. Here it is not a classical canon of questions that reigns; here it is not only questions which the system allows that are treated, not the elegant life, but rather life as it is forced upon us, the uneasy life.[9]

Rahner's is a biographical theology that "inscribes the mystical biography of religious experience, one's life-story before the hidden face of

God, into the doxography of faith."[10] As we saw in chapter 5, Rahner's starting point for his hermeneutic endeavor is the lived awareness of faith as it exists today.[11] It is in this context of people's spirituality that Rahner retrieves and enlivens doctrines that for too long had been elaborated only in scholastic manuals, doctrines in which believers were increasingly unable to recognize their own lives, doubts, pains, and struggles. According to Metz, the doctrines of the Church, mediated by Rahner's transcendental theology, could then potentially become again what they originally were: a public, ecclesial vocabulary in terms of which believers grasped, articulated, communicated, even argued about and acted upon their experiences of the breadth and length and height and depth of love experienced in following Jesus. In terms of my discussion of spirituality and theology in the first chapter, Rahner's theology is an attempt to retrieve the doctrines of the Church so that they can provide for believers the elements for making sense of and deepening their engagement in the practices of faith, drawing them ever more deeply into the mystery of discipleship. Instead of being technical jargon constructed by and for ecclesiastical or academic experts, they can become an invitation and initation into an art of living. In summary, again using my terminology, Metz is asserting—and he is surely correct in this—that Rahner's work exhibited the same dynamic interrelation of spirituality and theology that this book has sought to display in Metz's work.

It would take another book, perhaps even longer, to fully demonstrate and illustrate this facet of Rahner's theology. Here it must suffice to note that Rahner's theology could speak out of and to spirituality because he was at home in both worlds. Rahner's thought was shaped not only by the full breadth of the German intellectual tradition of the past two centuries, and nearly two millennia of Catholic theology, but also by contact with the great spiritual masters of the Christian tradition, from Origen to Ignatius.[12] Rahner himself argued that mystical theology, by which he meant the theology which reflects upon mystical experience, should be a part of dogmatic theology.[13] But, he did not mean that it is to be fitted into an omnicompetent, pre-given systematic structure. Rather, the whole structure of systematic theology has to be tested by whether or not it can do justice to what the saint or the mystic says. For example, in reflecting on the experience of spiritual consolation or desolation, treated in Ignatius's *Spiritual Exercises,* Rahner asserts that what is at issue for the theologian is whether or not he already has at his disposal in his theology the means really to bring explicitly before the mind the concrete experience in question, to make it more exactly comprehensible and to justify it. Or the fact is revealed that his theology would first have to be developed through contact with these works and what they say, and allow itself to be corrected by them.[14]

Hence, there are spiritual classics which give "a 'creative', original assimilation of God's revelation *in Christo*, . . . a new gift by God's Spirit of the ancient Christianity to a new age."[15] Using my own terminology, Rahner was well aware of the second way that spirituality influences theology, that a spirituality forms the theologian at a profound level—his or her way of being present to God, and consequently to him- or herself and to the world. Theology arises out of spirituality, and is judged by how well it articulates that spirituality. In turn, it communicates that spirituality, gives it breadth and living force in a complex world, experienced through an irreducible diversity of conceptual systems and meaning-producing practices (individual and institutional).

In the course of this book I have tried to show how crucial spirituality is in Metz's thought. We have seen how for Metz theological argument arises out of, and is at the service of, that basic way of being human before God that he calls a "mysticism of suffering unto God." He agrees that theology and spirituality must develop in intimate union with one another (and he acknowledges that it was precisely in this that Rahner was not only his teacher but his "father in faith.")[16] Yet it is at this point of deepest agreement that we find the point of disagreement. A bit further in the same essay cited above, in which Metz praised Rahner's theology for the way it intercalates the mystical experience of the everyday Christian with the content of Christian doctrine, Metz states that to be true to this fundamental insight for *today's* situation

> in the whole approach of a practical fundamental theology one would have to break out of this biographical conception of dogmatic theology and move in the direction of that theological biography of Christianity in which the mystical-political dual-structure of Christian faith—that is, that form of Christian faith which has taken up its social responsibility—is even more consistently taken into account and made into the moving force of theological reflection.[17]

The objection is that Rahner considers the "mystical dimension" of believers too much within the horizon of the individual, whose social dimension is confined to that of the I-Thou relationship. For Metz, Rahner's thought works too much out of a mystical-*existential* or mystical-*dialogical* correlation, whereas he wants a mystical-*political* correlation. It is attention to the political dimension and demands of Christian faith that prevents faith from being reduced to private religiosity. It is attention to the mystical dimension of faith that prevents the following of Christ from becoming merely a regulative ideal or cipher for what is already occurring on the political and social scene.[18]

Did not Rahner recognize this? In his introduction to Bacik's book on mystagogy, where he acknowledges Metz's critique, Rahner goes on to write "I gladly recognize that a concrete mystagogy must, to use Metz's language, be at the same time 'mystical and political.'"[19] Yet, again, he believes that his own appoach can move in such a direction. Much of Rahner's development after Vatican II can be understood precisely as such a move. Indeed, it may very well be that Metz provided not only some of the impetus for Rahner's further development but even some of the ideas that Rahner himself followed up on. For example, in his essay on the significance of Ignatius of Loyola for Jesuits today, it is significant that the only contemporary theologian that Rahner mentions (and recommends) is Metz. He cites Metz in talking about the social and political tasks facing the Society of Jesus, particularly in connection with the Jesuits' commitment to the promotion of justice as a constitutive element of their apostolic presence in today's world. In this regard Rahner uses Metz's notion of dangerous memory to talk about the social-political dimension of "following the poor and humble Jesus."[20] But, for his part, while Metz continued to praise Rahner's way of doing theology out of the spirituality of the everyday Christian, he was clearly not satisfied with *the way* that Rahner articulated the political dimension. Why did Metz not follow him? Indeed, why did he not follow his own initial attempts in the late fifties and early sixties to move in a similar direction? Why did he move off in a new direction? Have we arrived back at the same impasse?

My suggestion is that this is one of those moments in a theological career in which the choice is underdetermined by the concepts and themes that frame the choice. This is a point where a spirituality shows its presence as a deeper determining ground for a theological choice. The theologian is thrown back on his or her relationship to God, as it is incarnated in a specific way of following Jesus, and on how the world, with its points of crisis and of hope, shows up in light of that relationship. If we grasp that it was on the need to actualize a fruitful relationship between theology and spirituality (the mystical dimension) that the two were most deeply in agreement with each other, and further allow that each (Metz perhaps earlier than Rahner) understood that the *mystical* dimension must ultimately be open to and animate how one perceives and responds to the challenges of the *political* dimension, can we not then ask a further relevant question? What precisely was this mystical dimension that informed each man's thinking? Could a difference there help us to understand their difference on the political dimension? Might this not be the more fundamental root of their differences?

There is a wealth of material in the history of spirituality for exploring the question so posed. One of the most pervasive and important themes in that history is the relationship between prayer and action, classically formulated as the relationship between the *vita contemplativa* and the *vita activa*. It might be good at this point to consider this issue in terms of my earlier discussion of spirituality in chapter 1, so that we can make something explicit that was there given only implicitly; namely, both formally and substantively any Christian spirituality has ethical and political implications for the Christian in the world. The two *vitae* give rise to one another, and qualify one another in crucial ways, ways that must be examined if one is to understand the full depth of *either* a Christian spirituality *or* an authentically Christian ethics and politics.

This can be seen in a formal way by returning to my definition of spirituality. In my first chapter I proposed that we see a spirituality as made up of a set of practices, or, in Pierre Hadot's terminology, a set of *spiritual exercises,* which initiate one into a particular but comprehensive and comprehensively transformative way of life. These exercises are both nourished by, but also lend context and intelligibility to, a broad range of oral and literary materials. These materials, which may, and most often do, contain statements about the way the world is, and how in consequence one ought to act in the world, develop in dialectical relationship with the spiritual exercises. From this it can be seen that, insofar as engagement in a spirituality entails a transformation of the person and of how the person sees the world, then it will also entail a transformation of how the person acts in and towards the world. If the way I see the world and the goods that appear in and through the world changes, then so will my actions. Furthermore, just as those statements *about* the world which are included in a spirituality (as its "second dimension") cannot be fully understood apart from the spiritual exercises they are meant to nurture, so too the *actions in* the world—either those which are directly a part of the "exercises" that make up the first dimension of spirituality, or those which become intelligible and desirable because of the way the world is opened up to me (the second dimension)—cannot be understood apart from the spirituality that gives rise to them. Thus, even the most world-denying spirituality has consequences for how one acts in the world, even if admittedly they are largely negative.

To be sure, not much more can be said, formally speaking. To say more one must turn to the substantive character of a given spirituality. In my definition I made this move by arguing that the first dimension of a *Christian* spirituality comprises a set of practices that make up a mystagogical initiation into the mystery of discipleship. One need not read very far in Christian scripture to discover that a primary dimension of discipleship, if not the primary one, is love of neighbor—especially those we do not notice or do not want to recognize as neighbor—no matter what the cost. Thus, a transformation of the way we act in the world is not only entailed by Christian spirituality as mediated through the transformation of the way a Christian sees the world (as the relationship showed up in its "formal" dimension) but is at the very heart of the substance and goal of Christian spiritual exercises themselves. Indeed, in some ways the transformation in the way a Christian sees the world is mediated by this prior transformation, and not vice versa. Therefore, it is not without reason that Jon Sobrino has argued that we need to state something much more explicitly today (which was, to be sure, implicit in prior ages): Christian theology is not just or not even primarily a *fides quaerens intellectum,* but much more a *caritas quaerens intellectum,* an *intellectus amoris.*[21]

The great masters of the spiritual life, and of theology, have been well aware of this fact. Beginning with Origen, they took over the Greek concepts of *theoria* and *praxis* to articulate the connection between contemplation and action. Yet this pair, while enabling those who deployed it to express easily the more general formal relationship, was in many ways profoundly inadequate for expressing the substantive form of Christian spirituality's way of presenting this relationship.

On this issue the history of spirituality can be fruitfully read as a struggle to reconfigure the Greek philosophical concepts in order to adequately render the distinctively Christian way of defining the relationship between contemplation and action.[22] It is a history with a number of different approaches to solving this dilemma; the ways of relating contemplation and action, or (in our modern terminology) the spiritual and the ethical-political, are as diverse as the ways of understanding contemplation and spirituality in general. And this is a history that is by no means at an end, as the work of both Rahner and Metz illustrates.

In this light, if we examine the question of the relationship between Rahner and Metz, what we need to do is to understand how each sought to develop an understanding of a *vita mixta* (introduced into the history of Christian spirituality by Augustine) that is not some third way alongside the other two but that way of life in which the two are conjoined, one in which alone *both* Christian presence to God *and* Christian political action are genuinely possible, given the eschatological conditions of Christian life. Let us now return to Rahner and Metz in the light of these observations, first identifying their spiritualities; then considering how those spiritualities were reflected in, and continually transformed, their theologies; and finally deriving the ethical-political implications that they came to articulate in the process of that transformation.

Rahner never hesitated to articulate his own understanding of mysticism within the framework of his Ignatian heritage. Yet the Ignatian heritage is a complex one; the genealogy of the *Exercises* bears many names. Furthermore, Rahner's work brought him into contact with a great diversity of mystical traditions. So, we must look more carefully. Despite this complexity, few would contest the judgment that a careful reading of Rahner's theology makes it clear that he belongs to the apophatic neoplatonic tradition of Christian mysticism.[23] This is, of course, one of the elements of Ignatius's own mysticism, as in the neoplatonic imagery of the famous "Contemplation to Attain Love" with which the *Exercises* end.[24] As an early instance of Rahner's interpretation of Ignatius through a neoplatonic lens, consider Rahner's interpretation of "The Ignatian Mysticism of Joy in the World."[25] Rahner argues that Ignatius's piety is at once removed from the world and because of that open to engagement in the world. It is a "monastic piety," in which the monk puts on the crucified Christ as a way of putting to death the false self, of realizing his flight from the world.²⁶ Meditation on the cross detaches us from this world. Having attained detachment from the world, we can return to find God in the world wherever God wills to be found.²⁷ Thus, the central virtue of Ignatian mysticism is *indiferencia*:

> *Indiferencia* is possible only where the will to a *fuga saeculi* is alive, and yet this *indiferencia* in its turn disguises that love for the foolishness of the Cross into daily *moderation* of a *normal style of life* marked by *good sense*. Filled with such *indiferencia* Ignatius can even forego manifestations of mystical graces—after all God is beyond even the world of experience of the mystic.²⁸

This phrase cannot but remind one of Meister Eckhart, that great medieval mystic who tried to bring to expression a similar sort of movement into God, one that is marked by radical detachment (in his case, *abgeschiedenheit*). Meister Eckhart, too, insisted that a mysticism of the highest order could be lived out in a "normal style of life marked by good sense." Meister Eckhart's "democratization of mysticism"²⁹ is reflected in Rahner's aversion to any kind of elitism, an aversion that Metz notes in describing Rahner's theology as a mystical biography of the *everyday* Christian life. It is reflected in Rahner's insistence that mystical experience is not in principle different in form from the graced experience of any Christian. He did not deny the existence or possible value of paranormal mystical experiences (neither did the Meister), but he did deny any *theological* justification for the claim that they constitute the necessary pinnacle of a Christian life.³⁰

What of Metz? I have argued that the "mysticism of suffering unto God" is at the heart of Metz's theology. A case can be made that it fits the definition of spirituality I gave in my first chapter. There is certainly a set of "spiritual exercises" which are crucial for eliciting and nurturing this mysticism: a (Joblike) way of prayer, a eucharistic praxis centered around anamnesis ("do this in remembrance of me"), a *lectio divina* (allowing ourselves to be engaged, irritated, and transformed by the dangerous stories of scripture), unblinking attention to the history of suffering, and so on. Metz's theology itself is an elaboration of a view of the world, including basic ontological, anthropological, and theological (narrowly speaking) commitments that are entailed by and complement these practices. Yet can we also connect this "spirituality" with the history of spirituality, as we did with Rahner?

We can find sources in the Middle Ages for Metz's apocalyptic mysticism of *Leiden an Gott,* with its emphasis on a complaining, yet also hopefully expectant, presence to God in the midst of suffering and the stress on a radical following of Christ which is required and legitimated by the extraordinary character of the apocalyptic time in which we live. First, in the exfoliation of apocalyptic mysticism, beginning with Joachim of Fiore and continuing through the Spiritual Franciscans, Savanorola, and Radical Reformers like Thomas Münzer, we find a mysticism which was intensely aware of the unsettled, dangerous character of time. At the same time, as Ewert Cousins has noted, a new form of mysticism was born in the Middle Ages, launched by the towering figure of Francis of Assisi.[31] Unlike Christian Neoplatonism, which focuses on Christ's presence as Logos in the soul, or on the glorified risen Christ, this new form of mysticism focuses on the humanity of Jesus, humble and poor, stretched out between birth and death.[32] Cousins calls this a "mysticism of the historical event," in which "one recalls a significant event in the past, enters into its drama and draws from it spiritual energy, eventually moving beyond the event toward union with God."[33] New methods of meditation, in which one enters imaginatively into the events of Christ's life in order to realize personal transformation, enter into the stream of Christian spirituality, beginning as early as Bernard of Clairvaux, drawing strength from St. Francis's mysticism, maturing with Bonaventure's *Lignum Vitae,* and continuing in works like the *Meditations on the Life of Christ* in the late thirteenth century and Ludolph of Saxony's *Vita Jesu Christi,* which, finally, was the book upon which Ignatius meditated during his convalescence and conversion. This mysticism of the historical event formed a great alternative to the flowering of speculative and affective neoplatonic mysticism in the High and late Middle Ages. Indeed, some of the great classics of spirituality from the Middle Ages through the Reformation and beyond are attempts to synthesize the two streams: Bonaventure's work being the first, Ignatius's *Spiritual Exercises* certainly not the last.

If we use Cousins's historical typology, the difference between Rahner and Metz emerges quite strikingly. In Metz's early period the language and imagery he uses are very close to the mystical tradition that his teacher, Karl Rahner, utilized. In an early work on the beatitudes Metz defines poverty of spirit in terms of detachment and trusting surrender to God—very Rahnerian themes, as we saw above.[34] It is

Jesus' last words as reported by Luke's Gospel that are at the center of a Christian spirituality of poverty of spirit.[35] A quarter-century later the same mystical virtue finds its historical roots in "Israel's incapacity to be consoled [in the face of suffering] by myths and ideas that are far-removed from history"[36] and for Christians is nurtured by presence to the crucified Christ. And now this is no longer the Christ whose last words are "Father, into your hands I commend my spirit" but the crucified Christ of that most apocalyptic of the Gospels, Mark's, and the last words of Jesus reported there: "My God, my God, why have you abandoned me?"[37]

Metz's emphasis on the centrality of the imitation (*Nachfolge*) of Christ is found also in the Radical Reformers, for whom this virtue (more precisely, the following of the "bitter" or suffering Christ) was even more important than the Lutheran *fides*.[38] For them as well this mystical presence to God engendered a powerful sense of imminent expectation that often flowered in apocalypticism. But this apocalypticism did not necessarily imply a *fuga saeculi*:

> Although most of the Radicals despaired of political transformation of the world and opposed the structures of temporal power as themselves demonic in their violent *modus operandi,* they nevertheless resisted the ultimate temptation of quietism and political indifference. In their efforts to maintain a faithful witness in this present, provisional aeon, they forged a spirituality that was at once profoundly otherworldly and yet unswervingly committed to the purposes of God within history.[39]

This description could equally serve Metz's theology. We may conclude then that Metz's mysticism of *Leiden an Gott* stands in the traditions of apocalyptic mysticism and the mysticism of the historical event.

If we may thus identify the differences between the mystical stances of Rahner and Metz in terms of these two great streams of Christian mystical tradition, we should expect that the ontological conceptualities within which the two will labor to articulate the meaning and implications of their mysticisms—what I in my first chapter named "theology" in the narrower sense—will differ as well. It should come as no surprise that Rahner, with his Eckhartian consciousness of God's presence in the world, found the ontological conceptuality of German Idealism, and particularly that of Martin Heidegger, extremely attractive. Eckhart stands as one of the great founders of German theology and philosophy; his "rediscovery" in the early nineteenth century had a powerful impact on thinkers like Schelling, Hegel, and Hölderlin. John Caputo has convincingly demonstrated this "mystical element" in Heidegger's thought by showing clear parallels between Heidegger and Eckhart.[40] While Rahner was educated in the intricacies of Thomism, and took much from it in constructing his metaphysics and epistemology, he was also very much influenced by mystical traditions in Christianity, as I argued above. Even from the beginning, in *Geist in Welt* and *Hörer des Wortes*, Rahner's foundational metaphysics of knowledge and anthropology represent an attempt to draw out the ontological and epistemological commitments entailed by this mystical experience and to show its connaturality with the rest of our experience. I would contend that this explains, at least in part, his attraction to thinkers like Hegel, Schelling, and Heidegger. As noted above, however, all such attempts will be unsatisfactory to the mystic, or to the theologian trying to make use of the mystic's experience. Hence, one would expect precisely what one finds in Rahner's thought: a dynamism, a searching movement for ever more adequate uses of language and ever more precise ontological formulations.[41]

Early in his career we find Rahner speaking of God as the horizon of being, as pure being, or as that being with unlimited "possession of being" (*Seinshabe*). This is what we would expect of a good Thomist. But, later Rahner turned more and more to language of absolute mystery; he speaks of our fundamental presence to God as a "transcendence of transcendentality beyond the conceivable that is grasped (a transcendence into apparent emptiness)."[42] Furthermore, we find the same pairing of the incomprehensibility at the ground of the human soul and the incomprehensibility of the ground of God, upon which Eckhart insisted. Rahner struggled to express the more radical formulations of the later period within the language of the earlier period. For example, in considering the mystical notion of a "consolation without prior cause" from Ignatius's *Exercises,* Rahner speaks of it as an

> inexpressible, non-conceptual experience of the love of the God who is raised transcendent above all that is individual, all that can be mentioned and distinguished, of God as God. There is no longer "any object" but the drawing of the whole person, with the very ground of his being, into love, beyond any defined circumscribable object, into the infinity of God as God himself.[43]

This type of experience does not fit easily into the epistemological-metaphysical framework of *Spirit in the World,* in which there is no unmediated experience, no knowledge without images or concepts. Indeed, as we saw above, the notion of this sort of unmediated presence was precisely what transcendental Thomists like Emerich Coreth and Metz himself, early in his career, had criticized in Heidegger's ontological phenomenology.[44] Even in the context of this passage—laying out the anthropological basis for Ignatian discernment of spirits—Rahner labors mightily to explain how this type of "experience" is correlated with the concrete experiences of goals and desires, which form for Ignatius the raw materials of discernment.

In general Rahner struggles to find a place for mystical experience, and it is not clear to what degree it is not a sort of *tertium quid* between the mediated experience of the transcendent proper to the human knower in this life and the unmediated experience of divine incomprehensibility, which Rahner reserves for the next life.[45] Without plunging into a full-scale investigation of Rahner's mystical theology, one can at least observe that the "experience" or "consciousness" of God's presence is, in the later Rahner, at least as much an experience of *absence.* The "absence" or "silence" of God, loudly proclaimed by atheists and death-of-God theologians, is for the later Rahner God's most potent form of presence.[46] In the tradition of negative theology, Rahner's anthropology and epistemology now serve to map out the conceptual structure in which the consciousness of God's presence/absence as Holy Mystery can at least be located in the gaps and interstices, if it cannot be described. Rahner's greatness as a theologian lies in his willingness to live and work within the tensions between the mystical consciousness that he is trying to bring to expression and the linguistic, hermeneutical, and metaphysical tools within which he is struggling to articulate and communicate it.

What of Metz? One of the virtues of the interpretation I am offering here is its ability to explain the startling shift in Metz's thought during the sixties. I have argued that Metz was searching to grasp and articulate a mode of presence to God that would not be shattered by, but would emerge out of, experiences of radical evil and suffering, of the sort that Metz himself experienced in World War II, and that he finds all around us in our contemporary world. If I am right about the difference in mystical stance, then it is no surprise that he could not long feel at home with Rahner. He began exploring new concepts and strategies which could map out or locate the space within which one is conscious of the presence-in-absence of God in the sort of world that was and is Metz's.

Ultimately, therefore, he could not follow the Rahnerian path of rooting the conceptual structure more deeply in the spirituality in which it was already rooted. He needed something new, but how would he find it if he did not have the concepts to articulate it? It was his encounter with the Marxists that catalyzed this discomfort and opened up new conceptual resources for addressing and remedying his dissatisfaction. He took up philosophies that emphasize the primacy of praxis in order to grasp and articulate a mystical stance that stresses *Nachfolge,* a stance that does not focus so much on the presence of the Logos in the soul, but on presence (through *memoria* and *imitatio*) to the historical Jesus. Consider again Metz's interlocutors: Ernst Bloch, whose second important and formative text was an interpretation of the life and thought of the radical reformer Thomas Münzer;[47] Walter Benjamin, who, influenced by the apocalyptic mysticism of Jewish Kabbalah, sought a materialist (!) notion of time in which "every second in time [is] the strait gate through which the Messiah might enter."[48]

Apocalyptic and Franciscan mysticisms have been fertile sources for new understandings of history that are strongly in tension with the traditional soteriology and theology of history that spring from Augustine, or the individualized and cosmologized eschatology of Thomas (and the tradition of his interpreters), with its emphasis on the *ordo scientiae* over the *ordo historiae.*[49] It is thus no surprise that the fundamental ontological system for Metz is no longer a transcendental metaphysics reflecting on the existential and moral experience of the individual but rather a transcendental anthropology which reflects on the coherence and meaning of our finite, often fragmented experience of acting in society and history. Metz's long journey toward a revised fundamental theological anthropology is thus to be read as the struggle to find the adequate words to bring to light this apocalyptic mysticism of the historical event and to work out its implications for the whole of Christian theology.

Finally, can we use this difference in spirituality to illuminate the differences between Rahner and Metz on the political dimension of Christian faith? What ethical-political consequences flow from their mystical stances? An important result, hinted at above, that comes with Rahner's mysticism of the everyday has to do with what Charles

Taylor has identified as one of the most central strands of the modern identity: the affirmation of everyday life.[50] This emphasis on everyday goods (those associated with the goods of survival and procreation) over and against the sorts of "hypergoods" that one finds in ancient Mediterranean and Northern European societies (heroic virtue or philosophical contemplation), has a powerful influence on the understanding of the self and of the sorts of goods we ought to pursue both individually and collectively. This affirmation of the everyday is so pervasive today that it forms a sort of moral horizon against which particular choices are made. However, it is not self-evident, as Taylor has shown. It does have sources. In Rahner's theology, as an articulation of a certain mystical stance toward the world, we find a powerful vision of God, world, and self that holds open or "clears" such a horizon. This ethical-political dimension of Rahner's thought was particularly important in his work—with others—to open the Catholic Church to a greater appreciation of the everyday work of the laity in the world as the expression and implication of an authentically mystical-religious life.

Second, there is an anti-ideological reserve of Christianity that follows from the grounding of immanent meaning in the transcendent, ultimately incomprehensible God. As we saw in Rahner's explication of the mystical virtue of *indiferencia,* the Ignatian mystic enters into the world only as one who has already fled from it, through his or her identification with Christ crucified. No element of the world or human history can claim his or her unconditional allegiance. To be sure, he or she is sent back into the world, but only on the will of God, and only when and where God is to be found. God *can* be found in all things, and thereby engage all the energies of the Ignatian mystic; but, God is found in all things *only* by virtue of God's sovereign, loving will, and not by virtue of any purely immanent intelligibility or value. Hence, there is what Metz and others called an *eschatological proviso* that obtains in the Christian's political commitments.[51] In the final analysis, no one human conception of the future, with the ethical and political commitments it entails, can make an unconditional claim on the obedience of the Christian.[52]

All in all, however, there is a positive attitude toward the world and involvement in the world in Rahner's theology. In the final analysis, God *does* graciously will to be found in all things. The Christian who has allowed her or himself to "let go" and fall into the mystery of God, will consequently be "found" in the world in a similar way. He or she will "co-actualize" God's loving descent into the world.[53] The Christian's eschatological reserve is accompanied by faith in God's victorious gift of self, as that is attested in the event of Jesus the Christ. There is, to be sure, suffering and contradiction in the world, but for the Christian this suffering is finally like "echoes of a clap of thunder from a departing storm."[54]

To begin with, this was the avenue that Metz took as well. In an essay that dates from 1966 (Metz's "transitional period") on "The Theology of the World and Asceticism" he writes that authentic Christian mysticism

> does not proceed from an arbitrary denial of men and the world, in order to seek to rise towards a more immediate nearness to God. For the God of the Christian faith is found only in the movement of his love towards men, the "least," as has been revealed to us in Jesus Christ. Christian mysticism finds, therefore, that immediate experience of God which it seeks precisely in daring to imitate the unconditional involvement of the divine love for man in letting itself be drawn into the *descensus* of God, into the descent of his love to the least of his brothers.[55]

Here we can already begin to see some movement, insofar as Metz puts in the qualifier "the least"—alluding no doubt to that favorite parable for liberation theologians in Matthew 25. But Metz keeps moving; he becomes increasingly uncomfortable with that attitude towards suffering which sees it as ultimately "echoes of a clap of thunder from a departing storm." Evil and suffering are much more frighteningly and interruptively present to him, and had been ever since his traumatic experiences at the end of World War II. On the whole, this is also true of the tradition under which I have subsumed his thought. Francis's insistence on the radical, bodily imitation of Christ's poverty was in part a protest against the materialism that attended the growth of a money economy in Italy in the thirteenth century. The growing emphasis on the need for this sort of radical *Nachfolge Christi* grew in part from the sense of God's absence in the new economic, political, and even ecclesial orders.[56] This was an absence felt in the academy as well. We find in the later Middle Ages a growing mistrust of words and of their ability to mediate the sacred. Intellectually this distrust finds expression in the birth and growth of nominalism. In vernacular theology and mysticism[57] we find it in works like the *Imitation of Christ*, Marguerite Porete's *Mirror of Simple Souls*, and *The Cloud of Unknowing*. While this distrust of what passes as rational could and did find expression through a more radical "apophaticization" of the existing neoplatonic tradition, or by stressing the affective character of the dynamism toward God (as in the "love mystics"), it also produced the apocalyptic mystics of the Middle Ages and the Reformation. Their response was much more directly a political one. To be sure, this mysticism did not necessarily lead to revolutionary violence (although it could), but, particularly in the Radical Reformers, it did lead to an ethical-political stance of resistance, which took shape in the formation of communities that witnessed against the current age, living in imminent expectation of a new age.

We have already discussed the centrality of apocalpytic to Metz's political theology. In Rahner's thought, God is both absent and present as the absolute holy mystery that is at the same time the ground of all things and yet withdrawn from all things. This way of articulating God's presence and absence leads to the attitude of trusting abandonment to the risk of historical action which we saw above. Metz's way of articulating God's absence and presence is in terms of the apocalyptic expectation of one who is now absent. It engenders the sense that one lives in extraordinary times—filled with danger and hope—eliciting and justifying in turn an extraordinary ethical-political response: one of holding back, of resistance, of a radical questioning of what is and of what passes for reasonable and prudent.

This interpretation of Rahner and Metz also helps us to understand their profound disagreement over the status and meaning of apocalyptic imagery and language. It was over the issue of their "demythologization" that the two men were most divided in the closing years of Rahner's life.[58] Metz believed that in so concentrating eschatology on the death of the individual Rahner was weakening the political sting of Christianity. Metz is certainly correct about Rahner's focus on the death of the individual but there was also a "political" dimension to his thought. As I have hinted above, Rahner reflected and wrote a great deal on political issues, both ecclesial and secular, in his last years. Nonetheless, his fundamental stance was different from Metz's, and Metz would not, will not, recognize that mystical stance, with its ethical-political implications, as forceful enough for the needs of the present. For his part, Rahner objected that Metz's retrieval of apocalyptic could not finally be brought off, that it could not be rendered as a credible response in terms of the consciousness of modernity. This is, of course, Metz's point. It is precisely the canons of reasonableness of modernity that have to be called into question.

But it should be clear by now that Rahner's own position, with its own dynamic, cannot be made fully intelligible within the horizon of modernity either, and Rahner was well aware of this. In his later exposition of Ignatian mysticism, he has Ignatius say of his conviction of having experienced God without mediation that

> at root it is an outrageous claim, and this both from my perspective, where it is possible to experience the incomprehensibility of God in a wholly different way, and from the point of view of the godlessness of your own time, in which this godlessness has really only abolished the gods which the previous age, so innocently and yet at the same time so devastatingly, had identified with the unspeakable God. What should stop me from saying: godlessness even in the Church itself, if after all, in the final analysis the Church, throughout its history, in unity with the crucified one, is supposed to be the event of the overthrowing of the gods?[59]

Rahner insists that it is the task of every Jesuit, including Jesuit theologians, to guide persons into such an experience or, better, into grasping that this "experience" is at the very root of every truly human experience.[60] What better description by this committed Jesuit and skilled theologian of his own theological career? There is a certain mystical *excessus* that drives his own thought, as well as Metz's. The difference, as I have tried to demonstrate it here, is that the articulation of the experience of this *excessus* is rooted in two different strands of Christian mystical tradition, and it is this difference that is most crucial in understanding the differences between these two theologians.

Yet, while their thought is different, both theologians were (and in Metz's case, continues to be) provoked and fructified by the other. As I noted above, Rahner took Metz very seriously indeed, and Metz continues to speak of Rahner as his inestimable teacher, from whom he has learned everything that he holds of value. There is more to this than just the deep friendship and mutual respect between two men. On the one hand, the most important thing that Metz learned from Rahner was the need to mend the tear between spirituality and theology for the sake of Christian life and action in the world today, even if the precise way he carried that out differed from Rahner's way. On the other hand, the two strands of tradition upon which Metz and Rahner draw are not hermetically sealed one from the other. Some of the great classics of Western Christian theology and spirituality attempted to bring these two strands together, beginning with the theologian who gave Francis a theological voice, Bonaventure. Ignatius too is not just the mystic and theologian of the "Contemplation to Attain Love," with its Neoplatonic imagery and language of God's presence in all things. He is also the mystic of the cross, as his vision of the crucified Christ at La Storta shows, as well as the prominence of the crucified Christ in the *Spiritual Exercises*. Finally, he was no stranger to apocalyptic imagery, as the "Meditation on the Two Standards" or "The Call of the King" show.

This suggests that we can use Ignatius's spirituality as a map to locate Rahner and Metz in relation to one another. The heart of that spirituality is the *Spiritual Exercises,* a complex whole made up of four parts or "Weeks." For Rahner, as I have argued, the hermeneutical key for interpreting the whole was the Fourth Week, with its strongly neoplatonic "Contemplation to Attain Love" and the transformation that follows upon finding God in all things. Yet, this is not the only "part" out which one can approach the whole, and, *pace* Heidegger, perhaps it does make a difference how one enters into the hermeneutical circle of the spirituality of the *Exercises*. The difference *and* the connection between Rahner and Metz emerges more clearly if we look at liberation theologians, not an unreasonable move, since Metz himself has said that he finds in liberation theology the most forceful and thoroughgoing application of the insights and intentions of his own "post-idealist" paradigm.[61] In the Jesuit liberation theologians Jon Sobrino and Ignacio Ellacuría, as well as, I am suggesting, for Metz, it is not the transformation elicited in the Fourth Week's "Contemplation to Attain Love" that provides the driving force but a different, although related, transformation. It is found in the Third Week, in which one meditates on Jesus' passion, or in the meditations on sin during the First Week of the *Exercises*, in which one puts oneself in the presence of the full drama of divine redemption: the human world, wracked by sin, the divine compassionate response, and finally the cooperation of a paradigmatic disciple (Mary).[62] This sets the stage for a person to reflect on his or her *own* part in this drama, concluding with a conversation ("colloquy") with the various actors in this drama, from the foot of the cross. I believe that Ellacuría's paraphrase of that colloquy describes the locus for understanding the mystical-political structure of Metz's theology as well:

> I only want—I am trying not to be too demanding—two things. I want you to set your eyes and your hearts on these peoples who are suffering so much—some from poverty and hunger, others from oppression and repression. Then (since I am a Jesuit), standing before this people thus crucified you must repeat St. Ignatius's examination from the first week of the Exercises. Ask yourselves: what have I done to crucify them? What do I do to uncrucify them? What must I do for this people to rise again?[63]

The power of this spirituality is witnessed by the liberation movements and theologies which risk this sort of transformation.

Ultimately, Rahner was too good a Jesuit not to hear the voice of the First and Third Weeks in the work of his student. Metz, for his part, never denied the importance of the hope and confidence engendered by the resurrection and the sense of God's presence in all things. In the light of the interpretation offered here, Metz's continuing insistence that his is a "corrective" to Rahner's theology manifests his recognition of the more optimistic stance toward God and the world, which emphasizes the "already" of God's Kingdom more than it does the "not yet." But he wants to make sure that this hope arises out of the dangerous memory of suffering, that it embraces not just the disruptive sense of my own impending end but the reality of the crucified peoples who fill our world today. He does not want believers and theologians to stop speaking about the resurrection of Christ and the future glory that this event reveals; but he does want us not to speak about this in such a way that "the cry of the crucified becomes unhearable."[64] Here he continues to praise his teacher, because he senses that Rahner's optimism was not cheaply won or superficial; using the language of the *Exercises* we might say that Metz understands that Rahner came to the Fourth Week (as Ignatius insists one must) only by laboring, perhaps better, laboring along with God, through the First, Second, and Third Weeks, both in one's interior life and in one's life in the world:

> Rahner never interpreted Christianity as some sort of bourgeois domestic religion, which has been purged of every hope that is threatened by death and of every vulnerable and stubborn longing. I never

felt his understanding of faith to be a kind of security ideology. There was always a homelessness; through everything there remained a longing which I never felt to be sentimental, nor pollyannishly optimistic. This was not a longing that would storm the heavens, but much more a hushed sigh of the creature, like a wordless cry for light before the hidden face of God.[65]

Finally, then, both had a deeply rooted intuition that their distinctive mystical-political positions, just like the Weeks in the *Spiritual Exercises,* are part of a greater whole, that both are initiations into the breadth and length and height and depth of the love of Christ, which surpasses all knowledge (including that of theological systems!). Metz would agree wholeheartedly with Rahner that "even in your theology you are pilgrims who are seeking in an ever renewed exodus the eternal homeland of truth."[66] In and because of this, each always listened to and learned from the other with the utmost seriousness, even love, that obtains between kindred spirits, even while each also continued to "drink from his own well," nourishing his theology from the specific spirituality which had come to incarnate discipleship for each— as men and as theologians.

CRITICAL APPRECIATION AND QUESTIONS

Under the assumption that there is no omnicompetent, "perennial" theology, and that (at least for Rahner and Metz) a theology is ultimately judged according to how well it brings to the surface the mystical-political dimension of Christian faith, how well does Metz's theology do? In terms of my earlier discussion of the relationship between spirituality and theology, it is clear by now that Metz's theology is indeed nurtured by a particular spirituality, and that it gains much of its force, its interest, and often arresting grandeur to the degree that it evokes and nourishes that spirituality. Does his theology, in turn, bring out the implications of that spirituality, make explicit the implicit ontological and ethical commitments entailed by its advocacy? I have tried to show some of the ways that it does, but in concluding our discussion of Metz it may be worthwhile to consider some of the common criticisms of Metz's theology in the light of its relationship to spirituality.

There have been a surfeit of these criticisms. Some of them can be traced back to the occasional, intuitive, often frustratingly aphoristic style of much of his writing. One purpose of this study has been to draw together the full range of Metz's writing, centered on a construction of the understanding of the subject, and thereby to fill in some of the gaps in Metz's work. Whether or not this construction reads too much into Metz's thought, or violates his own dictum that "the system" is not the place to work out theological truth today, has to be left to the reader to decide. One virtue of this approach, however, is that in placing Metz's writings within the constellation of elements that make up his thought, and in trying to develop from out of that the underlying structure, one can answer or at least qualify some of the principal criticisms that have been made of his theology.

R. R. Reno has articulated a common criticism that Metz's thought is so focused on the crucifixion, negativity, and suffering, that it never reaches the resurrection and fails to articulate Christian hope for redemption.[67] This is primarily a criticism of Metz's Christology, or perhaps better, of the underdeveloped nature of his Christology. It points out the more general character of Metz's work: he does not write extensively on the themes of systematic theology, including Christology. In his defense one could respond that Metz's most important work, particularly *Faith in History and Society,* is not intended to be a systematic theology but a practical *fundamental* theology; but, insofar as Metz himself has questioned the adequacy of any hard-and-fast divisions between fundamental and systematic theology, this response does not suffice. In my reading of Metz I have chosen to allow a relative distinction between fundamental and systematic theology and to interpret his work as a fundamental theology which, like that of his teacher, takes as its primary conceptual and systematic focal point a revised theological anthropology, even though it is interwoven with many other themes from systematic theology.[68]

In this light, then, the criticisms of Metz's incompleteness in certain areas of systematic theology could be completely answered only by taking up the basis that I have attempted to sketch here and working out in more detail the interpretation of other doctrines of Christian faith, including a fuller Christology. Just as there is an implicit Christology in Rahner's *Hörer des Wortes* which became explicit and was fleshed out in his later work, could not the same be true of Metz's work? There are some places in that work where he does hint at what his Christology would be.[69] Given Metz's definition of Christian faith as solidaristic *hope*, and his assertion that the God of Jesus Christ is the God before whom even, and especially, the dead are called to the dignity of human subjecthood, it is difficult to see how the Christology that would be derived from such a theology would be one that ignored the resurrection or the divine power that is manifested in Jesus Christ, whose memory we reenact and enflesh narratively, liturgically, and in radical praxis of imitation. He does say that it is the *memoria passionis, mortis et resurrectionis* that defines the "dangerous memory" of Christians.[70] The issue is how to formulate the latter within the constellation which always includes the other two.

As we have seen in the comparison with Rahner, Metz will allow talk about the resurrection, but only in a way that does not make "the cry of the crucified unhearable." This does not satisfy his critics. But here I think it is important to remember the context, both in terms of the spirituality of which Metz speaks and in terms of the society in and to which he speaks. Metz's theology is addressed to a society that tends either to deny the crucified peoples who live on its margins or (perhaps like Benjamin's angel) to look on with horror, despair, or cynicism (but ultimately, without taking action), at the wreckage piling up at its feet. It is, in short, a society that seems increasingly unable to recognize and to respond hopefully to the danger that is all around. Just as in Mark's apocalyptic Christology (for, after all, Mark's Gospel too was originally without resurrection narratives), Metz wants to convince us that we live in extraordinary times. The times are full of danger but also, if we *recognize that* and turn to the God of Jesus Christ, full of hope. But this hope is available to us *only* if we hope with the victims of Auschwitz, Wounded Knee, My Lai, El Salvador, and all the other places where the crucified peoples are.

Here it is illuminating to turn again to Christian mysticism, drawing a parallel with the imagery of the dark night in that tradition— something that Metz does not do, although the liberation theologian Gustavo Gutiérrez does.[71] According to this imagery, the person does not finally arrive at a pure, unmediated bliss of union with God that sidesteps the finitude, fragility, and sinfulness of our present existence. Rather, the union with God in this life, which adumbrates that final consummation of all things that has been won in the cross and resurrection, occurs within a dark cloud of unknowing. The weakness, pain, and longing of this life are not left behind but become the very medium in which God is found. It is entirely appropriate to tarry in this "dark cloud," and in certain circumstances it may be the one thing necessary. If we "transpose" this into the political key, the hope of resurrection, which has as its ultimate object and horizon the full consummation of the kingdom of God, is experienced in this life, with all of its fragility, its evil, its "endangeredness" (to use one of Metz's favorite terms), in the "dark night" of laboring with the victims, of solidarity with those who suffer. This insight is particularly important for understanding the Third World, where, as Sobrino points out, *the* most significant and amazing Christological datum is the emergence of the liberating and empowering force of the *crucified* Christ.[72] It is equally necessary, as I noted above, in the First World. This approach to Metz's articulation of Christian hope in—and *only* in—the memory of suffering, also suggests that the Christological implications of Metz's approach are being worked out by liberation theologians. This is a possibility that Metz himself has allowed. Only time will tell if it is true.

It does seem fair to say, however, that if political theology is to have a future, then it must undertake the patient and difficult labor of elaborating the implications of political theology for the various themes of systematic theology, the work that took up so much of Rahner's life. This is especially crucial with regard to what is in my view a more serious problem: Metz nowhere elaborates the Trinitarian implications of his theology or of a mysticism of *Leiden an Gott*. The lack of any reflection on the Trinity is one of the most conspicuous lacunae in Metz's theology. This is particularly striking given his evaluation and appreciation of Rahner's Trinitarian theology as rooted in salvation narrative and history.[73] There is certainly no lack of Trinitarian speculation in the traditions of apocalyptic spirituality, although they are usually dismissed with a few disparaging remarks about Joachim of Fiore. It is Moltmann who has done the most to recover that tradition.[74] But Metz has voiced hesitancy about Moltmann's Trinitarian theology as being too speculative, as "onto-logizing" suffering too much.[75] It is also true that in his thinking on God he has been greatly concerned to refute the thesis, first proposed by Erik Peterson, but also often a tacit or explicit premise of much postmodern religious thought, that monotheism, simply taken, supplies an ideological justification for authoritarian political cultures.[76] This is all well and good, but Metz's theology eventually must undertake the task of retrieving, elaborating, and refining Trinitarian theology, both for the sake of its own Christian identity and for the sake of bringing it into dialogue with other Christian spiritualities and theologies.

Perhaps these observations might also help us to begin to respond to the other common criticism of Metz's theology: that he offers few practical guidelines as to what might count as a concrete, positive Christian response to the dilemmas of the contemporary world. His theology, for all its claims that we must attend to the specific social and political contexts within and for which Christian theologians labor, is curiously devoid of social analysis,[77] and never makes the crucial step to developing specific, theologically warranted practical steps that follow from the fundamental practical theology.[78] There is a good deal of truth to this complaint. Religion for Metz is "interruption" as a necessary prelude to action. He is less interested in developing concrete suggestions for action than he is in creating the sense of urgency, of danger, that will move Christians to act. He has been satisfied with the social and political theory of the early Frankfurt School, which was itself notorious for its highly abstract theoretical style and lack of methods for empirical verification of its results. He shares that approach's continuing distrust of "instrumental reason" and of the totalizing tendencies of scientific rationality when applied to the human. On this count it is true that much of modern social and political theory has no place for the person as the uniquely self-interpretive, self-creative subject of his or her history.[79] Even a thinker as sympathetic to religion and Christianity as Jürgen Habermas has little room in his impressive and sweeping social theory for the disclosive and transformative power of narrative and memory.[80]

Nevertheless, new understandings of human rationality, even and especially within the sciences, are coming on the scene which deserve attention from the perspective of Metz's political theology.[81] Just as Metz's fundamental theology could profit from an *Auseindandersetzung* with other theologians' attempts systematically to retrieve the symbols of Christian faith, so too must political theology seek out conversation partners in those social sciences which are open to its understanding of the human subject. This will better enable political theology to offer rigorous analyses of the social and political structures which make the work of defending and cultivating the processes and contents of memory and narrative so difficult but also so important in the increasingly computerized, highly industrialized late capitalist societies of Western Europe and North America.[82]

Political theology cannot dispense from this sort of dialogue, for reasons that come from Metz's own understanding of the dual structure of solidarity. Universal solidarity with the victims of the past who stand on the margins of our histories must be complemented with preferential solidarity with today's victims. Universal solidarity calls into question the circle of persons with whom we feel solidarity now and broadens it. On the other hand, we concretely make our own the horizon of hope of the past's victims insofar as we live and act out of that hope today, that is, in preferential solidarity with the present's victims. Universal solidarity, and the disturbing, destabilizing guilt that is woven into our own histories, can overwhelm and paralyze us, can lead to apathy or cynicism, if it is not complemented by criteria for establishing and working out preferential solidarity in the present. The circle of universal solidarity, which brings with it the recognition of the scope of our guilt, *can* be taken up hopefully for Metz, just as for Luther the Christian can live joyfully in the recognition that he or she is *simul justus et peccator*. But, just as for Luther, this recognition is only possible for the Christian if she or he is living within the circle of faith working through love, so too for Metz is universal solidarity a positive force, within which persons are able to live identities endangered by guilt for the death of the other, to the degree that one is living in preferential solidarity now. Unless, then, political theology can move from fundamental theology to theological ethics, it will not achieve its aim of evoking and articulating liberative praxis. On the other hand, theological ethics can profitably reflect on the ways that Metz's existential of preferential *and* universal solidarity articulates the forceful, interruptive power of the prophetic and apocalyptic traditions within Christianity.

Does Metz's theology of the subject succeed as a fundamental theological anthropology? On inner-theological grounds it would have to serve as a basis for offering an understanding of the contents of Christian faith that meets the needs of the Church in a particular social and historical setting. I believe that the theological anthropology outlined in this work does offer such a basis, particularly if one takes seriously the exigencies of doing theology "after Auschwitz." Most fundamentally, as I observed in chapter 5, a fundamental theological anthropology tries to show how our day-to-day struggles to find and make meaning in a world that often appears meaningless are grounded in a deeper ontological relationship to God. Metz works out a view according to which the human person as subject is constituted and sustained by memory of God's promises and that apocalyptic future that these promises disclose: a future in which all are called to be subjects in God's promise. He expresses this relationship negatively by asserting that the "death of God" is soon followed by the "death of the subject." Besides articulating this fundamental relationship between God and the human person (as Rahner did in *Hörer des Wortes*) Metz's fundamental theological anthropology has enabled him to find and offer new and challenging interpretations of Christian doctrines and practices. He has been able to show the disclosive and transformative possibilities of apocalyptic texts and traditions that too often and too hastily have been dismissed as curious anachronisms, left over from an age of ignorance and superstition.

Has Metz's theological anthropology succeeded in the apologetic task (*ad extra*) of defending the categories of (dangerous) memory and narrative as authentically cognitive categories in a world dominated by technical rationality and positivism? Here Metz's style often works against him. His tendency to offer extremely condensed, often one-sided, characterizations of the positions he opposes produces confrontation more than it does genuine conversation or productive argument.[83] His stance toward postmodern thinkers is a case in point. Metz reads these thinkers (primarily citing Michel Foucault, Jean-François Lyotard, and Odo Marquard) as executing the final step in the progression from the death of God to the death of the subject, as it was laid out by Friedrich Nietzsche a century ago.[84] It is certainly true that these thinkers, and other postmodernists as well, have made the critique and deconstruction of modernity's "subject" into a cornerstone of their project. It is also true that their style is often even more aphoristic and antisystematic than Metz's, so that they can be read as almost completely nihilistic.

On the other hand, it is helpful to borrow a methodological premise from Michael Buckley's work on atheism. He points out there that atheism in its denial of God is often parasitic on the theism that it attacks, that it depends on that theism for much of the positive, but often only implicit and assumed, content and force of its critique.[85] In evaluating atheism one must be careful to ask what "God" is being attacked and denied; indeed, the theologian can learn much from the atheist about how the theologian's method, and the "God" that such a method articulates and defends, not only creates the vocabulary, logic, and rhetoric that is turned against it but perhaps richly deserves such a critique. The same is true, I would suggest, of postmodern critiques of the subject. Those theologians who would still make use of some variety of transcendental analysis, and would still appeal to some understanding of the subject upon which such analysis depends, would do well to reflect on the extent to which the "subject" which they articulate, defend, and depend upon in such argumentative strategies creates the vocabulary, logic, and rhetoric that is used, often with justice, to critique it. On the other hand, those postmodern critics of the subject who would dispense with it altogether need to ask to what degree the quite worthy passion which often animates such critiques is vitiated by their results.[86]

Metz has given a great deal of thought to the concept of the subject that he would defend, the understanding of which then serves as the cornerstone for his fundamental theology. In this he has shared some of the central concerns of the very postmodern thinkers he has criticized. With Foucault he has shared the concern that modernity's subject might be a cipher for the socially enthroned master of relations of exchange of knowledge and power. With Lyotard he has shared the suspicion of the "metanarratives" that cover over the dark underside of history and legitimate our continuing disavowals of responsibility to its victims. Metz is as ferocious a critic as any of a concept of the subject which is atemporal, already constituted apart from or before social and historical relations, immune from the disruptive catastrophes that interrupt history. On the other hand, he recognizes the unparalleled critical and liberative power that the concept of the subject lends to Christian faith, as an instrument for articulating the biblical tradition of the unsated hunger and thirst for justice.

In short, Metz's theological anthropology offers to theologians a way of continuing to reap the fruits that have been gained by past generations of theologians and their "turn to the subject," while also being responsible to the justified critiques made of this turn. Metz's theology, with its attention to the death of the other as the negative horizon for our attempts to find and create meaning, yields an understanding of the subject that is related from its very roots to the other. His emphasis on the narrative depth-structure of the subject opens his thought to this century's sensitivity to the linguistic dimension of human subjectivity. His emphasis on *dangerous* memory and narrative enables him to affirm the constitutive role of history and tradition without surrender-

ing the critical and liberative stance of humans toward history and tradition. His focus on the subject does not cover over the dangers of ego-
ism, both individual and institutional, and the guilt that comes from
our involvement in history and society. Rather, in his insistence on the
capacity for guilt that is a part of the dignity of the subject's freedom,
and his formulation of the apocalyptic character of being a subject,
Metz offers an analysis of the subject, and of its authentic existentiell stance of poverty of spirit—of a *Leiden an Gott*—in which even in
such guilty failure we are able to continue to pray, hope, and act as
women and men who are called by God to be the subjects of our lives
and histories.

CONCLUSION: THE MYSTICAL-POLITICAL DIMENSION OF CHRISTIAN FAITH

In his book on the origins of atheism, Michael Buckley has documented the momentous development in which the theologians who
came forward in the sixteenth and seventeenth centuries to give a defense of the hope that is in Christians, of their faith in a God of nature
and history, cosmos and person, prescinded from Christians' *experience* of God, mediated by an encounter (individual and corporate)
with Jesus Christ, and articulated, communicated, and argued over
conceptually in Christology and pneumatology:

> [N]either Christology nor a mystagogy of experience was reformu-
> lated by the theologians to present *vestigia et notae* of the reality
> of god—as if Christianity did not possess in the person of Jesus a
> unique witness to confront the denial of god or as if one already had
> to believe in order to have this confrontation take place. In the rising
> attacks of atheism, Christology continued to discuss the nature of
> Christ, the unity of his freedom and his mission, the precisely consti-
> tuting factor of his person, the consciousness of the human Jesus, the
> nature of his salvific act; but the fundamental reality of Jesus as the
> embodied presence and witness of the reality of god within human
> history was never brought into the critical struggle of Christianity in
> the next three hundred years. . . . In the absence of a rich and com-
> prehensive Christology and a Pneumatology of religious experience
> Christianity entered into the defense of the Christian god without
> appeal to anything Christian.[87]

Whatever its reasons, this strategy proved disastrous over the next two centuries, as Buckley shows. If we take up Gutiérrez's distinction between the challenge posed to theology by the nonbeliever and the challenge posed by the "nonpersons" of modernity, then, mutatis mutandis, Buckley's story could be recapitulated for the latter challenge. On questions of power, wealth, and justice, on the nature and scope of the human city in relation to the city of God, the ground of argument was in large measure surrendered to the new "political philosophy" and "social sciences." This contributed to the increasing privatization of spirituality on the one hand and the secularization of Christian political theory and practice on the other. In the face of the challenge presented by practical atheism or, even worse, by a practical idolatry of the gods of efficiency, production, possession, and consumption, the Church responded without engaging explicitly the very substance of its experience and understanding of the presence of God in Christ and in the Spirit.[88]

The story has been documented from a different perspective by John Milbank.[89] His cautionary "metanarrative" of theology in modernity captures in a sweeping (if not always fair) overview the ways that modern theologians, including political and liberation theologians like Metz and Gutiérrez, took over concepts and argumentative strategies from secular reason, thereby running the danger of becoming fatally entangled in the world and the implicit historical metanarrative of history projected by those concepts and arguments. His cautions are well taken. Perhaps what he misses, however, are the ways that many of these theologians modified these "borrowings" in crucial respects in the process of using them to express, nurture, and communicate a particular Christian religious experience: spiritualities like Metz's painful but inspiriting mysticism of *Leiden an Gott,* or a spirituality centered on the radically transformative encounter with Jesus in and with the poor. Certainly we saw that even when it came to the language of his favorite "secular" theory, the critical theory of the early Frankfurt School, Metz was always using it to try and limn, as a suggestive possibility, a way of tarrying with the suffering and injustice of our histories, and finding there, even there, especially there, the possibility of redemption.

Perhaps the lesson to be learned in these histories is that liberation and political theologies, indeed, all theologies, will not and cannot be successful if they are not first and foremost invitations into an art of living that transcends them, founded in an experience out of which both the necessity and the inadequacy of speech emerges. In this they are not so unlike the theologies crafted by the early Fathers of the Church, who attempted to articulate the radical experience of God's offer of salvation in Jesus within and to the conceptualities of the Greek world.[90] The effort to craft such invitations is not without risk; one may complain with the prophets that one lacks the power of thought or speech for the task. When all is said and done, one may perhaps even be left, like Thomas Aquinas, in stunned silence at the inadequacy of one's words to the experience.[91] This does not so much invalidate the attempt, as it shows its animating source and its limits. We today are in the debt of those who have taken this risk before us, and we owe those who come after us nothing less.

If they are to continue in our "postmodern," "postchristian" world, theology and spirituality need one another, and the Church needs both together. Friedrich von Hügel recognized this at the beginning of our century when he argued that the vitality and force of the Church depended upon the existence and cooperation of three elements: the historical-institutional, the intellectual, and the mystical-volitional.[92] The first presents and safeguards the facticity, the givenness of religion; the second elaborates and correlates this given with other givens of our experience, for the sake of understanding and communication, while the third represents an individual's appropriation of what is given, in the depth and subjectivity of his or her own heart, from whence alone it transforms his or her whole way of acting and understanding. The intellectual element needs the mystical; otherwise it becomes, to recall again Hadot's devastating indictment, "the construction of a technical jargon reserved for specialists."[93] Furthermore, as Buckley so forcefully reminds us, if theology ignores the evidentiary power of the experience of the mystery of discipleship as this experience has irrupted into human history in classic figures and movements, it risks constructing the very god which stands at the origins of the history of modern atheism.

Finally, if theology becomes obsessed only with the coherence of its concepts, or their collective correspondence to a reality "out there," then it risks losing its eyes for the new movements of the Spirit in our midst. Metz himself reminds us forcefully of this, in reporting his most basic conviction during his recent visit to Latin America:

> One of the phrases that I used over and over during this visit, in an almost instinctive way, was "the eyes of theology." That is to say,

time and again I was struck by the suspicion, perhaps naive but persistent, that particularly here in Europe what we need in theology is not so much ideas as it is the eyes which would first learn and then teach us to see what is of absolute theological significance. At times what I was seeing brought my familiar ways of thinking to a standstill. It checked the flood of ideas and the mostly hasty seeming theological interpretations. . . . Perhaps in this I came back "poorer" than I could have foreseen. Yet I think that this "poverty" is one of the presuppositions and conditions for grasping at all what "Latin America" means."[94]

Such poverty is essential for understanding what any of the challenges that face us in theology today mean. What we need are the eyes to see the power of the risen Christ shining through the "failure" of an Oscar Romero, or the gifts of the Spirit to the whole Church offered in the Maya people of Chiapas, in the new churches of Africa and Asia, as well as in the voices of women everywhere. New spiritualities have always begun in people who saw farther and better, and theology lives off of what they have seen. This will become even more important for us to understand and recognize as we make our way from a predominantly monocultural Eurocentric Church to a polycentric global Church.

On the other hand, the mystical element needs the intellectual; spirituality needs theology. Otherwise, a spiritual experience becomes a moment of purely private and ineffable religiosity; it does not sink roots into the greater tradition (von Hügel's historical-institutional element), with its enriching variety of spiritualities and its variegated history of theological labor that has elaborated the broader implications of following Jesus under the classic topoi of Christology, ecclesiology, eschatology, and so on. These topoi may appear differently when illuminating, and illuminated by, new spiritualities, but they *must* appear, if those spiritualities are to be gifts to the whole Church and are to have lasting vitality and effect in the world. It is when a new gift of the Spirit is elaborated, however tentatively and inadequately, by the work of theology, and is embraced and proclaimed courageously within the broader institutional Church, that the Church most fulfills its evangelical mission. In the Roman Catholic Church this can be seen in an exemplary fashion in the history of religious life. Today it can be seen vividly in the history of the Latin American Catholic Church, in which the powerful—and, it must be insisted, *mystical*—experience of encountering Christ in and with the poor was *both* elaborated theologically and *at the same time* became a part of the historical-institutional reality of the Church, at Medellín, at Puebla, and then at the world synod of bishops in 1971. The theological labor here is one of making connections between the new spirituality and the riches of scripture and tradition; the institutional labor is to take the risk—a very real one, as the history of martyrs in Latin America shows—of discerning and embracing this new spirituality. Both are necessary, and they reinforce one another. If there is to be a new evangelization in Latin America, or in North America for that matter, it will only progress if theologians and church leaders have both the eyes to discern these gifts and the patience and courage to appropriate them.[95]

This important work needs doing in the First World too, and is being taken up by, for instance, feminist and Hispanic theologians in North America and by at least some segments of the institutional Church. Here we face the further danger that the creativity being exhibited in the proliferation of new spiritualities is being co-opted by a consumer culture and packaged for placement in yet another aisle in the great supermaket of choice—more palliatives and opiates for easing our growing and desperate sense that the optimistic culture of enlightenment is becoming a culture of death. Thus, here just as tenaciously as in the Third World, we must attend to Metz's insistence that every spirituality, every articulation of the mystical dimension of Christianity, be developed in terms of its *political* implications.[96] This too is a theological labor without which spirituality will become little more than a matter of individual taste, simply another lifestyle choice.

Ultimately, the whole Church needs the labor of elaborating the mystical-political dimension of Christian faith as it enters into its third millennium, facing a transformation as radical as that of its first two centuries. As the Church changes from a monocultural Eurocentric Church to a polycentric world Church, Christians and Christian theologians are less and less united by a common cultural matrix, much less by a universal foundational philosophical method. We *are* united by a common conviction that we are striving to embrace the mystery of discipleship in our different societies and cultures with their different (albeit interconnected) histories. All of these particular cultural traditions, with their distinctive memories and narratives, are wombs in which new gifts of the Spirit are in gestation. We should expect, we *need* new spiritualities. While there are many gifts, however, there is but one Spirit, and one God who activates them all in everyone (1 Cor 12:4–6). How will we (Europeans, North Americans, Latin Americans, Africans, Asians) learn to speak in solidarity with and to one another, as believers and theologians who belong to *one*, holy, catholic, and apostolic church, unless we learn both to root ourselves in our own particular contexts of following Christ but also learn to articulate those theological, ontological, and ethical-political commitments and claims that flow from that following, so that we can talk to one another and act with one another across these contexts? This requires an openness to the broadest spectrum of spiritualities within Christianity, as that is being made available to us by historical work. It also involves the the eyes and the courage to perceive new possibilities of incarnating the *imitatio Christi,* as these become available in the new cultures and traditions in the global Church. To "test everything and hold fast to what is good" (1 Thes 5:21) requires the sociological, anthropological, hermeneutical tools which render a "thick description" of social and cultural traditions and practices. It also needs the sort of ontological investigation found in the transcendental reflection, as carried on by Rahner and Metz, which opens up the particular to a solidarity of memory, hope, and yes, argument, but leads to action that crosses the boundaries of particular traditions and brings to light the mystical riches of a polycentric world Church in a way that the whole Church can be enriched by them. In a global Church which is challenged both by the potentially enriching diversity of newly retrieved or created spiritual and intellectual resources, and by the dangers which are so prominent in our troubled age, Metz's elaboration of the mystical-political Christian response may not be the only one possible, but it is certainly paradigmatic of the kind of labor that all theologians must undertake.

ABBREVIATIONS

CA   *Christliche Anthropozentrik*, J. B. Metz

EC   *The Emergent Church*, J. B. Metz

FHS   *Faith in History and Society* (translation of *GGG*),
            J. B. Metz

GGG   *Glaube in Geschichte und Gesellschaft*, J. B. Metz

HdW1   *Hörer des Wortes*, 1st ed., Karl Rahner

HdW2   *Hörer des Wortes*, 2d ed., Karl Rahner, edited for
            republication by J. B. Metz

HG   *Handbuch theologischer Grundbegriffe*, 2 vols., edited by
            Heinrich Fries

HPM   "Heidegger und das Problem des Metaphysik," J. B. Metz

LK   *Lexicon für Theologie und Kirche*, 10 vols., edited by Karl
            Rahner

PG   *A Passion for God: The Mystical-Political Dimension of
            Christianity*, J. B. Metz

TW   *Theology of the World* (translation of *ZTW*), J. B. Metz

TI   *Theological Investigations*, 23 vols., Karl Rahner

ZTW   *Zur Theologie der Welt*, J. B. Metz

NOTES

INTRODUCTION

1. "The Defense of the Subject: The Problem of Anthropology in Johann Baptist Metz" (Ph.D. diss., University of Chicago, 1993).

2. See "On the Way to a Post-Idealist Theology," in J. B. Metz, *A Passion for God: The Mystical-Political Dimension of Christianity,* trans. and ed. J. Matthew Ashley (Mahwah, New Jersey: Paulist Press, 1998), henceforth abbreviated *PG.*

3. See "Do We Miss Karl Rahner?" and "Karl Rahner's Struggle for the Theological Dignity of Humanity" in Metz, *PG.*

4. This is the position maintained by Andrew Tallon in his account of Rahner's development: "Personal Becoming: Karl Rahner's Christian Anthropology," in *The Thomist* 43 (Jan. 1979): 1–177.

5. For examples of this approach, see Mary Maher, "Historicity and Christian Theology: Johannes Baptist Metz's Critique of Karl Rahner's Theology" (Ph.D. diss., Catholic University of America, 1988), and Titus Guenther, *Rahner and Metz: Transcendental Theology as Political Theology* (Lanham, Md.: University Press of America, 1994). This also seemed to be Rahner's own assessment, as expressed in his Introduction to James Bacik, *Apologetics and the Eclipse of Mystery: Mystagogy According to Karl Rahner* (Notre Dame: University of Notre Dame Press, 1980), ix–x.

6. For just one example, see "Theology as Biography," in *Faith in History and Society,* 219–28, which is a version of a tribute to Rahner written on the occasion of his seventieth birthday, "Karl Rahner—ein theologisches Leben: Theologie als mystische Biographie eines Christenmenschen heute." The subtitle of that original address conveys the heart of Metz's praise: "Theology as a mystical biography of a Christian today."

7. Ibid., 227. The most familiar introduction of this claim is in the first volume from the international journal *Concilium* devoted to liberation theology, Claude Geffré and Gustavo Gutiérrez, eds., *The Mystical and Political Dimension of Christian Faith, Concilium* 96 (New York: Herder and Herder, 1974).

8. In his Introduction to Bacik's book (see n. 5 above), x; also, "The Spirituality of the Church in the Future," *Theological Investigations* 20, trans. Edward Quinn (New York: Crossroad, 1986), 145f.

9. *Faith in History and Society*, trans. David Smith (New York: Crossroad, 1981). This book is a translation of *Glaube in Geschichte und Gesellschaft* (Mainz: Matthias-Grünewald, 1977). Since the translation is quite uneven, I will frequently give my own translations. The German original will be abbreviated *GGG* and the English translation *FHS*.

1. THE RELATIONSHIP BETWEEN SPIRITUALITY AND THEOLOGY

1. Phyllis Tickle, *Re-discovering the Sacred: Spirituality in America* (New York: Crossroad, 1995), 17f.

2. For an overview of the topics currently being published, see ibid., 35–52. Specifically on the "spirituality" of physics: Fritjof Capra and David Steindl-Rast, *Belonging to the Universe: Explorations on the Frontier of Science and Spirituality* (San Francisco: HarperSanFrancisco, 1995); Diarmuid O'Murchu, *Quantum Theology: Spiritual Implications of the New Physics* (New York: Crossroad, 1997).

3. Philip Rieff, *The Triumph of the Therapeutic: Uses of Faith after Freud* (Chicago: University of Chicago Press: 1987).

4. Robert Wuthnow, *God and Mammon in America* (New York: The Free Press, 1994), 5f.

5. For overview of this trend, see Sandra Schneiders, "Spirituality in the Academy," *Theological Studies* 50 (1988): 676–97 and Bernard McGinn, "The Letter and the Spirit: Spirituality as an Academic Discipline," *Christian Spirituality Bulletin* 1/2 (Fall 1993): 1–4. On historiographical problems involved in drawing on spirituality as a resource for current reflection, see Philip Sheldrake, *Spirituality and History: Questions of Interpretation and Method* (New York: Crossroad, 1992). An invaluable resource for the study of mysticism is the ongoing multivolume history of mysticism, Bernard McGinn's *The Presence of God*, of which the first two volumes are now available: *The Foundations of Mysticism: Origins to the Fifth Century* (New York: Crossroad, 1991) and *The Growth of Mysticism: Gregory the Great through the 12th Century* (Crossroad, 1994). The appendix to the former volume contains a wide-ranging overview of theoretical approaches to mysticism (265–343).

6. *Dictionnaire de spiritualité* (Paris: Beauchesne, 1932–); *The Classics of Western Spirituality* (Mahwah, N.J.: Paulist Press, 1978–).

7. I shall have more to say about Rahner later, but for a start, see Harvey Egan, "The Devout Christian of the Future Will . . . Be a 'Mystic': Mysticism and Karl Rahner's Theology," in *Theology and Discovery:*

Essays in Honor of Karl Rahner, S.J., ed. William J. Kelly (Milwaukee: Marquette University Press, 1980, 139–58. On von Balthasar, see the relevant essays (along with the eulogies in the appendices) in David L. Schindler, ed., *Hans Urs von Balthasar: His Life and Work* (San Francisco: Ignatius Press, 1991), especially: Werner Löser, "The Ignatian *Exercises* in the Work of Hans Urs von Balthasar," and Antonio Sicari, "Hans Urs von Balthasar: Theology and Holiness." For a specific study of the way that von Balthasar correlated mystical resources with his Christology, see Mark McIntosh, *Christology from Within: Spirituality and the Incarnation in Hans Urs von Balthasar,* Studies in Spirituality and Theology, no. 3 (Notre Dame: University of Notre Dame Press, 1996).

8. "Conversation with David Tracy," an interview conducted by Todd Breyfogle and Thomas Levergood, in *Cross Currents* 44/3 (Fall, 1994), 293. For Tracy's own turn to the mystics, see his *Dialogue with the Other: The Inter-religious Dialogue* (Grand Rapids: Eerdmans, 1990).

9. In this category I would include all those theologies which make liberative praxis the central concern of their theologies: hence, early on, Latin American liberation theology, political theology in Europe and North America, as well as feminist and black theologies; but also, more recently, Hispanic, womanist, and Latina theologies in the United States, and the emerging force of liberation theologies on the continents of Africa and Asia. For an impressive survey, see Alfred T. Hennelly, *Liberation Theologies: The Global Pursuit of Justice* (Mystic, Conn.: Twenty-Third Publications, 1995). Hennelly, too, notes the importance of spirituality to these theologies (211–15).

10. Gustavo Gutiérrez and Claude Geffré, eds., *The Mystical and Political Dimension of the Christian Faith.* That this first volume of *Concilium* devoted to Latin American liberation theology focused on the role that Christianity's mystical dimension plays in the struggle for liberation is indicative of liberation theology's early and constitutive concern for spirituality.

11. See, Gustavo Gutiérrez, *A Theology of Liberation: History, Politics and Salvation,* rev. ed., trans. and ed. Sister Caridad Inga and John Eagleson (Maryknoll, N.Y.: Orbis, 1988), xxxii, 74, 116–20. His next book (*The Power of the Poor in History* is a collection of essays) was a work on spirituality: *We Drink from Our Own Wells* (Maryknoll: Orbis, 1984).

12. James Cone, *My Soul Looks Back* (Maryknoll: Orbis, 1992), 61.

13. James Cone, *The Spirituals and the Blues* (Maryknoll: Orbis, 1972).

14. The classic text here has to be Virgilio Elizondo's *The Future is Mestizo: Life Where Cultures Meet* (New York: Crossroad, 1988). It is true that the debate is framed around the issue of the status (or lack of status!) of so-called "popular religiosity" of Hispanic communities and its

relationship to a theological orthodoxy which is allegedly impartial with regard to any form of popular religion, be it Hispanic or Anglo (if there is such a thing). This is, however, a very close analogue to the debate over the relationship between spirituality and theology that is occupying us in this chapter. A clear overview of the former debate, which also suggests its close parallels to the cognate that we are examining here, is found in Orlando O. Espín, "Tradition and Popular Religion: An Understanding of the *Sensus Fidelium*," in Allan Figueroa Deck, ed., *Frontiers of Hispanic Theology in the United States* (Maryknoll: Orbis, 1992), 62–87.

15. For a powerful example of such a reformulation of the doctrine of God, see Elizabeth A. Johnson, *She Who Is: The Mystery of God in Feminist Theological Discourse* (New York: Crossroad, 1992). In this book Johnson forges a new way of talking about God based on underutilized resources from the past, often from Christianity's mystical tradition, particularly the apophatic traditions. This is correlated with women's "lived experience," interpreted through a classic *topos* of spirituality: conversion (see 61–65).

16. For just one example, see Joan Nuth, *Wisdom's Daughter: The Theology of Julian of Norwich* (New York: Crossroad, 1991). For a provocative example of the kinds of resources being uncovered by research into women mystics, see the last two essays in Caroline Walker Bynum's *Jesus as Mother: Studies in the Spirituality of the High Middle Ages* (Berkeley: University of California Press, 1982). See also the essays in Bernard McGinn, ed., *Meister Eckhart and the Beguine Mystics: Hadewijch of Brabant, Mechthild of Magdeburg, and Marguerite Porete* (New York: Continuum, 1994).

17. *Spirituality of the Third World: A Cry for Life,* ed. K. C. Abraham and Bernadette Mbuy-Beya (Maryknoll: Orbis, 1994), 1.

18. From the classic account of this danger in Robert Bellah et al., *Habits of the Heart: Individualism and Commitment in American Life* (San Francisco: Harper & Row, 1985) 221, 235.

19. A good example of this phenomenon can be found in the closely related debate over the relationship between theology and popular or indigenous religion noted above (see n. 14).

20. In a very provocative study, George Schner has mapped out the ambiguities of the appeal to experience and the ways that it often reproduces the very presuppositions of modernity that it is overtly employed to subvert: "The Appeal to Experience," *Theological Studies* 53 (1992): 40–59.

21. I owe this insight to lectures given by David Tracy at the University of Chicago in the fall of 1991. On the distinctive and innovative character of the spirituality initiated by Francis of Assisi and on the

gradual, but radical, impact of that spirituality on theology, see the works of Ewert Cousins on Francis and on those figures, culminating in St. Bonaventure, who worked out the theological implications of his life: "Francis of Assisi: Christian Mysticism at the Crossroads," in Stephen Katz, ed., *Mysticism and Religious Traditions* (New York: Oxford University Press, 1983), 175–88.

22. Thomas S. Kuhn, *The Structure of Scientific Revolutions*, 2d edition, enlarged with a postscript (Chicago: University of Chicago Press, 1970). The term "paradigm," variously defined, by which Kuhn denoted this set of variables, and his "paradigm shift," were soon taken over by other disciplines, theology included. For reflections on this change in theology, see Hans Küng and David Tracy, eds., *Paradigm Change in Theology: A Symposium for the Future* (New York: Crossroad, 1989). Stephen Toulmin's essay therein, "The Historicization of Natural Science: Its Implications for Theology" (233–42), offers a helpful overview and critical analysis.

23. For a recent installment in the so-called "commensurability debate" that was ignited by Kuhn's book, see Hiley, Bohman, and Shusterman, eds., *The Interpretive Turn: Philosophy, Science and Culture* (Ithaca: Cornell University Press, 1991), particularly the articles by Bohman and Shusterman, who argue persuasively against those (like Richard Rorty or Paul Feyerabend) who draw radically skeptical conclusions from the hermeneutical turn in the epistemology of science.

24. The initial volumes of the *Christian Spirituality Bulletin,* published biannually by the Society for the Study of Christian Spirituality, chart this debate, with contributions from advocates of various approaches. Besides the material cited in note 5 above, see the essays by Walter Principe, Bradley Hanson, Sandra Schneiders, and Philip Sheldrake in vol. 2, no. 1 of that bulletin. William Thompson has dealt with these issues in *Fire and Light: The Saints and Theology* (New York: Crossroad, 1987) and in the opening chapters of *Christology and Spirituality* (New York: Crossroad, 1991). See also, Walter Principe, "Toward Defining Spirituality," *Sciences Religieuses* 12/2 (Spring 1983), 127–41; Lawrence S. Cunningham, "*Extra Arcam Noe*: Criteria for Christian Spirituality," *Christian Spirituality Bulletin* 3/1 (Spring 1995), 5–10. The essays in vol. 3, no. 2 of the *Bulletin*, by myself, Philip Endean, Mark McIntosh, and Anne M. Clifford explicitly consider the relationship between spirituality and theology. My reflections in this chapter are based on ideas I developed in that issue, and I am grateful to its editor, Douglas Burton-Christie, for inviting me to write on the topic and for allowing me to use that material in this book.

25. These three approaches are identified and described by McGinn in "The Letter and the Spirit" 4–7.

26. Here I am relying principally on Walter Principe's short but very helpful historical overview in "Toward Defining Spirituality," 130–35. See also Philip Sheldrake's *Spirituality and History,* 34–53, and Bernard McGinn, "The Letter and the Spirit," 3f.

27. On Aquinas's usage of the noun *spiritualitas,* see Principe, "Toward Defining Spirituality," 131. He notes that it appears some seventy times, the majority having the more traditional usage but a significant number reflecting the new, more dualistic one.

28. The concept of secularization has had a stormy career in the history of sociology as a whole and in the sociology of religion in particular. For a brief overview, as well as for the concept of secularization I will draw on here, see Casanova, *Public Religions in the Modern World* (Chicago: University of Chicago Press, 1994), 11–39.

29. On the "discovery" of the individual in the Middle Ages, see Caroline Walker Bynum's critical overview of the literature: "Did the Twelfth Century Discover the Individual?" in *Jesus as Mother,* 82–110. On the growing interest in itineraries and methods of prayer, see Philip Sheldrake, *Spirituality and History,* 40–44.

30. On monastic theology, see Jean Leclerq's classic: *The Love of Learning and the Desire for God: A Study of Monastic Culture,* 2d rev. ed., trans. Catherine Misrahi (New York: Fordham University Press, 1974). For a brief description of "vernacular theology," see Bernard McGinn, "Meister Eckhart and the Beguines in the Context of Vernacular Theology," in *Meister Eckhart and the Beguine Mystics,* 1–14.

31. Casanova, *Public Religions in the Modern World,* 15, 20.

32. Michel de Certeau, *The Mystic Fable,* trans. Michael B. Smith (Chicago: University of Chicago Press, 1992), 2.

33. This, I would suggest, is the gist of Wuthnow's warnings (see n. 4 above).

34. See David Tracy, *The Analogical Imagination: Christian Theology and the Culture of Pluralism* (New York: Crossroad, 1986), esp. chaps. 3–5.

35. It is also possible to see Franciscan spirituality as a more constructive attempt to come to terms with the demands of following Christ in the growing mercantile economies of medieval Europe. Thus, Lester Little argues that new interpretations and practices of poverty emerged in the Middle Ages because of the need to integrate the practice of poverty with a changing set of social and economic practices. See Lester K. Little, *Religious Poverty and the Profit Economy in Medieval Europe* (Ithaca: Cornell University Press, 1978).

36. On the other hand, particularly in modernity, it is quite possible to conceive of a person who has mastered the themes, metaphors and symbols, and rhetorical strategies of a given spiritual tradition but either does

not have the deeper sense of what they "mean" that can be provided only by taking up a stance toward the practices which contextualize them or who distorts them by interpreting them within the particular regime of practices into which "academics" are formed.

37. Pierre Hadot, "Forms of Life and Forms of Discourse in Ancient Philosophy," in *Philosophy as a Way of Life: Spiritual Exercises from Socrates to Foucault*, edited with an introduction by Arnold I. Davidson, translated by Michael Chase (Chicago: University of Chicago Press, 1995), 64.

38. Hadot, "Philosophy as a Way of Life," in ibid., 272. Hadot also notes, drawing on Leclercq, that from its beginnings and through the Middle Ages, monasticism took over the task of ancient philosophy; it was frequently presented as the true *philosophia* in this sense: that is, as proposing a way of life (ibid., 128–30).

39. This is my own way of rendering the distinction that Walter Principe draws between a "*real* or *existential* level" and "*the formulation of a teaching about the lived reality,*" in "Toward Defining Spirituality," 135f.

40. "[W]e ought not to forget that many a philosophical demonstration derives its evidential force not so much from abstract reasoning as from an experience which is at the same time a spiritual exercise" (Hadot, *Philosophy as a Way of Life*, 107).

41. This is an amended version of the definition offered by Roger Haight in *Dynamics of Theology* (Mahwah, N.J.: Paulist, 1990), 1 (repeated in variant forms on 83, 143, 216f.). Haight's book offers a sustained defense and elaboration of this definition, which I have found very helpful.

42. See David Tracy, *The Analogical Imagination*, 3–46.

43. Here following David Tracy: *Blessed Rage for Order: The New Pluralism in Theology* (Minneapolis: Winston-Seabury Press, 1975), esp. 45–46, 79–81.

44. Here I follow Haight's criteria for theology in his *Dynamics of Theology*, 210–12.

45. See Mark McIntosh, *Christology from Within*.

46. The classic here is Caroline Walker Bynum, "Jesus as Mother and Abbot as Mother," in her *Jesus as Mother*, 110–69. On the general issue of the significance of this kind of imagery for Christology, see Elizabeth Johnson, *She Who Is*, 101–2, 150–54. For a theological study related to one key figure, see Joan Nuth, *Wisdom's Daughter*, 65–69, 92–94, and passim.

47. Karl Rahner, *The Dynamic Element in the Church*, trans. W. J. O'Hara (London: Burns & Oates, 1964), 86.

48. From *Une Ecole de Théologie: Le Saulchoir*. Cited in Gustavo Gutiérrez, *We Drink from Our Own Wells*, 147 n. 2.

49. Frederick Ferré, *Hellfire and Lightning Rods: Liberating Science, Technology and Religion* (Maryknoll: Orbis, 1993), 13f.

50. See the materials noted above (n. 20). For Francis's role in the shift from the classical topos of "cosmos" to the modern scientific topos of "nature," see Louis Dupré, *Passage to Modernity* (New Haven: Yale University Press, 1993), 36–41. Note here that what Francis and his first followers introduced was not a new theology or cosmology, but the *practices* which fostered a form of devotion to the concrete individuality and physicality of Jesus. It was up to later disciples (Bonaventure in particular) to articulate the vision that corresponded to this new spirituality and that was (as Dupré notes) of decisive importance for the development of the modern, scientific worldview.

51. See John Caputo's wonderful book, *The Mystical Element in Heidegger's Thought* (New York: Fordham University Press, 1990). Here Caputo is very careful to note that Heidegger's thought is not mystical per se but has a mystical *element,* and further suggests that the abstraction of the mystical terminology from its own spiritual horizon shifts that terminology in significant, indeed, dangerous, ways (xvii–xviii, 245–54).

52. They may shift meaning so much that they break down or even backfire. For instance, Michael Buckley has demonstrated that when theology attempted to mount arguments for the existence of God without reference to religious experience (in my terms, without reference to specific spiritualities), it ironically (to say the least) generated its own antithesis in atheism. See Michael Buckley, *At the Origins of Modern Atheism* (New Haven: Yale University Press, 1987).

53. On the theology's task of placing a given spirituality within the broader compass of the Christian tradition (and at times of expanding that compass), see Lawrence S. Cunningham, *"Extra Arcam Noe:* Criteria for Christian Spirituality," 6–9.

54. See Bernard McGinn, "The God beyond God: Theology and Mysticism in the Thought of Meister Eckhart," *The Journal of Religion* 61 (1981): 1–19.

55. Here the situation is analogous to one found in that other difficult relationship: between theologians and scripture scholars. Here, paraphrasing Sandra Schneiders' formulation, we have come to the paradoxical state that while we study and interpret the texts because they are "the Word of God," that fact makes almost no difference at all for the interpretation of the texts themselves. See, Sandra Schneiders, *The Revelatory Text: Interpreting the New Testament as Sacred Scripture* (San Francisco: HarperCollins, 1991), 2.

56. This much at least is demonstrated in John Milbank's contentious book, *Theology and Social Theory: Beyond Secular Reason* (Cambridge,

Mass.: Blackwell, 1990), whether or not one agrees with the particular construal of the history that Milbank presents.

57. Certainly the language is Rahnerian. But even in its secular usage—in Heidegger and the existential and hermeneutical traditions—it does not escape this influence. Again, see Caputo, *The Mystical Element in Heidegger's Thought*.

58. Gustavo Gutiérrez has stated that Ignatian spirituality has formed his theology in *The Truth Shall Make You Free: Confrontations*, translated by Matthew O'Connell (Maryknoll: Orbis, 1990), 45. James Cone has documented his own spiritual heritage, both more distantly in the spirituals and the blues, and more proximately in coming to terms with his upbringing in the African Methodist Episcopal Church, with its distinctive spirituality. See *My Soul Looks Back*.

59. Chenu, in Gutiérrez, *We Drink from Our Own Wells*, 147, n. 2.

2. DANGEROUS MEMORIES: THE DYNAMISM OF METZ'S THOUGHT

1. J. B. Metz, *Heidegger und das Problem der Metaphysik*. A very dense summary of this work is contained under the same title in *Scholastik* 28 (1953): 1–22.

2. See Herbert Vorgrimler, *Understanding Karl Rahner*, trans. John Bowden (London: SCM Press, 1986), 71. A helpful summary of these students' collaboration with Rahner follows: 71–87.

3. J. B. Metz, *Christliche Anthropozentrik: Über die Denkform des Thomas von Aquin* (Munich: Kösel Verlag, 1962).

4. Karl Rahner, *Geist in Welt: zur Metaphysik der endlichen Erkenntnis bei Thomas von Aquin*, neue bearbeitet von J. B. Metz (Munich: Kösel, 1957). Metz's revisions were minimal in this work. They were more substantial in the second: *Hörer des Wortes: Zur Grundlegung einer Religionsphilosophie*, neue bearbeitet von J. B. Metz (Munich: Kösel, 1963). For a discussion of the changes, see chapter 3.

5. See Vorgrimler, *Understanding Karl Rahner*, 76–78.

6. Bibliographical details from Titus Guenther, *Rahner and Metz*, 17f.

7. The first three of these books by Metz have been translated: *Theology of the World*, trans. William Glen-Doepel (New York: Herder and Herder, 1969); *Faith in History and Society: Toward a Practical Fundamental Theology*, trans. David Smith (New York: Seabury, 1980); *The Emergent Church: The Future of Christianity in a Postbourgeois World*, trans. Peter Mann (New York: Crossroad, 1987). Some of his shorter monographs are crucial for understanding his theology. For instance, *Followers of Christ*, trans. Thomas Linton (New York: Paulist Press, 1978),

is important for understanding his Christology, as well as his understanding of the dual mystical-political character of discipleship (the German original suggests this in its subtitle: *Zeit der Orden: Zur Mystik und Politik der Nachfolge*). Important later works include: J. B. Metz and F. X. Kaufmann, *Zukunftsfähigkeit: Suchbewegungen im Christentum* (Freiburg: Herder, 1987); J. B. Metz and H. E. Bahr, *Augen für die Anderen: Lateinamerika—eine theologische Erfahrung* (Munich: Kindler, 1991); J. B. Metz and T. R. Peters, *Gottespassion: Zur Ordensexistenz Heute* (Frieburg: Herder, 1991), a "sequel" to the earlier work on religious orders.

8. See *Unterbrechungen*, 7–9.

9. See, for instance, *Faith in History and Society*, 213.

10. Martin Jay, *Adorno* (Cambridge: Harvard University Press, 1984), 14f.

11. J. B. Metz, "Productive Noncontemporaneity," in *Observations on "The Spiritual Situation of the Age,"* ed. Jürgen Habermas, trans. with an introduction by Andrew Buchwalter (Cambridge: MIT Press, 1984), 171.

12. Ibid.

13. *FHS*, 16–22.

14. Twice he gave long addresses to meetings of major superiors of German men's religious orders, both of which have appeared as monographs: *Followers of Christ*, and "Passion for God," *PG*, 150–174.

15. In 1979 Metz's call to a post in fundamental theology in Munich was blocked by Joseph Ratzinger, then archbishop of Munich. In response, Karl Rahner wrote an impassioned protest. For the pertinent literature and Metz's own account, see the Epilogue, "On My Own Behalf," in *EC*, 119–23.

16. As in the title of the Habermas Festschrift: *Philosophical Interventions in the Unfinished Project of Enlightenment*, ed. Axel Honneth, Thomas McCarthy, et al., trans. William Rehg (Cambridge: MIT Press, 1992).

17. Recently, as Metz notes, the postmodern "mood" has penetrated more deeply into German philosophy, political thought, and cultural criticism. Yet Metz still stands resolutely with those, like Habermas, who believed that the Enlightenment can and must be redeemed. See, "Theology versus Polymythicism: A Short Apology for Biblical Monotheism," *PG*, 72–91.

18. For an introduction to this topic, see George L. Mosse, *Germans and Jews* (Detroit: Wayne State University Press, 1970), idem, *German Jews beyond Judaism* (Cincinnati: Hebrew Union College Press, 1985), Gershom Scholem, *On Jews and Judaism in Crisis: Selected Essays*, ed. Werner Dannhauser (New York: Schocken, 1976), and the essays in

Jehuda Reinharz and Walter Schatzberg, eds., *The Jewish Response to German Culture: From the Enlightenment to the Second World War* (Hanover, N.H.: University Press of New England, 1985).

19. "Christians and Jews after Auschwitz," in *EC*, 26.

20. Ibid., 26, 28.

21. See "Die Rede von Gott angesichts der Leidensgeschichte der Welt," in *Stimmen der Zeit*, 117/5 (May 1992): 314. Here his interest in Judaism is also evident.

22. Beginning in 1960, Metz participated with Karl Rahner in dialogues sponsored by the *Paulusgesellschaft*, a loose coalition of natural scientists and academics who began meeting to address the confrontation between religion and science but soon turned to other issues. See Vorgrimler, *Understanding Karl Rahner*, 73, 112f.

23. *Gaudium et Spes*, par. 19.

24. Martin Jay has splendidly captured both the creative tensions and ambiguities in these thinkers' attitudes toward theory and praxis in his *The Dialectical Imagination: A History of the Frankfurt School and the Institute of Social Research, 1923–1950* (Boston: Little, Brown, 1973), esp. 63–65, 77–85, 279–80.

25. This is a flaw, for instance, that mars Maher's otherwise fine survey. Metz's early work is often dismissed with reference to surveys covering that period, for example, in Roger Dick Johns, *Man in the World: The Theology of Johannes Baptist Metz* (Scholars Press: Missoula, 1976). The problem here is that the crucial developments of Metz's work only become fully clear in the light of their terminus in his mature thought. As I shall suggest below, Metz must be read *nach vorn*, looking toward his mature thought.

26. For instance, Nedjeljko Ancic, *Die "politische Theologie" von Johann Baptist Metz als Antwort auf die Herausforderung des Marxismus* (Frankfurt: Peter Lang, 1981). In fairness to such works, it should be noted that crucial clues to Metz's thought have become apparent only in the last decade.

27. Specifically, Metz tells us that he originally introduced it to answer those critics who asserted that his thought was fundamentally a-Christian, that it had no substantively Christian content, speaking, as it did, of the history of freedom and of hope in a still-outstanding, messianic future. With the category of memory Metz tied his thought to *the* dangerous memory of the passion and death of Jesus, thus giving it a specifically Christian content. See, J. B. Metz, "'Politische Theologie' in der Diskussion," in *Diskussion zur "Politischen Theologie,"* ed. Helmut Peukert (Mainz: Matthias-Grünewald, 1969), 284–96. For an example of this sort of critique (one which was not satisfied by Metz's introduction of the

category of memory), see Hans Urs von Balthasar, "Zu einer christlichen Theologie der Hoffnung," in *Münchner Theologische Zeitschrift* 32 (1981): 81–102.

28. J. B. Metz, "Communicating a Dangerous Memory," in *Communicating a Dangerous Memory: Soundings in Political Theology,* ed. Fred Lawrence (Atlanta: Scholars Press, 1987), 39f.

29. Ibid., 41f.

30. See "A Passion for God: the Existence of Religious Orders Today," (unpublished ms.). This is the text of an address to superiors of religious orders given in Vienna, in November 1991. Metz introduced this story by observing that the psychologist Eugen Drewermann criticizes his theology as a sort of theology for a broken-down, or neurotic, life. He relates the story so that his hearers can see "whether or not this shattering event has to do with the story of a sham existence or with the history of faith."

31. *"Leiden an Gott."* I will have much to say of this term below (for instance, see text, pp. 127–29, 153–63, 180f.). For the moment it can be illuminated by example. Metz refers to this mystical stance as that taken up by Job in the Old Testament or exemplified by Jesus' cry from the cross in Mark's Gospel: neither Job nor Jesus accepts suffering, attemps to explain it away (as Job's friends try to do), or ignores it; rather, each turns passionately, angrily, questioningly, expectantly, back to God within this suffering. Metz claims that this is the mystical stance of *resistance,* since it keeps my attention focused *hopefully, expectantly,* on suffering: "Mourning is hope in resistance—resisting the frenetic acceleration of time, in which we are increasingly losing ourselves . . . against the attempt to reduce to existentiell meaninglessness those who have disappeared and cannot be brought back" (*PG,* 160). The phrase presents difficulties for the translator as well. The German construction *"leiden an . . ."* normally translates as "to suffer from . . ." as in "to suffer from a fever." I have chosen the admittedly more peculiar translation of "suffering unto God" to capture the *dynamic* character of this relationship; "suffering before God" or "suffering in the presence of God" are other possible translations. It is best understood in terms of its biblical paradigms. See also, J. B. Metz, H-E. Bahr, *Augen für die Anderen* (Munich: Kindler Verlag, 1991), 21–23; J. B. Metz, "Die Rede von Gott angesichts der Leidensgeschichte der Welt," *Stimmen der Zeit* 117/5 (May 1992): 319–20.

32. J. B. Metz, "Gotteszeugenschaft," 8.

33. See, for instance, J. B. Metz, "Theology in the New Paradigm: Political Theology," in *Paradigm Change in Theology,* ed. Hans Küng and David Tracy, trans. Margaret Köhl (New York: Crossroad, 1989), 355–66.

34. "On the Way to a Post-Idealist Theology," *PG,* 32.

35. The literature attempting to describe and account for these shifts is immense. I have found the following most helpful: Louis Dupré, *Passage to Modernity*; Charles Taylor, *Sources of the Self: The Making of the Modern Identity* (Cambridge: Harvard University Press, 1989); Stephen Toulmin, *Cosmopolis: The Hidden Agenda of Modernity* (New York: The Free Press, 1990); Hans Blumenberg, *The Legitimacy of the Modern Age*, trans. Robert M. Wallace (Cambridge: MIT Press, 1983). For an account limited to the Enlightenment, see Peter Gay's *The Enlightenment: An Interpretation*, 2 vols. (New York: Norton, 1969).

36. Taylor, *Sources of the Self*, 186.

37. Ibid., 168.

38. Immanuel Kant, *Introduction to Logic*, cited in Franklin L. Baumer, *Modern European Thought: Continuity and Change in Ideas, 1600–1950* (New York: Macmillan, 1977), 161.

39. For a superb exploration of the fruits and tensions of Kant's approach to religion, see Michel Despland, *Kant on History and Religion* (Montreal: McGill-Queen's University Press, 1973). For a survey of nineteenth-century responses to modernity, see Claude Welch, *Protestant Theology in the Nineteenth Century*, 2 vols. (New Haven: Yale University Press, 1972).

40. As for instance in Karl Barth's *Protestant Theology in the Nineteenth Century*. The fundamentalist revolt in the United States at the end of the century stems at least in part from an analogous sense of alarm over the kinder, gentler Arminian Protestantism of liberal Christianity. See George Marsden, *Fundamentalism and American Culture: The Shaping of Twentieth-Century Evangelicalism, 1870–1925* (Oxford: Oxford University Press, 1980).

41. For the history of European Catholic theology during this period, see Gerald McCool's intellectual histories: *Catholic Theology in the Nineteenth Century: The Search for a Unitary Method* (New York: Seabury, 1977), and *From Unity to Pluralism: The Internal Evolution of Thomism* (New York: Fordham University Press, 1989). Also, see Thomas F. O'Meara, *Romantic Idealism and Roman Catholicism: Schelling and the Theologians* (Notre Dame: University of Notre Dame Press, 1982), and idem, *Church and Culture: German Catholic Theology, 1860–1914* (Notre Dame: University of Notre Dame Press, 1991).

42. McCool, *From Unity to Pluralism*, 200–233.

43. See Taylor, *Sources of the Self*, 417, 441–47.

44. For an anthology of key texts, as well as a helpful introduction, see Richard M. Rorty, ed., *The Linguistic Turn: Essays in Philosophical Method with Two Retrospective Essays* (Chicago: University of Chicago Press, 1992).

45. For an attack on the anthropological turn in theology (focusing on Karl Rahner), based on the linguistic turn as found in Ludwig Wittgenstein, see Fergus Kerr, *Theology after Wittgenstein* (Oxford: Basil Blackwell, 1986).

46. Michel Foucault, *The Order of Things: An Archaeology of the Human Sciences* (New York: Vintage Books, 1970), xxiii–xxiv.

47. Johann Baptist Metz, *Faith in History and Society,* 73 (translation slightly emended—see *Glaube in Geschichte und Gesellschaft,* 70).

48. Claude Welch, *Protestant Thought in the Nineteenth Century,* 1:47f.

49. Despland, *Kant on History and Religion.*

50. See, for instance, Emil Fackenheim's masterful reconstruction of Kant's argument in "Immanuel Kant," in Ninian Smart, et al., eds., *Nineteenth Century Religious Thought in the West,* 3 vols. (Cambridge: Cambridge University Press, 1985), 1:17–40.

51. Ibid., 23.

52. "I readily concede that no man can with certainty be conscious of *having performed his duty* altogether unselfishly." Kant, "On the Proverb: That may be true in theory but is of no practical use," in *Perpetual Peace and Other Essays,* trans. with an introduction by Ted Humphrey (Indianapolis: Hackett, 1983), 68.

53. Despland, *Kant on History and Religion,* 91f., 271, 275–77.

54. Kant, "An Answer to the Question: What Is Enlightenment," in *Perpetual Peace,* 44.

55. Relevant essays are found in *Perpetual Peace.* In addition, Kant did incorporate his philosophy of history into the apparatus of the three critiques, albeit in an appendix: "The Methodology of Teleological Judgment," in *The Critique of Judgment.* Of course, history was a far more central category for other thinkers like Lessing or Herder. What is interesting about Kant is that he developed his philosophy of history in close correlation with the apparatus of the three critiques. For instance, the "idea of history with a cosmopolitan intent" is a *regulative* ideal of reason, like the idea of the cosmos or the soul in Kant's first critique. Again, just as the concepts of immortality and the existence of God are arrived at in the second critique by a transcendental reflection on finite moral experience, so are the concepts of providence and the progress of reason arrived at by a transcendental reflection on the experience of morality in society and history (see Despland, *Kant on History and Religion,* 1–28).

56. Kant, *Perpetual Peace,* 39.

57. Ibid., 31f.

58. In *The Critique of Judgment* Kant qualifies this sort of public reason as that which is constitutive of a "culture of skill," in which the

threats of nature and other human beings are contained. This is different from a "culture of discipline" in which the pathological tendencies of reason itself (the "despotism of desires") are healed. The latter requires a qualitatively new development of reason; see Kant, *The Critique of Judgment*, translated with an introduction by Werner Pluhar (Indianapolis: Hackett, 1987), 319–21. One might ask what happens when humanity "stalls" in the first type of culture and defines its own rationality exclusively in terms of the reason required at this level: I suggest that the resulting situation would be precisely what was meant by Theodor Adorno and Max Horkheimer in their critique of the "dialectic of enlightenment" and the instrumental reason which underlies it.

59. Kant, "Idea for a Universal History," in *Perpetual Peace*, 32.

60. Kant, "Speculative Beginnings of Human History," in ibid., 49–60. Significantly, the first transition is not itself accessible to human reason, and Kant uses the Genesis narratives as a suitable representation or "map" to guide reason's reflections (p. 49).

61. Kant, "To Perpetual Peace: A Philosophical Sketch," in *Perpetual Peace*, 124.

62. "The End of All Things," in ibid., 96.

63. Kant, *The Critique of Judgment*, 323, 338.

64. Ibid., 319.

65. Ibid., 339, 342.

66. Ibid., 340. Here Kant picked up and clarified the distinction between nature and providence which he had introduced in earlier essays in his philosophy of history: "Idea of a Universal History," in *Perpetual Peace*, 39; "Perpetual Peace," ibid., 120.

67. "On the Failure of All Attempted Philosophical Theodicies," translated as an appendix to Despland, *Kant on History and Religion*, 290.

68. Kant, "On the Proverb: That may be true in theory but is of no practical use," in *Perpetual Peace*, 87; *The Critique of Judgment*, 340 n. 44.

69. Kant was acutely aware of the danger of a nihilistic cynicism attendant upon too close an examination of the course of history: "The reflective person feels a grief that the unreflective do not know, a grief that can well lead to moral ruination: this is a discontentedness with the providence that governs the entire course of the world; and he feels it when he thinks about the evils that so greatly oppress the human race, leaving it without (apparent) hope for something better. It is of greatest importance, however, *to be content with providence* . . . partly so that we can always take courage under our burdens and not neglect our own obligation to contribute to the betterment of others." From "The Beginning of Human History," in Kant, *Perpetual Peace*, 57f.

70. Despland, *Kant on History and Religion*, 91f., 276.

71. Kant, *Religion Within the Limits of Reason Alone*, trans. with an introduction and notes by T. M. Greene and H. H. Hudson (New York: Harper & Row, 1960), 54, 55, 77.

72. Ibid., 87–114; see also "The End of All Things," in *Perpetual Peace*, 102.

73. Kant, "The End of All Things," in *Perpetual Peace*, 102.

74. "On the Failure of All Philosophical Theodicies," 291–93.

75. Despland, *Kant on History and Religion*, 225.

76. "On the Failure of All Philosophical Theodicies," 293.

77. See Despland, *Kant on History and Religion*, 278.

78. For a discussion of Dilthey's attempt in comparison with the contemporary work of Bernard Lonergan, as well as their relationship to the problems of Metz's political theology, see Matthew Lamb, *History, Method, and Theology: A Dialectical Comparison of Wilhelm Dilthey's Critique of Historical Reason and Bernard Lonergan's Meta-Methodology* (Missoula: Scholars Press, 1978).

79. Here in Metz, for instance: "The subject is the human being who is involved in his own experiences and history, and is always able to identify himself anew in terms of them." *GGG*, 196; *FHS*, 220.

80. This is a central thesis of Metz's early work, *Christliche Anthropozentrik*, as well as of an address in Vienna in 1990, "Gott und Aufklarung."

81. "Communicating a Dangerous Memory," 40.

82. *Gottespassion*, 41f. (see *PG* 164f.).

83. "Kirchliche Autorität im Anspruch der Freiheitsgeschichte," in Metz, Moltmann, and Oellmüller, *Kirche im Prozeß der Aufklärung* (Munich: Kaiser-Grünewald Verlag, 1970), 63 (my translation). Metz goes on to cite the early Frankfurt School as an example of a source which does attempt to take seriously this side of Kant.

84. *GGG*, 21; *FHS*, 23.

85. Thus, in "On the Way to a Post-Idealist Theology" he lists as the first challenge that any contemporary theological paradigm must meet "the Marxist Challenge" (see *PG*, 34–39).

86. See the discussion of *Christliche Anthropozentrik* in the following chapter.

87. In this regard it is also intriguing to speculate that during the turbulent sixties Metz's shattering youthful experience could emerge as one more characteristic of modernity than previously, and this nascent spirituality as a more appropriate way of responding to that world.

88. This means the inner-historical and social coming to autonomy of human subjects. It is a more explicitly social and historical way of describing the "coming to itself" of reason.

89. The parallels with some of Kant's statements about belief in Jesus Christ "opening the portals of freedom" and concerning the Church as the public bearer of the good principle (i.e., the principle which leads to purification and perfection of practical reason) are very clear indicators of the shift that Metz has made.

90. *GGG*, 50 (my translation; cf. *FHS*, 53f.).

91. Here he was usually compared with Carl Schmitt's infamous political theology of the thirties, which served as an ideological justification for fascism. Metz, in this view, was merely replacing an ideology of the right which masqueraded as theology with an ideology of the left. See, for instance, Hans Maier, "'Politische Theologie'? Einwände eines Laien," in *Diskussion zur "politischen Theologie,"* 1–25. References to Schmitt's work may be found in Maier's essay and in the general bibliography to the whole collection.

92. *GGG*, 53; *FHS*, 56.

93. *GGG*, 57; *FHS*, 60.

94. That is, in terms of those "stars" in Metz's "constellation" that I describe in the text, pp. 29–34.

3. METZ AND THE TRANSCENDENTAL METHOD

1. On the transcendental method, see Otto Muck, *The Transcendental Method,* trans. William Seidensticker (New York: Herder and Herder, 1968); also, the introductions to Rahner's thought by Carr, Roberts, and Weger have helpful sections on this issue. An assessment of the use of and response to Heidegger by Thomists can be found in John Caputo, *Heidegger and Aquinas: An Essay on Overcoming Metaphysics* (New York: Fordham University Press, 1982).

2. *Scholastik* 28 (1953): 1–22. Henceforth, *HPM*. All translations are my own.

3. Out of the vast domain of literature on Heidegger, the following works have proven the most helpful to me: John Caputo, *The Mystical Element in Heidegger's Thought;* Hubert Dreyfus, *Being-in-the-World: A Commentary on Heidegger's Being and Time, Division I* (Cambridge: MIT Press, 1991). Michael Gelvin, *Heidegger's Being and Time,* revised edition (Dekalb: Northern Illinois University Press, 1989); Otto Pöggeler, *Martin Heidegger's Path of Thinking,* trans. Daniel Magurshak and Sigmund Barber (Atlantic Highlands, N.J.: Humanities Press, 1989); Frederick Olafson, *Heidegger and the Philosophy of Mind* (New Haven: Yale University Press, 1987). For summaries and analyses of Heidegger's attack on metaphysics, see, inter alia, Caputo, 47–96; Olafson, 3–27, 206–20.

4. Later even this task of "overcoming metaphysics" ceded too much for Heidegger's comfort. He began to speak simply of "leaving meta-

physics be," since the attempt to overcome it determines one's own think-ing too much in terms of the very metaphysical categories which one had intended to overcome. See Caputo, *Mystical Element,* 1–9.

5. See, for example, the work of Emerich Coreth: *Metaphysik,* 2nd ed. (Innsbruck: Tyrolia Verlag, 1964), especially 41–42, 64f.; idem, "Hei-degger und Kant" in *Kant und die Scholastik Heute,* ed. J. B. Lotz, vol. 1 of *Pullacher philosophische Forschungen,* ed. W. Brugger & J. B. Lotz (Munich: Verlag Berchmanskolleg, 1955), 207–55.

6. *HPM,* 20.

7. *HPM,* 16–17 n. 14^a. For a brief summary of this argument, see text, pp. 74–76.

8. For example, Metz's critique (which he shares with Coreth) of Heidegger's "transcendental empiricism," according to which Heideg-ger allegedly searches for an immediate "appearing" or "visibleness" of being, is also found in Bernard Lonergan's critique of those modern theo-ries of knowing which model knowing as "taking a good look." See Ber-nard Lonergan, *Insight: A Study of Human Understanding* (London: Philosophical Library, 1958).

9. *HPM,* 20, 22.

10. Ibid., 12 n. 11.

11. Rahner's dependence upon Heidegger's thought always remained relatively opaque, and he seemed to have little interest in clarifying it for himself or for his readers. See Carr, *Theological Method,* 18–35.

12. *Lexicon für Theologie und Kirche,* 10 vols., ed. Karl Rahner (Freiburg: Herder, 1957–1965). Henceforth, *LK.*

13. Metz, *Zeitschrift für katholische Theologie* 83 (1961): 1–14. The text originated in an address given to the sixth German Philosophy Con-gress in Munich, in October of 1960. An English translation is available: "The Theological World and the Metaphysical World," trans. Dominic Gerlach, in *Philosophy Today* 10 (Winter 1966): 253–63. I will use my own translations and cite from the German original.

14. This is the same approach taken in Rahner's *Hörer des Wortes.* Indeed, during the same period in which he wrote this article Metz was working on the revised edition of Rahner's work, to which we will turn in the following section.

15. Metz, "Theologische und metaphysische Ordnung," 1.

16. Ibid., 3 n. 3.

17. Ibid., 3–4.

18. Translated, somewhat misleadingly, by Macquarrie and Robinson as "state-of-mind." See Martin Heidegger, *Being and Time,* trans. J. Mac-quarrie and E. Robinson (San Francisco: Harper and Row, 1962), 172–82. See also Metz's article, "Befindlichkeit," in *LK,* 2:102–4.

19. Heidegger, *Being and Time,* 331. Although I will return to this concept later (pp. 154–56), I cannot hope to do more than hint at the possibilities and problems with Heidegger's idiosyncratic appropriation of such terms as guilt, anxiety, and being-toward-death. The reader should consult the literature cited above. I am also indebted to a series of lectures on this book given by Professor Robert Pippin of the University of Chicago in the fall of 1992.

20. Metz, "Theologische und metaphysische Ordnung," 4.

21. Ibid., 4.

22. Ibid.

23. Ibid., 9 n. 16. It is interesting to note that Metz cites approvingly Rahner's article on eschatology, "The Hermeneutics of Eschatological Assertions," *TI* 4:323–46, as an instance of the last function of philosophy. This is a position he will exactly reverse by the end of his career. While he will continue to accept the first function of philosophy, he will reformulate the second and third to the point of dialectically inverting them.

24. Ibid., 7 n. 7.

25. Ibid., 7. Metz repeats this critique in "Freiheit als theologische-philosophische Grenzproblem," in *Gott in Welt: Festgabe für Karl Rahner,* ed. J. B. Metz et al. (Freiburg: Herder, 1964), 304, 308.

26. This is the position advocated in Heidegger's "The Question Concerning Technology" and the "Letter on Humanism."

27. Bernstein, "Heidegger's Silence?" *The New Constellation,* 133. Bernstein's citation of Habermas is from "Work and Weltanschauung: The Heidegger Controversy from a German Perspective," *Critical Inquiry* 15 (Winter 1989): 55–56. Habermas had voiced his protest as a student, levelling the following question—which Heidegger never answered: "Can even the planned mass murder of millions of people, about which all of us know today, be made understandable in terms of the history of Being, as a fateful error? Is it not a factual crime of those who were responsible for carrying it out—and the bad conscience of an entire people?" ("Zur Veröffentlichung von Vorlesungen aus dem Jahre 1935," *Frankfurt Allgemeine Zeitung,* July 25, 1953, cited in Bernstein, *The New Constellation,* 141 n. 55). For some of the literature in the growing controversy over Heidegger and the Nazis, see *The Heidegger Controversy: A Critical Reader,* ed. Richard Wolin (Cambridge: MIT Press, 1993). It is puzzling that, to my knowledge, Metz has never added his own voice to this debate, as much as one would expect it given his early reservations concerning Heidegger's philosophy, as well as the way postmodern philosophy (which Metz attacks ferociously at almost every opportunity) has been implicated in the debate (see Wolin's introduction to the above-named text).

28. Metz, "Theologische und metaphysische Ordnung," 8.

29. Ibid., 12–14.

30. The celebrated "turn" in Heidegger's thought seems to signal some sort of awareness of this problem in Heidegger himself. He stopped trying to make the existential analytic serve as a prolegomenon for a general ontology, and looked elsewhere (to poetry, to even more radically disruptive neologism, etc.) to try to find the correct path to thinking. Whether or not this move by Heidegger succeeds is outside the scope of this work. See Olafson, *Heidegger and the Philosophy of Mind*, esp. 153–60.

31. Metz commonly uses two terms to speak of the existential character of our being as incarnate: *Leiblichkeit* and *Leibhaftigkeit*. I believe that the terms are essentially synonymous, but to preserve his usage I will translate the first term with "bodiliness" and the second with "embodiedness."

32. For instance, in this passage, which is actually a prelude to a strong *critique* of the failure of Rahner's theology to do justice to the catastrophe of the holocaust: "I had the good fortune to learn that Catholic theology which in my eyes was the best of that time, and to it I owe everything that I can do theologically myself. I mean the theology taught by Karl Rahner" ("Facing the Jews: Christian Theology after Auschwitz," in *Faith and the Future*, 40). This evaluation never wavers.

33. See text, p. 40f.

34. On the transcendental method, see Otto Muck, *The Transcendental Method*. On the foundations of Rahner's method, see Anne Carr, *The Theological Method of Karl Rahner* (Missoula: Scholars Press, 1977); Louis Roberts, *The Achievement of Karl Rahner*, with a foreword by Karl Rahner (New York: Herder, 1967). For a more biographical introduction, see Herbert Vorgrimler, *Understanding Karl Rahner*, trans. John Bowden (New York: Crossroad, 1986). For a survey of Rahner's appropriation of his Neo-Scholastic tradition, see Gerald McCool, "Karl Rahner and the Christian Philosophy of St. Thomas Aquinas," in *Theology and Discovery: Essays in Honor of Karl Rahner*, ed. William Kelly (Milwaukee: Marquette University Press, 1980), 63–93. All of the essays in the latter book give engaging reviews of selected aspects of Rahner's thought, as well one version of Metz's critique: "An Identity Crisis in Christianity? Transcendental and Political Responses," 169–78.

35. "Theology and Anthropology," in *TI* 9:28. This was originally a lecture given in Chicago in 1966.

36. Ibid., 29.

37. The first was Rahner's doctoral dissertation, completed in Freiburg while he sat in on Martin Heidegger's seminars, from 1934 to 1936.

It was rejected by his director, Martin Honecker, for being "too Heidegger-
gerian" (see Vorgrimler, *Understanding Karl Rahner*, 58–62). The work
was nonetheless published in 1937. It was republished twenty years later
under Metz's supervision. Metz's revisions were minor. An excellent
English translation is available: *Spirit in the World*, trans. William Dych
(New York: Herder, 1968). The provenance of his second work is more
complicated. Originally a series of lectures delivered by Rahner in the
late thirties, then collected and published (Munich: Kösel-Pustet, 1941),
it was republished under Metz's supervision with extensive and, for
some, controversial changes (Munich: Kösel, 1963). No adequate English
translation exists of the second edition, but there is a very good translation by Joseph Donceel of the first edition: Karl Rahner, *Hearer of the
Word: Laying the Foundation for a Philosophy of Religion*, translated by
Joseph Donceel, edited, and with an introduction by Andrew Tallon
(New York: Continuum, 1994). I will work from the German editions,
abbreviating them as *HdW1* and *HdW2* respectively, and give my own
translations.

38. For closer, more synchronic interpretations, see the literature cited
above: Carr, *Theological Method*, 60–88; Roberts, *The Achievement of
Karl Rahner*, 18–44. See also Andrew Tallon's interpretation of Rahner's
theological anthropology in "Personal Becoming: Karl Rahner's Christian Anthropology," with a foreword by Karl Rahner, in *The Thomist* 43
(January 1979): 1–177.

39. Carr, *Theological Method*, 66.

40. This is the classic definition of human being and autonomy in the
German tradition, from Kant on. Freedom and rationality are defined in
terms of the degree to which my own existence—including the conditions
of my existence and the decisions I make—is transparent to me as my
own. Much of the history of German thought (at least) since Kant can be
seen as an attempt to harmonize this ideal of human existence, freedom,
and rationality with the experience of the heteronomous presence of exigencies of nature and human society.

41. This does not represent an unfortunate "fall" of spirit into matter,
but the mode of being which is characteristic of human being. We can
only distinguish the pairs spirit/world, intellect/sensibility, because they
are present in an original unity in each act of human knowing.

42. Comparison with Heidegger is illuminating. For Heidegger, too,
human Dasein is characterized by the fact of presence, so that its Being is
an issue for it. Yet the ultimate ground for this self-presence in the world
is Dasein's temporality, by which Dasein always *is* ec-statically, outside of
itself in the three temporal ecstases of future, having-been, and present.
But, whereas for Rahner the ultimate term of this transcendence is the

fullness of being (God), for Heidegger it is the nothingness of pure possibility.

43. This is the meaning for Rahner of Aquinas's requirement of the *conversio ad phantasma*. There is no knowledge without a turning to the sensible image. But, whereas for Kant this disallows any speculative knowledge of the transcendent, Rahner argues that a more careful transcendental analysis of human knowing, taking into account both the constitutive role of abstraction, as well as the dynamism of knowing, allows one to overcome Kant's strictures.

44. *HdW1*, 106; *HdW2*, 107.

45. *HdW1*, 125, *HdW2*, 123. As Tallon notes, it is at this point, when speaking of God, that Rahner first uses the term "person," absent from *Geist in Welt*. See Tallon, "Personal Becoming," 77–85.

46. "Man is spirit in such a way that in order to become spirit he engages in and according to his being is always already engaged in otherness, in *materia* and thus in the world." *HdW1*, 161; *HdW2*, 159.

47. Compare this with Heidegger's belief that silence, and the existential stance of reticence from which it comes, is a genuine mode of discourse—indeed, perhaps the most authentic mode. See, for instance, *Being and Time*, 208, 318.

48. Rahner tells us that such a question (what a philosophy of religion would look like if in fact a word of revelation had not come to us in history) is not existentially interesting: see *HdW1*, 17, 219; *HdW2*, 22f., 211f. See also Carr's discussion of the ambiguity: *Theological Method*, 104–9. By the *end* of his career, however, this mode of revelation (in silence) has become much more interesting for Rahner: indeed it has become the crucial mode of God's revelatory presence to modernity. See text, p. 182f.

49. *HdW2*, 212 n. 7.

50. Rahner comments on these in a short foreword to the second edition (9–10). In a survey which covers Metz's early work, *Man in the World: The Theology of Johannes Baptist Metz*, Roger Johns lists the additions and gives an example of one that responds to a critique by von Balthasar (p. 72).

51. Andrew Tallon, who is on the whole rather hostile to the changes Metz made, agrees on this point. See "Personal Becoming," 29 n. 22.

52. *HdW2*, 10–12. Johns, in *Man in the World*, gives exhaustive lists of the changes made in *Hörer des Wortes* (as well as *Geist in Welt*): 83–84 nn.

53. See *HdW1*, 24–41. It is perhaps easier to see the second case as a debate over the relationship betwen philosophy of religion and theology. As Gerald McCool notes (*Catholic Theology in the Nineteenth Century*),

that debate pitted a Thomistic position, with its clear and almost exclusive priority of the *ordo scientiae* over the *ordo historiae,* against those who were attempting to make use of German Idealism to develop a *Wissenschaft der Offenbarung* that was more sensitive to history. But the locus of the battle, and the point on which the Neo-Thomists were able to carry the day, was the ability of their systems to deal adequately with Roman Catholic teachings on the relationship of grace and nature and the derivative relationship of faith and reason. The Neo-Thomists' triumph was encoded at Vatican I, in the decree *Dei Filius,* and in Leo XIII's encyclical *Aeterni Patris. This* is the history within which Rahner wrote *HdW1,* and which defines its intent.

54. *HdW2,* 10.

55. For surveys of these critiques, see David Held, *Introduction to Critical Theory: Horkheimer to Habermas* (Berkeley: University of California Press, 1980), 160–74; Martin Jay, *The Dialectical Imagination,* 271–75.

56. Some key passages where Metz does this (reference to *HdW1* given first, then *HdW2*): 22, 27f.; 22f., 28f.; 133, 130; 140, 139; 221, 214; 224, 215.

57. *HdW2:* 24 n. 11; 35 n. 3; 139 nn. 2, 3; 144 n. 5; 159 n. 5; 180 n. 3; 193 n. 4; 207 n. 5; 213 n. 8; 220 n. 11.

58. All of Part IV is devoted to this task: *HdW1,* 138–211.

59. *HdW2,* 88 n. 13; 164 n. 2; 170–71 n. 6; 175–76 n. 2; 180–81 n. 3.

60. Ibid.; 88 n. 13.

61. Thus we find a strongly Thomistic argument and an Aristotelean understanding of time as a function of motion. See chapter 10: "Der Mensch als materielles Wesen," *HdW1,* 150–62; *HdW2,* 150–60.

62. *HdW2,* 159 n.

63. *HdW1,* 178; *HdW2,* 175. The order (*Mitwelt* before *Umwelt*) is not accidental. In two other notes Metz asserts that however much our everyday experience, even of ourselves, is first an experience of a world of things (*Umwelt*), in fact this experience is only possible in terms of a more primordial experience of our world as a world of persons, a *Mitwelt:* see 170–71 n. 6; 164 n. 2.

64. *HdW2,* 35 n., 144 n., 180–81 n., 193 n.

65. *HdW1,* 164; *HdW2,* 163.

66. *HdW1,* 164–66; *HdW2,* 163–65.

67. *HdW2,* 164 n.

68. This argument is in *HdW1,* 103–14; *HdW2,* 117–26. See Carr, *Theological Method,* 99.

69. *HdW2,* 175 n.

70. *HdW2,* 88 n. 13. The text of this note is given above, p. 79.

71. Tallon, "Personal Becoming," 7, 66–68, 75–94.

72. This is, in essence, Tallon's evaluation of Metz's changes (ibid., 90 n.). It is an evaluation with which I am in agreement, although I am, as mentioned above, less convinced that the position in *Geist in Welt* unfolds harmoniously into Rahner's later position.

73. As evidence for this consider how many times he cites this historical argument in his revisions of *Hörer des Wortes*. This is especially true in the final chapters, which discuss the historicity of thinking and the relationship between philosophy of religion and theology proper: see, for instance, *HdW2*, 180 n.; 206 n. 2; 207 n. 5.; 213 n.; 220 n. (referring to Metz's earliest elaboration of the historical argument in "Die 'Stunde Christi,'" in *Wort und Wahrheit* 12 [1957]: 5–18).

74. *HdW2*, 88 n. 13. See text, p. 79f.

75. Besides the ten articles he wrote for Karl Rahner's *Lexicon für Theologie und Kirche*, he produced three articles for Heinrich Fries, ed., *Handbuch theologischer Grundbegriffe*, 2 vols. (Munich: Kösel, 1962), henceforth *HG*.

76. J. B. Metz, *Christliche Anthropozentrik: Über die Denkform des Thomas von Aquin* (Munich: Kösel, 1962), henceforth, *CA*. Still in print in Germany, no English translation has ever been published. Metz tells us (p. 21) that his interest in investigating the "thought-form" of Thomas Aquinas was engendered by his investigation of the Thomistic concepts of concupiscence and integrity—key concepts in Metz's theological anthropology as we shall see below.

77. "Leib," in *LK* 6:902; cf., "Leiblichkeit," *HG* 2:30. These concepts occupied Metz for almost a decade. He had already begun to work out his understanding of bodiliness in "Zur Metaphysik der Leiblichkeit," *Arzt und Christ* 4 (1958): 78–84. In the middle sixties Metz wrote a long article with Francis Fiorenza on theological anthropology, in which he treated the same material, although the eschatological focus of his later thought is clearly evident: "Der Mensch als Einheit von Leib und Seele" in *Mysterium Salutis: Grundrisse heilsgeschichtlicher Dogmatik*, 6 vols. (Cologne: Benziger, 1967), 2:584–636.

78. "Befindlichkeit," *LK* 2:102–4, dating from 1958.

79. *LK* 7:491–92, from 1962.

80. Ibid., 492. This refers to Rahner's second method discussed above of deriving historicity in *Hörer des Wortes*.

81. "Leiblichkeit," *HG* 2:35–37.

82. See, J. B. Metz, *Poverty of Spirit*, trans. John Drury (New York: Newman Press, 1968), 6–8, 27–29, 33, 46, 52. For Heidegger's understanding of anticipatory resoluteness, see *Being and Time*, 343–48, 351, 378. Metz will shift dramatically on this, as I will show in chapter 6.

83. *Gescheht*. Note that this is the verb that Heidegger uses to speak of the temporal "stretching out" which is proper to human existence. Macquarrie and Robinson, accordingly, translate it "historize." See, *Being and Time*, 40 n. 424–34.

84. "Leiblichkeit," 37.

85. "Konkupiszenz," *HG* 1:843–51.

86. Ibid., 848.

87. Ibid., 848, cf. Metz, *Poverty of Spirit*, 15–18.

88. Francis Fiorenza, "The Thought of J. B. Metz," *Philosophy Today* 10/4 (1966): 248–49.

89. See Rahner's early article, "The Theological Concept of Concupiscentia," *TI* 1:347–82. The original of this text first appeared in 1952. It is interesting to compare the treatment of concupiscence in this text with a later treatment in *Foundations of Christian Faith*, trans. William Dych (New York: Crossroad, 1978), 90–115. The later treatment is much closer in vocabulary and meaning to Metz's than it is to Rahner's early article. This suggests that the influence between Rahner and Metz ran both ways.

90. *CA*, 26.

91. He does refer to a forthcoming book that would defend this assertion (ibid., p. 28 n. 5), but this book never appeared. As we shall see, Metz's intellectual agenda was soon to shift dramatically.

92. Ibid., 31.

93. The *Seinsfrage* and the *Seinsverständniss* that it implies function in Heidegger's work in the same way as *Denkform* in this chapter of Metz's work: see, for instance, Heidegger, *Being and Time*, 28–35.

94. Ibid., 36. He uses language that is very close to that of Hans-Georg Gadamer, whose *Wahrheit und Method* (Tübingen: J. C. B. Mohr, 1960) was published just prior to the publication of *Christliche Anthropozentrik*. Metz does not cite Gadamer's work in his bibliography, but one suspects that he had read it by the time he worked through the final draft of his dissertation.

95. *CA*, 47, 49. Metz adds that Thomas's thought is *ontically* theocentric: that is, the most preeminent entity is God, not the human being. Here one could argue that with Thomas, and with Rahner, since *this* entity (God) is absolutely unique in being pure *esse* (Aquinas) or self-presence (Rahner), then ontic theocentricism will lead to a specific, and unique, ontological form.

96. *Vorhandenheit*, a key Heideggerian concept which Macquarrie and Robinson translate as "presence-at-hand" (Heidegger, *Being and Time*, 48 n. 1). For Heidegger too this sort of presence of beings to us is a derivative one, dependent on certain modes of human self-presence.

97. *CA*, 53. Like Rahner, Metz associates self-presence, *Beisichsein*, with Thomas's *reditio subjecti in seipsum completa*.

98. Ibid., 68.

99. Ibid., 57, 66, 72f., 89.

100. Ibid., 92-94.

101. Ibid., 114, cf. 101.

102. Hence Metz suggests (131 n. 18) that Greek philosophy, with its ground in Greek religion, was never able to become even relatively autonomous because it did not have the proper thought-form with which to attain that relative autonomy. He cites J. Pieper, *Was heißt Philosophieren* (Munich: 1948) in support of this view.

103. *CA*, 123.

104. Ibid., 126.

105. Ibid., 130.

106. Ibid., 125.

107. This evaluation of secularization is found very early in Metz's theological career: see "Die 'Stunde Christi'. Eine geschichtstheologische Erwägung," in *Wort und Wahrheit* 12 (1957): 5-18.

108. *CA*, 128. He does not name them, but in the early sixties Metz must have been thinking of the antimodern "Christian philosophies" of Neo-Thomists like Jacques Maritain and Etienne Gilson.

109. Ibid., 128, 135-36.

110. See, for instance, Ernst Cassirer's vigorous rejection of Heidegger's "interpretation" of Kant, in "Kant und das Problem der Metaphysik: Bemerkungen zu Martin Heidegger's Kant-Interpretation," in *Kant-Studien* 36/1: 167-99. For a critique of Rahner's reading of Aquinas, see Denis J. M. Bradley, "Rahner's *Spirit in the World*: Aquinas or Hegel?" *The Thomist* 41/2 (April 1977): 167-99, and the literature cited therein.

111. See *CA*, 28 n. 5; "Theologische und metaphysische Ordnung," 11 n. 18. Metz's work on integrity and concupiscence gave rise to the book on Thomas's thought-form. Metz himself avers that the latter would not be fully justified until complemented by a careful analysis of the material contents of the former: *CA*, 21f.

112. Hans Blumenberg, *Die Legitimität der Neuzeit* (Frankfurt: Suhrkamp, 1966), translated as *The Legitimacy of the Modern Age*, trans. Robert Wallace (Cambridge: MIT Press, 1985). To be sure, Blumenberg's primary opponent was Karl Löwith, who argued that modern notions of progress were fundamentally secularized Christian eschatology, and thereby flawed and "illegitimate." However, the general form of Blumeberg's counterattack also encompassed Metz's argument.

113. Hence, Metz's last work that lies fully within the sphere of transcendental Thomism was a contribution to the Rahner Festschrift that con-

sidered the issue of human freedom: "Freiheit als philosophisch-theologisches Grenzproblem," *Gott in Welt: Festgabe für Karl Rahner,* 2 vols, ed. J. B. Metz et al. (Freiburg: Herder, 1964), 1:287–311.

114. This will be the central argument of chapter 5.

115. See Rahner's "Ignatian Mysticism of Joy in the World," *TI* 3: 277–93. This work will be discussed in greater detail in chapter 6.

4. THE BIRTH AND DEVELOPMENT OF POLITICAL THEOLOGY

1. "Tremendum" is Arthur Cohen's naming of this, in some ways unnameable, catastrophe: *The Tremendum: A Theological Interpretation of the Holocaust,* with a foreword by David Tracy (New York: Crossroad, 1988).

2. Metz was aware that these new initiatives were not without risk. But they must be run, he argued, if the Church is to fulfill its mission. He came to say that what is needed is a "second courage" to follow the "first courage" exhibited at Vatican II. See "Do We Miss Karl Rahner?" *PG,* 95–99.

3. See "On the Way to a Post-Idealist Theology," *PG,* 33; Metz, "Theology in the New Paradigm: Political Theology," in *Paradigm Change in Theology,* ed. H. Küng and D. Tracy (New York: Seabury, 1989), 355–66.

4. J. B. Metz, *Theology of the World,* trans. William Glen-Doepel (New York: Herder, 1969) is a translation of *Zur Theologie der Welt* (Mainz: Matthias Grünewald, 1968). The translation has some problems. Where it follows the German original it is quite adequate. But in at least one instance (Chapter 3: "An Eschatological View of the Church and the World") it makes use of an English translation of the original essay which does not incorporate the changes that Metz made when he collected the essays for publication. In some places text in the German original is not translated and included in the English. For these reasons, the German original will be consulted and referenced when an emended translation is required. The German and English texts will be abbreviated as *ZTW* and *TW* respectively.

5. See, for instance, John Macquarrie's review in *The Journal of Ecumenical Studies* 7 (Spring 1970): 355–56.

6. See my chapters 2 and 5.

7. See Metz's interview with Peter Rottländer, "Politische Theologie und die Herausforderung des Marxismus," in *Theologie der Befreiung und Marxismus,* ed. Peter Rottländer (Munich: Edicion Liberación, 1986), 178. Also J. B. Metz, "On the Way to a Post-Idealist Theology," *PG,* 34–39.

8. See text, pp. 52–55.

9. For the relationship between German theology and the "second phase" of the Enlightenment, see Jon Sobrino, *Christology at the Crossroads,* trans. John Drury (New York: Seabury, 1978), 19, 26f., 29f., 348.

10. J. B. Metz, "On the Way," *PG,* 36. He calls this "the real Copernican revolution in philosophy" (*FHS,* 53).

11. *ZTW,* 48f., emended translation; cf. *TW,* 54. This part of the book dates from 1965. See also *TW,* 109.

12. Metz, "Herausforderung des Marxismus," 177; "On the Way," *PG,* 33. See also his "Theology in the New Paradigm," 358–62.

13. On ideology and ideology critique, see Paul Ricoeur, *Lectures in Ideology and Utopia,* ed. George Taylor (New York: Columbia University Press, 1986); Raymond Geuss, *The Idea of a Critical Theory* (New York: Cambridge University Press, 1981). For a summary of Marx's application of this approach to Christianity, see Van A. Harvey, "Ludwig Feuerbach and Karl Marx," in Ninian Smart et al., eds., *Nineteenth Century Religious Thought in the West* (New York: Cambridge University Press, 1985), 1:291–328.

14. See Geuss, *The Idea of a Critical Theory,* 12–22; 26–44; 69f. As Geuss points out, these claims and procedures are exceedingly difficult to sustain. The history of critical theory, from its origins through Habermas, is a history of a research program that has sought to do precisely that.

15. See, *TW,* 108–111; *GGG,* 56–59; "On the Way," *PG,* 35f.

16. *TW,* 149–55.

17. *ZTW,* 107 (the relevant passage is missing in the translation), 118. See also "'Politische Theologie,' in der Diskussion," in *Diskussion zur "Politischen Theologie,"* ed. Helmut Peukert (Mainz: Matthias-Grünewald, 1969), 275.

18. See text, pp. 112–15, and chap. 5.

19. See "Ernst Bloch—im Spiegel eines theologisch-politisches Tagebuchs" (henceforth, "Ernst Bloch"), in *Unterbrechungen: Theologische-politische Perspektive und Profile* (Gütersloh: Gütersloher Verlagshaus, 1981), 58, and *Trotzdem Hoffen: Mit Johann Baptist Metz und Elie Wiesel im Gespräch,* ed. Ekkehard Schuster and Reinhold Boschert-Kimmig (Mainz: Matthias-Grünewald, 1993), 30–32. At this meeting Metz also met another important future friend and collaborator: Jürgen Moltmann.

20. *GGG,* 149 (this sentence is missing from the translation).

21. The central work in Bloch's opus is his massive multivolume undertaking, *The Principle of Hope,* trans. Stephen Plaice and Paul Knight (Oxford: Basil Blackwell, 1986). A helpful collection of those of his writings which bear more directly on religion may be found in *Man on His*

Own: Essays in the Philosophy of Religion, trans. E. B. Ashton (New York: Herder, 1970). Bloch wrote a summary of his philosophy of religion, as well as of his interpretations of the biblical traditions of Judaism and Christianity and the subsequent history of Christianity, in *Atheism in Christianity: The Religion of the Exodus and the Kingdom,* trans. J. T. Swann (New York: Herder, 1972). This book, as we shall see, made a great impact on Metz. For a helpful summary of Bloch's career and work, as well as a close reading of *The Principle of Hope,* see Richard H. Roberts, *Hope and Its Hieroglyph: A Critical Decipherment of Ernst Bloch's "Principle of Hope"* (Atlanta: Scholars Press, 1990); see also Wayne Hudson, *The Marxist Philosophy of Ernst Bloch* (London: Macmillan, 1982).

22. Bloch, *Atheism in Christianity,* 82.

23. Ibid., 94.

24. Ibid., 26, 114–15.

25. Ibid., 180.

26. Bloch's second major book laid this latter thesis out in detail: *Thomas Münzer als Theologe der Revolution* (Munich: Kurt Wolff, 1921).

27. *Atheism in Christianity,* 9.

28. See J. B. Metz, "Gott vor uns statt eines theologischen Argument," in *Ernst Bloch zu ehren,* ed. Siegfried Unseld (Frankfurt: Suhrkamp, 1965), 300; see also *TW,* 81. This is the definition of theology with which he begins *Faith in History and Society* (p. 3).

29. This shift can be seen within *Theology of the World* itself by comparing its first chapter (esp. 32–41), which dates from 1962, with Appendix II, "On the Hiddenness of the Problem of the Future in Metaphysics," 98–100 (which dates from 1966).

30. Metz, "Gott vor uns," 297. Cf. *TW,* 84–87.

31. *ZTW,* 83. The corresponding passage in the English translation is substantially different—cf. *TW,* 90.

32. See "On the Hiddenness of the Problem of the Future in Metaphysics," *TW,* 98–100. This essay originally appeared in *Stimmen der Zeit* in 1966.

33. Ibid., 99. Here lie the beginnings of Metz's critique of using development or evolution as the model upon which to base one's understanding of human temporality and history. This critique became more radical with Metz's reading of Benjamin.

34. *TW,* 94f.; cf. 112f. Like Bloch, Metz's favorite passage from Marx is the famous eleventh thesis on Feuerbach: see Metz, "Gott vor uns," 227. This may be the place to point out that much of Metz's work during the sixties parallels Moltmann's, who published a far more systematic

Auseinandersetzung with Bloch's philosophy of hope in the early sixties: *Theology of Hope,* trans. James Leitch (New York: Harper & Row,
1967).

35. See, for instance, J. B. Metz, "The Controversy about the Future
of Man, an Answer to Roger Garaudy," *Journal of Ecumenical Studies*
4/2 (1967): 227–34.

36. "Ernst Bloch," 6. For Bloch's own critique, see his *Atheism in
Christianity,* 25, 36–42.

37. "Ernst Bloch," 66. This is from an entry dated 1974. Note that
Metz explicitly uses the Heideggerian term for the authentic existentiell
mode of being toward death: *Vorlauf.*

38. "On the Way," *PG,* 47.

39. *GGG,* 149–58; *FHS,* 169–79.

40. *GGG,* 154; *FHS,* 175. The "cunning of evolution" is an allusion
to Hegel's infamous invocation of the "cunning of reason" (*List der Vernunft*) in his philosophy of history, according to which even history's
catastrophes turn out to be further stages in Spirit's self-realization. The
irony would not have been lost on Bloch, who saw in Hegel a final, titanic
effort to tame the subversive power of hope, not with a *Deus absconditus,*
but with a *Ratio absconditus.*

41. For a historical introduction, see Martin Jay, *The Dialectical
Imagination.* For an introduction to the issues with which critical theory
grapples, see Geuss, *The Idea of a Critical Theory.* A good general survey
that highlights the differences between the different representatives of
critical theory is found in David Held, *Introduction to Critical Theory.*
On Adorno see Martin Jay, *Adorno;* also, Susan Buck-Morss, *The Origin
of Negative Dialectics* (New York: The Free Press, 1977), which has good
material on Benjamin as well; Gillian Rose, *The Melancholy Science: An
Introduction to the Thought of Theodor W. Adorno* (New York: Columbia University Press, 1979). A discussion of the relationship between
Metz and the Frankfurt School may be found in Joseph Colombo, *An
Essay on Theology and History: Studies in Pannenberg, Metz, and the
Frankfurt School* (Atlanta: Scholars Press, 1990).

42. Metz cites the following works most often: Theodor Adorno and
Max Horkheimer, *Dialectic of Enlightenment,* trans. John Cumming
(New York: Continuum, 1989); Max Horkheimer, *The Eclipse of Reason*
(New York: Oxford University Press, 1947); Theodor Adorno, *Negative
Dialectics,* trans. E. B. Ashton (New York: Continuum, 1973); and Her-
bert Marcuse *One-Dimensional Man* (Boston: Beacon Press, 1964).

43. For a survey of this family of philosophical and sociological theories, see Gregory Baum, *Religion and Alienation: A Theological Reading
of Sociology* (New York: Paulist Press, 1975).

44. See, for example, Horkheimer's essay "On the Problem of Truth," in A. Arato and E. Gebhardt, eds., *The Essential Frankfurt School Reader* (New York: Continuum, 1988), 407–43. Adorno was just as opposed to a simple, in his view naive, appeal to praxis: see Buck-Morss, *The Origin of Negative Dialectics*, 24–41.

45. Horkheimer understood this problem quite clearly; see "Traditional and Critical Theory" in his *Critical Theory: Selected Essays* (New York: Continuum, 1986). See also Geuss, *The Idea of a Critical Theory*, 83f.

46. Metz, "The Controversy about the Future," 230. Cf. Metz, "Gott vor uns," 301.

47. *TW,* 68, 74.

48. Ibid., 132.

49. *GGG,* 93; *FHS,* 107. The essay dates from 1971. The first explicit mention of these thinkers is from 1968, in Metz, "'Politische Theologie,' in der Diskussion," 278 n. 28 (he cites *Dialektic der Aufklärung*).

50. *GGG,* 6–8; *FHS,* 5–8.

51. J. B. Metz, "Wider die zweite Unmündigkeit," in *Die Zukunft der Aufklärung,* ed. Rüssen, Lämmert, and Glotz (Frankfurt: Suhrkamp, 1988), 81–87.

52. J. B. Metz, *EC,* 70. Cf. Metz, "Wider die zweite Unmündigkeit," 86f.

53. As several critics have noted, this universalization of a particular manifestation of reason (e.g, instrumental or "positive" reason), which was originally evaluated in terms of the economic and social conditions of modernity, paralyzes critical theory. It can no longer be a critical theory of history since its universalized concept of instrumental reason undercuts any grounds for positive proposals for the present. This is the thesis of Rose's book on Adorno, *The Melancholy Science*. See also the conclusions in Buck-Morss's study, *Negative Dialectics*, 185–90.

54. For instance, Metz raised this objection in 1967 in his debate with Roger Garaudy: "The Controversy about the Future of Man," 231. Cf. Metz, "Gott vor uns," 304.

55. Metz, "Die Herausforderung des Marxismus," 185. Cf. Metz, "Wider die zweite Unmündigkeit," 83.

56. The two most important statements of this crucial conceptualization of Metz's philosophy and theology of history are: "Redemption and Emancipation," chap. 7 of *GGG,* 104–19; *FHS,* 119–35; "Vergebung der Sünde," *Stimmen der Zeit,* 195/2 (February 1977): 119–28. The germs of this idea are to be found in the document for the German bishops' conference which Metz helped author: *Unsere Hoffnung: Ein Beschluß der gemeinsamen Synode der Bistümer in der Bundesrepublik Deutschland* (1975), 9–11.

57. *GGG*, 110; *FHS*, 124.

58. *GGG*, 112f.; *FHS*, 127.

59. As Horkheimer recognized. See "On Traditional and Critical Theory," in *Critical Theory: Selected Essays*, 188–243.

60. Geuss calls this situation, which resembles more Huxley's *Brave New World* than Orwell's *1984*, "the nightmare which haunts the Frankfurt School," *Critical Theory*, 83f.

61. *One-Dimensional Man*, 98. Metz cites this passage in *GGG*, 171; *FHS*, 193f.

62. "'Politische Theologie,' in der Diskussion," 286.

63. *GGG*, 154; *FHS*, 175. Cited above, 152.

64. *GGG*, 177; *FHS*, 201.

65. The two key works cited by Metz are Walter Benjamin, "The Storyteller: Reflections of the works of Nikolai Leskov" and "Theses on the Philosophy of History." They may be found in *Illuminations*, trans. by Harry Zohn, edited with an introduction by Hannah Arendt (New York: Schocken, 1968), and will be cited from that edition. For an introduction to Benjamin's life and work see Richard Wolin, *Walter Benjamin: An Aesthetic of Redemption* (New York: Columbia University Press, 1982); see also Arendt's introduction to *Illuminations*, as well as Gershom Scholem's remembrances and interpretations in *Walter Benjamin: The Story of a Friendship* (London: Faber & Faber, 1982), and the two essays on Benjamin, "Walter Benjamin," and "Walter Benjamin and His Angel" in Gershom Scholem, *On Jews and Judaism in Crisis*, ed. Werner Dannhauser (New York: Schocken, 1976), 172–236. On the implications of Benjamin for theology, see Ottmar John, "Forschrittskritik und Erinnerung: Walter Benjamin, ein Zeuge der Gefahr," in Ottmar John, Peter Rottländer, Edmund Arens, *Erinnerung, Befreiung, Solidarität: Benjamin, Marcuse, Habermas und die politische Theologie* (Düsseldorf: Patmos, 1991).

66. Benjamin, "Theses on the Philosophy of History," 256.

67. Ibid., 258.

68. Ibid., 264.

69. See John, "Fortschrittskritik und Erinnerung," 31–57.

70. See Benjamin, "Theses on the Philosophy of History," 261–63.

71. From Metz, "Hope as imminent expectation, or the struggle for the time that has vanished: untimely theses on apocalypticism," a chapter in *GGG*, 150; *FHS*, 170. Not by chance, these reflections on time are given as theses, just as Benjamin's theses on history. It should be noted that the English translation of these theses is particularly uneven.

72. Ibid., 151/172 (Citing from these theses I will give the citation from *GGG* first and then the page number from the translation, *FHS*. The translations are all my own.).

73. Metz, "Hope as Imminent Expectation," 150/170.

74. Metz refers to Nietzsche as the one who most clearly foresaw the consequences of the sort of temporal continuum into which the "death of God" would thrust human beings. See "Die Verantwortung der Theologie in der gegenwärtigen Krise der Geisteswissenschaften," in *Wissen als Verantwortung*, Hans-Peter Müller, ed. (Stuttgart: Kohlhammer, 1991), 120f.

75. Metz, "Ende der Zeit," in *Frankfurter Allgemeine Zeitung* 160 (July 13, 1991). Cf., Metz's *Followers of Christ*, 75–77.

76. *Followers of Christ*, 76. Metz is quoting the last line of Benjamin's theses on history, cited above, n. 65.

77. See, for instance Metz, "Theology versus Polymythicism: or, a brief Apology for Biblical Monotheism," in *PG*, 72–91.

78. To be sure, the exact nature of this response will vary. As the radical reformers showed, the extraordinary response could involve heroic patience and nonviolent following of Christ, or it could involve (as in Thomas Münzer) revolution.

79. Metz, *Followers of Christ*, 76.

80. This German neologism could also be translated by a corresponding English one: "remembrancing." The term invokes a liturgical context. See text, p. 161f.

81. See Benjamin's essay, "The Storyteller," in *Illuminations*, 83–109. Metz was particularly interested in Buber's and Scholem's retrieval of the art and content of Hasidic storytelling: *GGG*, 183–85; *FHS*, 207f.

82. *GGG*, 189f.; *FHS*, 212. Metz insists over and over again that he does not mean to exclude argument from theology (e.g., *GGG*, 186, 190, 194; *FHS*, 209, 213, 216), an issue to which we will return later.

83. Later, Metz calls this a "theological respect for the nontransferable, negative mystery of human suffering," and gives it his highest praise by saying that it was at the heart of Rahner's theology. See, "Karl Rahner's Struggle for the Theological Dignity of Humankind," in *PG*, 116–120.

84. *GGG*, 185; *FHS*, 208.

85. *GGG*, 190; *FHS*, 213.

86. Metz, "Ernst Bloch," 63f.

87. See Schuster and Boschert-Kimmig, *Trotzdem Hoffen*, 20.

88. This is amply documented by the essays collected in *Jenseits bürgerlicher Religion: Reden über die Zukunft des Christentums* (Munich: Kaiser, 1980); translated by Peter Mann as *The Emergent Church: The Future of Christianity in a Postbourgeois World* (New York: Seabury, 1981). See in particular, "Christians and Jews after Auschwitz," "Christianity and Politics," and "Transforming a Dependent People: Toward a Basic-Community Church." In addition to these essays, in the late seven-

ties Metz participated in ecumenical discussions which included Jewish-Christian dialogue, and coedited a book on the implications of the holocaust for Christianity and Christian theology: E. Kogon, J. B. Metz, eds., *Gott nach Auschwitz: Dimensionen des Massenmordes am jüdischen Volk* (Freiburg: Herder, 1979).

89. J. B. Metz, "Facing the Jews. Christian Theology after Auschwitz," in *The Holocaust as Interruption*, ed. Elisabeth Schüssler Fiorenza and David Tracy, *Concilium* 175/5 (1984): 27f. Cf. Metz, "On the Way to a Post-Idealist Theology," *PG*, 39–42.

90. J. B. Metz, "Theology in the New Paradigm: Political Theology," in *Paradigm Change in Theology*, 363.

91. Jon Sobrino, "The Crucified Peoples: Yahweh's Suffering Servant Today," in *1492–1992: The Voice of the Victims*, ed. Leonardo Boff and Virgil Elizondo, *Concilium* Special Edition (London: T. & T. Clark, 1990), 120.

92. It is first mentioned by Metz in relation to Ernst Bloch, "Ernst Bloch," 66. It also appears in Metz's essay on the dialectic of emancipation and redemption (*GGG*, 109f.; *FHS* 124). The most concise statement of this issue in his mature work is "Theology as Theodicy?" in *PG*, 54–71.

93. Metz, "Vergebung der Sünde," 120.

94. The parallels with the "question of being," the *Seinsfrage*, as articulated and proposed by Heidegger, but also by transcendental Thomists like Emerich Coreth, are very illuminating, and will be argued in greater detail in the next chapter. For the moment, let us simply note that for Heidegger part of the task of philosophy is to "deconstruct" the history of metaphysics as a history of false "solutions" to the question. So too for Metz and the question of suffering.

95. Recall that for Metz the "theodicy-question" is not solved by atheism, which gets rid of God. This only transforms it into a question of *anthropodicy*—justifying whatever notion of the subject of history one puts in God's place. This is what he means when he says that the theodicy question cannot be "transferred to human jurisdiction" ("Vergebung der Sünde," 120, quoted on p. 125). It can no more be solved there, but ends up being suppressed and then generates the catastrophic dialectic of enlightenment. A final tactic in this regard would be to continue following the strategy of the atheists with regard to God: now one simply denies that it is meaningful to speak of *any* subject in history. This is Metz's interpretation of postmodernism, an interpretation to which we will return in the final chapter.

96. Metz, "Ernst Bloch," 66f.

97. "Theology as Theodicy", *PG*, 58–63.

98. See, for instance, "Anamnestic Reason: A Theologian's Remarks on the Crisis in the *Geisteswissenschaften*," in *Cultural-Political Interventions in the Unfinished Project of Enlightenment*, ed. Thomas McCarthy et al. (Cambridge: MIT Press).

99. "Theology as Theodicy," *PG*, 66. The theme of poverty of spirit is a guiding thread in Metz's theological writings. He dealt with it in *Poverty of Spirit* in 1962, again in the late seventies (*Followers of Christ*), and yet again in 1990 ("A Passion for God"). We shall return to this thread in the final chapter.

100. "Theology as Theodicy," *PG* 67. The story, taken from the opening pages of Wiesel's classic novel, *Night*, is worth citing in full:

"'Man raises himself toward God by the questions he asks Him,' he [Moché the Beadle] was fond of repeating. 'That is the true dialogue. Man questions God and God answers. But we don't understand His answers. We can't understand them. Because they come from the depths of the soul, and they stay there until death. You will find the true answers, Eliezer, only within yourself!'

"'And why do you pray, Moché?' I asked him.

"'I pray to the God within me that He will give me the strength to ask Him the right questions'" (Elie Wiesel, *The Night Trilogy* [New York: Noonday Press, 1988], 15).

101. *TW,* 106, 114–18, 153.

102. See Metz, "Messianic or Bourgeois Religion?," in *The Emergent Church*, 1–16.

103. *GGG,* 71; *FHS,* 73.

104. See Jon Sobrino, "Awakening from the Sleep of Inhumanity," Introduction to *The Principle of Mercy: Taking the Crucified People from the Cross*, trans. Dimas Planas (Maryknoll: Orbis, 1994), 1–14.

105. See the discussion of the tasks of theology in chap. 3.

106. *GGG,* 190; *FHS,* 213.

107. *GGG,* 199–203; *FHS,* 223–28.

108. *GGG,* 193f.; *FHS,* 218. We can say in his defense that he did try to set up an interdisciplinary faculty at the University of Bielefeld which would encourage this sort of interchange between theology and the human sciences. It failed due in large part to ecclesial resistance. For Metz's vision of this project, see J. B. Metz, "Zu einer interdisziplinär orientierten Theologie auf bikonfessioneller Basis," in *Die Theologie in der interdisziplinär Forschung,* ed. J. B. Metz and T. Rentdorff (Düsseldorf: Bertelsmann Universitätsverlag, 1971), 10–23.

109. *GGG,* 131; *FHS,* 148. This is not far from what liberation theology understands as the task of conscientization. As an exemplar of this

theological labor Metz cites Ernesto Cardenal and his work in Solenti-name: see *EC*, 100–106.

5. METZ'S THEOLOGY: IN DEFENSE OF THE HUMAN

1. To be sure, Metz often accuses transcendental method of aspiring to occupy such a stance. Rahner would be subject to such a critique if all he did was "transcendental method." But, as both Rahner and Metz insisted, he does not apply a philosophical method after the fact to the contents of Christian faith. Metz, correctly in my view, maintains that in fact Rahner's theology arises from out of the life-world of the every-day Christian and can only be understood in terms of that life-world. It has, in short, the very narrative depth-structure that Metz advocates for any adequate contemporary theology. See, inter alia, *GGG*, 141–48, 199–203; *FHS*, 159–63, 223–27.

2. "Danger is in my eyes 'the' category for history and historical con-sciousness in theology." "Politische Theologie und die Herausforderung des Marxismus," 182. Cf. "Theology in the New Paradigm: Political The-ology," 365.

3. Martin Heidegger, *Being and Time*, 195.

4. Ibid., 363.

5. Ibid., 195.

6. Ibid., 191.

7. Ibid., 67. On the "fore-structure" of Heidegger's interpretation of human being I am following Dreyfus, *Being-in-the-World*, 198–201.

8. "Reflections on Methodology in Theology," *TI*, 11:81.

9. Ibid., 82.

10. *GGG*, 51; *FHS*, 54.

11. "Theology in the New Paradigm: Political Theology," 365.

12. *GGG*, 46f.; *FHS*, 49f.

13. Ibid., 196/220 (here, as usual, the German is cited first, followed by the corresponding passage in the English translation).

14. Ibid., 56/53.

15. See, for instance, ibid., 42f./46.

16. Ibid., 53f./56f.

17. Here one could perhaps cite Angelus Silesius' Eckhartian celebra-tion of the rose which blooms without a why, a passage that was also important for Heidegger in *Der Satz von Grund*.

18. *GGG*, 54; *FHS*, 57.

19. Ibid. 146 n. 20/167f. n. 15.

20. This is the root of Metz's resolute resistance to any conceptual theodicy which attempts to construct a comprehensive structure of mean-

ing which can "absorb" the surd of evil in history. Here Metz is not so far, after all, from Kant's statement "On the Failure of All Attempted Philosophical Theodicies," trans. in Michel Despland, *Kant on History and Religion* (see text, p. 48).

21. *GGG,* 66; *FHS,* 66.

22. Metz, "Communicating a Dangerous Memory," in Fred Lawrence, ed., *Communicating a Dangerous Memory: Soundings in Political Theology* (Atlanta: Scholars Press, 1987), 43.

23. See "The Question Concerning Technology," in *Martin Heidegger: Basic Writings,* edited with introductions by David Farrell Krell (San Francisco: HarperSanFrancisco, 1977), 287–317.

24. It is true for Metz that the salvific event is an apocalyptic one, that it in no way can be projected or forced from the current course of events. One can only struggle and prepare hopefully for it. Here he runs parallel to Heidegger: "Only a god can save us." But whereas in Heidegger it seems that there is nothing that humans can do to bring about a new dispensation of being, that there is really no justification for hope, in Metz's thought hope is justified because history is not finally the random play of being but belongs to the God of Abraham, Isaac, Jacob, and Jesus Christ. On danger and human response to it in Heidegger, see Caputo, *The Mystical Element in Heidegger's Thought,* xvii–xviii, 261–69.

25. This is so both outside of the Church and within it. Metz points to basic Christian communities in Latin America as the prime instance of such a transformation of old political and ecclesial structures. See, for instance, *EC,* 62–65.

26. *GGG,* 202; *FHS,* 206.

27. For instance, Heidegger argues that being-in-the-world for Dasein is always a being-with other beings which have Dasein's mode of being. But Heidegger's usage of *Mitsein* is sporadic, and plays a diminishing role in *Being and Time,* especially in the second division. See Olafson, *Heidegger and the Philosophy of Mind,* 70–74, 96–97.

28. *GGG,* 159; *FHS,* 183.

29. *GGG,* 162; *FHS,* 185.

30. Ibid., 166–72/188–94.

31. Ibid., 169/191.

32. Ibid., 172/194. This discussion recalls the well-known "Habermas-Gadamer" debate. The former sees in Gadamer's hermeneutics the danger of an uncritical submission to the past; Gadamer, on the other hand, accuses Habermas of being yet another instance of the Enlightenment attempt to gain mastery over tradition by means of method. Metz offers his own solution to the debate in his advocacy of dangerous memory.

33. This is why two of the functions of theological theory and argument are to critique these abuses of narrative and to elicit the narrative power of people who have lost it. See text, p. 132f.

34. *GGG*, 204; *FHS*, 229.

35. Ibid., 204f./229.

36. Ibid., 71/73.

37. Metz, "Communicating a Dangerous Memory," 40. See text, p. 52.

38. *GGG*, 205, 208; *FHS*, 230, 233.

39. *Being and Time*, 163–69, 210–24.

40. See Karl Rahner, *Foundations of Christian Faith: An Introduction to the Idea of Christianity*, trans. William V. Dych (New York: Crossroad, 1984), 90–115.

41. See text, pp. 112–15.

42. This is the dilemma that Heidegger identifies at the beginning of Division II of *Being and Time*, 279–81.

43. Ibid., 279–311. My attempt to understand this exceedingly complex facet of Heidegger's thought has been greatly aided by Gelven, *A Commentary on Heidegger's Being and Time*, 136–55, and Dreyfus, *Being-in-the-World*, 304–40.

44. "Thus death reveals itself as that *possibility which is one's ownmost, which is non-relational, and which is not to be outstripped* [unüberholbare]" (*Being and Time*, 294).

45. *Sein-zum-Tode*. Gelven translates this helpfully as "to-be-going-to-die," *Commentary*, 147.

46. Heidegger, *Being and Time*, 228–35, 295.

47. Ibid., 378; see the more detailed exposition on pp. 349–58.

48. Ibid., 343.

49. Rahner, *Foundations of Christian Faith*, 107.

50. We have seen this understanding of the primordial guilt of original sin and concupiscence in Metz's early work as well.

51. Rahner, *Foundations of Christian Faith*, 268–71, 296–98, 436–41. Rahner even uses Heideggerian distinctions such as the difference between "demise" and "death" (269f.), Heideggerian language like "being unto death" (270), and the notion that the consciousness of death can be suppressed; see also his "Christian Dying," *TI*, 17:226–256.

52. Rahner, "Following the Crucified," *TI*, 18:165.

53. Ibid., 169–70. Cf., Rahner, *Foundations of Christian Faith*, 296–98.

54. Metz, "Vergebung der Sünde," 126.

55. See text, p. 113f.

56. Metz, "Facing the Jews. Christian Theology after Auschwitz," 28.

57. "Theology as Theodicy, *PG*, 56 (translation slightly emended).

58. See text, pp. 127–29.

59. As far as I have been able to determine, Rahner's theology of the crucifixion and resurrection always hinges on Luke's version of the last words of Jesus. One can trace the shift in Metz's thought quite precisely by comparing his early understanding of poverty of spirit, expressed in *Poverty of Spirit* (1962), and his later understanding, expressed in "A Passion for God" (1990). The former is virtually identical to Rahner's approach: Metz tells us that one's *own* death is the "lodestone" for all forms of poverty of spirit, and uses Lk 23:46 as the center of a Christian interpretation of death (46f.). In the latter, Mark's passion predominates, and it is the meaningless death of *the other* that is the "lodestone" which orients authentic poverty of spirit.

60. "Verantwortung der Theologie in der gegenwärtigen Krise der Geisteswissenschaften," in *Wissen als Verantwortung: Ethische Konsequenzen des Erkennens,* ed. Hans-Peter Müller (Stuttgart: Kohlhammer, 1991), 122f.

61. *GGG,* 173; *FHS,* 196. The aporia intrinsic to *both* of the traditions which attempt to be critiques of historical reason (see text, pp. 149–50) are avoided: the "submissive attitude toward the past" that is the danger of Gadamer's hermeneutics, or the "or in an attitude toward the past that approaches it only in terms of ideology-critique" of critical theory.

62. Jon Sobrino, "The Crucified Peoples: Yahweh's Suffering Servant Today," in *1492–1992: The Voice of the Victims,* ed. Leonardo Boff and Virgil Elizondo, *Concilium* Special Edition (London: SCM Press, 1990), 120.

63. *GGG,* 207; *FHS,* 232.

64. Metz, "Politische Theologie und die Herausforderung des Marxismus," 181.

65. Metz, "Theology versus Polymythicism: or, a Short Apology for biblical Monotheism," *PG,* 87 (translation slightly emended).

66. Metz, "Die Rede von Gott angesichts der Leidensgeschichte der Welt," 319.

67. "Theology versus Polymythicism," *PG,* 85.

6. THE MYSTICAL-POLITICAL STRUCTURE OF CHRISTIAN FAITH AND THEOLOGY

1. Metz, "Die Verantwortung der Theologie," 122f., given above, p. 000.

2. Thus the title of a pair of interviews with Metz and Elie Wiesel: *Hope Against Hope* (forthcoming, Paulist Press). The German title is *Trotzdem Hoffen,* which could also be rendered "hoping in spite of it all."

3. One of the first mentions of *Leiden an Gott* comes in a little book on prayer that he wrote with Karl Rahner, published in 1977: *The Courage to Pray*, translated by Sarah O'Brien Twohig (New York: Crossroad, 1980). Metz's part of this book goes back to sermons he preached in the Münster Cathedral in 1976 (see the preface to the German original, *Ermütigung zum Gebet* [Freiburg im Br.: Herder, 1977], 5). In the central chapter, "What Is Prayer?" Metz uses the technical terms of *Rückfragen an Gott* and *Leiden an Gott*. They are somewhat veiled in the English translation (see pp. 12–14), but can be easily found in *Ermütigung zum Gebet*, 19–21. It is also found, at about the same time, in the text of an address he gave to the superiors of men's religious orders in West Germany in 1976: see his *Followers of Christ: The Religious Life and the Church*, trans. Thomas Linton (New York: Paulist Press, 1978), 64, where it is translated as "suffering from God." (On the translation issue, see above, chap. 2, n. 32.) Thus, 1976, the same year he was assembling *Glaube in Geschichte und Gesellschaft* for publication, is the crucial year.

4. Besides the literature cited in the Introduction (n. 5), see Joseph Colombo, "Rahner and His Critics," *The Thomist* 56/1 (January 1992): 71–96. It should be conceded at the outset that much in Metz's own writings suggests this approach: for instance, see, "An Identity Crisis in Christianity? Transcendental and Political Responses," in William Kelly, ed., *Theology and Discovery: Essays in Honor of Karl Rahner, S.J.*, 169–78.

5. Karl Rahner, Introduction to James Bacik, *Apologetics and the Eclipse of Mystery: Mystagogy According to Karl Rahner* (Notre Dame: University of Notre Dame Press, 1980), ix.

6. Ibid., x.

7. Ibid. This is the view that Titus Guenther tries to elaborate and justify in his book, *Rahner and Metz*. While it goes a long way in showing how Rahner's theology *does* indeed have a political dimension, it does not finally succeed in explaining the difference between the two, for reasons I will go into below.

8. Among others, see Metz, "Theology in the New Paradigm: Political Theology," *Paradigm Change in Theology*, esp. 357f.; "Toward a Post-Idealist Theology," *PG*, 30–34.

9. *GGG*, 200; *FHS*, 224.

10. Ibid., 196/220.

11. See text, p. 142.

12. See Harvey Egan, "The Devout Christian of the Future will . . . be a Mystic," in W. Kelly, ed., *Theology and Discovery*, 139–58.

13. Rahner, "The Theology of Mysticism," in *The Practice of Faith*, ed. Karl Lehman and Albert Raffelt (New York: Crossroad, 1986),

70–77. This is in opposition to its standard neoscholastic placement as a part of moral theology.

14. Rahner, *The Dynamic Element in the Church*, trans. W. J. O'Hara (London: Burns & Oates, 1964), 109. Rahner concludes that the "theology of the schools" is not up to this task.

15. Ibid., 86.

16. Metz, "Do We Miss Karl Rahner?" *PG*, 99–101.

17. *GGG*, 203; *FHS*, 227.

18. Metz, *Followers of Christ*, 42–44.

19. Introduction to Bacik, x.

20. See Karl Rahner, "Rede des Ignatius von Loyola an einen Jesuiten von Heute," *Schriften zur Theologie XV: Wissenschaft und christlicher Glaube* (Zürich: Benziger, 1984), 389, 391 [translated by Rosaleen Ockenden as "Ignatius of Loyola Speaks to a Modern Jesuit," in Karl Rahner and Paul Imhof, *Ignatius of Loyola* (London: Collins, 1979]. Citations will be made to the German; any translations are my own. Rahner alludes to the address that Metz gave to German superiors of men's religious orders in 1976 (eventually translated as *Followers of Christ*).

21. Jon Sobrino, "Theology in a Suffering World: Theology as *Intellectus Amoris*," in *The Principle of Mercy* (Maryknoll: Orbis, 1994), 49–57.

22. Excellent literature is available on this history, although we still lack a careful *modern* history of this struggle. On the philosophical history of theory and praxis up to and including Marx, with a very readable account of its Greek origins, see Nicholas Lobkowicz, *Theory and Practice: History of a Concept from Aristotle to Marx* (New York: University Press of America, 1967). For a treatment of the *vita contemplativa* and *vita activa* in spirituality and theology, up through the late Middle Ages, see Dietmar Mieth, *Die Einheit von Vita activa und Vita contemplativa in den deutschen Predigten und Traktaten Meister Eckharts und bei Johannes Tauler* (Regensburg: Friedrich Pustet, 1969); Brian Vickers, ed., *Arbeit Musse Meditation: Betrachtungen zur Vita activa und Vita contemplative* (Zürich: Verlag der Fachvereine, 1985). For a treatment of the history of the typological interpretation of Martha and Mary, which almost through the Reformation formed the scriptural *locus classicus* for working out this issue, see Giles Constable, "The Interpretation of Martha and Mary," in *Three Studies in Medieval Religious and Social Thought* (Cambridge: Cambridge University Press, 1995), 1–141.

23. As Bernard McGinn puts it: "No theologian of the modern era has been a more powerful spokesman of the apophatic tradition. . . . For Rahner God always remains the ultimate mystery, even in the beatific vision. Like Gregory of Nyssa and many other Christian mystics, he holds

that progress toward perfection consists in the ever-deepening and more direct awareness of the divine incomprehensibility" (*The Foundations of Mysticism*, 286).

24. *The Spiritual Exercises*, nos. 230–37; see Ignatius of Loyola, *The Spiritual Exercises of Saint Ignatius: A Translation and Commentary*, translated, with commentary by George Ganss, S.J. (St. Louis: Institute of Jesuit Sources, 1992), 94f. It is certainly true that Ignatius's *Spiritual Exercises* are highly kataphatic. Yet there are good reasons to posit connections to the neoplatonic tradition, particularly as it culminated in the great Rhineland mystics. First, as already noted, there is Ignatius's use of sun and light imagery—a classic neoplatonic motif. Second, Ignatius never recommended the contemplation of images in the *Exercises* as a means to union with God, or as the culmination of one's spiritual life. He always maintained a certain reserve toward images and the consolations that came with them; they were to be rigorously tested in order to determine how well they contributed to the real end of spiritual exercises: the union with God that comes through service under the banner of Christ. In seeking the greater glory of God one recapitulates and is united with God's presence in salvation history, and so achieves a type of union with God that is different from, but not inferior to, the union with God achieved through meditation or contemplative rapture. In this reading, Ignatius is close indeed to Meister Eckhart, who articulated a spirituality of the active life which does not see the active life as a preliminary stage to, or an outflow from, contemplative union with God, but a type of loving union with God in its own right. See Mieth, *Einheit*, 223–36.

25. Rahner, "The Ignatian Mysticism of Joy in the World," *TI*, 3:277–93. This text originated in a paper first published in 1937, coinciding with Rahner's preparation of *Geist in Welt* for publication. Rahner gave another interpretation of Ignatian Spirituality forty years later in "Rede des Ignatius von Loyola an einen Jesuiten von heute," 373–408. In this later essay there are also strong neoplatonic themes; indeed, now it is Meister Eckhart who looms large in the background.

26. Ibid., 282–84. Furthermore, the place of the cross is very similar to Bonaventure's treatment of the crucifixion in the *Itinerarium*. Rahner dealt extensively with Bonaventure in his early work. Note further that in this article the two Fathers he cites are the great early representatives of neoplatonic Christian mysticism: Origen and Clement of Alexandria.

27. Ibid., 287. This position seems to verge upon nominalism. The world and history are stripped of inherent meaning; any meaning they have subsequently is due only to "God's sovereign will upon which everything depends" (p. 287).

28. Ibid., 291.

29. The phrase is Bernard McGinn's.

30. Rahner, "The Theology of Mysticism," *The Practice of Faith,* 75, 77. He does state that an empirical study and description (e.g., developmental psychology) of the life of a Christian might provide such a justification, but he is ambiguous about what this might mean *theologically.*

31. The exact relationship between the rebirth of vivid forms of apocalyptic mysticism and Franciscan spirituality (along with its descendants) is a controversial issue. For the role of John's Apocalypse in the Mendicant orders, see David Burr, "Mendicant Readings of the Apocalypse," in *The Apocalypse in the Middle Ages,* ed. Richard Emerson and Bernard McGinn (Ithaca: Cornell University Press, 1992), 89–102.

32. See Ewert Cousins, "The Humanity and Passion of Christ," in *Christian Spirituality II: High Middle Ages and Reformation,* ed. Jill Raitt (New York: Crossroad, 1989), 375–91; also, "Francis of Assisi: Christian Mysticism at the Crossroads," in Stephen Katz, ed., *Mysticism and Religious Traditions* (New York: Oxford University Press, 1983). This devotion went beyond mere recollection to reenactment. Hence the explosion of practices like pilgrimage, veneration of the child Jesus in reenactments of his birth, as well as reenactments of his crucifixion.

33. Cousins, "Francis of Assisi: Christian Mysticism at the Crossroads," 165.

34. See Metz, *Poverty of Spirit,* 33–36, 46–48.

35. Ibid., 46. This approach to Jesus' death is *always* the one that Rahner takes up; see above, chap. 5.

36. Metz, "A Passion for God," *PG,* 158. In the same work Metz reflects consciously on the evolution of his views on the central mystical virtue: "I admit that the contemplation of this beatitude permeates the entirety of my theological biography" 157.

37. For a slightly different interpretation, which traces back the difference sketched here to the difference between Rahner's favorite narrative of salvation, also the favorite of all neoplatonic thinkers, John's Gospel, and Metz's (as well as Sobrino's) preferred text, Mark, see David Tracy's response to Metz's contribution in Willaim Kelly, ed., *Theology and Discovery,* 184–87. Here as in so many other ways, Tracy's own penetrating insights have guided my work on Metz at crucial points.

38. See Timothy George, "The Spirituality of the Radical Reformation," in *Christian Spirituality II,* 344–71, esp. 338–41.

39. Ibid, 358. See also Robert Friedman, *The Theology of Anabaptism* (Scottdale, Pa.: Herald Press, 1973), 103.

40. See Caputo, *The Mystical Element in Heidegger's Thought.*

41. Indeed, the famous turn in Heidegger's thought may represent something quite similar, although one must (following Caputo) be quite

clear that what is at issue in Heidegger's thought is a mystical *element*, not a mysticism per se. Heidegger himself always insisted on the neutrality of his system with regard to the question of God, and his use of mystical themes and language (especially after his "turn") has aroused considerable controversy. On this, see Caputo, *Mystical Element*, 1–46.

42. Rahner, "The Incomprehensibility of God in Thomas Aquinas," *Journal of Religion, Supplement* 58 (1978): 122. Compare this with the ambiguity in Eckhart's thought concerning which transcendental (*esse, unum, verum, bonum*) has precedence in the divine nature, as well as Eckhart's propensity for speaking of God's "ground" as a desert or waste (*Wüste*), into which "the soul cannot look."

43. Rahner, *The Dynamic Element in the Church*, 135. Cf. his "Rede des Ignatius," 381–83.

44. See text, p. 61f. To be sure, in his early works Rahner talks of a *Vorgriff* of the infinite horizon of Being (which we call God) that is always entailed and coaffirmed *with and by* every finite experience, but Rahner is claiming more in these later works cited here.

45. See McGinn, *Foundations*, 287.

46. Rahner, "Rede des Ignatius," 374, 377, 380. This makes a fascinating contrast to Rahner's early work. In *Hearer of the Word* the silence of God is entertained as a possibility, but it is the fact that God *has* indeed spoken a constituting word to the human hearer that is the structural key to the work.

47. Ernst Bloch, *Thomas Münzer als Theologe der Revolution*, (Munich: Kurt Wolff, 1921). Metz's reliance on Jewish thinkers raises the question as to how much he draws his mystical resources from the Christian tradition. Of course, in the instance of Bloch, there is a presence at second remove from Christian sources. In any event, I have tried to argue above that the sort of mystical stance that Metz writes from does have a history within Christianity, but there is no doubt that Metz's own expression of that stance is deeply marked by the mystical and messianic traditions within Judaism.

48. Benjamin, *Illuminations*, 264.

49. See Karl Löwith, *Meaning in History* (Chicago: University of Chicago Press, 1949), especially his chapter on Joachim of Fiore, 145–59. See also Bernard McGinn's analysis of Joachim's Trinitarian theology of history, as well as (in the final chapter) the responses of Bonaventure and Aquinas, in *The Calabrian Abbot: Joachim of Fiore in the History of Western Thought* (New York: Macmillan, 1985), esp. 161–237.

50. Charles Taylor, *Sources of the Self* (Cambridge: Harvard Univ. Press, 1989), 211–305.

51. See Metz's *Theology of the World*, 114–20, 153. Metz developed and applied this notion before he had fully abandoned the "transcenden-

tal approach" of his mentor. Not surprisingly, in light of the thesis I am arguing here, the term is no longer a central focus of his political theology after 1970.

52. For the application of this principle in Rahner's thought, see, inter alia, "A Fragmentary Aspect of a Theological Evaluation of the Future," *TI*, 10:235–41; "Marxist Utopia and the Christian Future of Man," *TI*, 6:59–68.

53. Rahner, "Rede des Ignatius," 380–84. Once again there are striking parallels with Eckhart's notion of the soul that is a virgin and a wife, detached from the world but *precisely because of this* fruitful in the world, because in such a soul a "third" birth of the Word (besides the eternal begetting within the Trinity and the birth into time of the Son of God) occurs, thus recapitulating God's primordial, and world-constituting, descent into the world. Here it is tempting to speculate that Rahner was decisively influenced by his brother Hugo Rahner, with his seminal essay on the history of the controversial notion of a "birth of the Word" in the soul: "Die Gottesgeburt: Die Lehre der Kirchenvätern von der Geburt Christi aus dem Herzen der Kirche und der Gläubigen," in *Symbole der Kirche: Die Ekklesiologie der Vätern* (Salzburg: Müller, 1964), 13–87. For a helpful summary of Eckhart's teaching, see Caputo, *Mystical Element*, 113–18.

54. This is one of Rahner's favorite phrases. See Vorgrimler, *Understanding Karl Rahner*, 128–30. This serene confidence in the face of suffering is one of the elements of Rahner's thought that Metz found most disturbing, particularly when the suffering is that of Auschwitz.

55. Metz, *TW*, 104.

56. In *The Mystic Fable,* Michel de Certeau argues that one of the most important factors driving the development of Christian mysticism in early modernity is precisely this sense of God's absence.

57. Using McGinn's terminology: see text, p. 11.

58. When asked, a few months before Rahner's death, to pinpoint the difference between his theology and Rahner's, Metz said "Some day Rahner will die, and he will be greeted by God the Father with this question: 'My dear great Karl Rahner, what have you done to the apocalyptics of my son.'" Rahner's response: "You may be right, you may be right; *but,* how are you going to get this across [*durchsetzen*]?" From Mary Maher, "Historicity and Christian Theology," 12, 110.

59. Rahner, "Rede des Ignatius," 374.

60. Ibid., 377, 380.

61. See, for instance, Metz, "On the Way to a Post-Idealist Theology," *PG*, 32, 34, 35; also, his "Thesen zum theologischen Ort der Befreiungstheologie," in J. B. Metz, *Die Theologie der Befreiung: Hoffnung oder Gefahr für die Kirche* (Düsseldorf: Patmos, 1986), 147–57. Another brief

but significant justification of the affinity between Metz and particularly the Jesuit theologians Jon Sobrino and Ignacio Ellacuría can be adduced from their common preference for the final words of Jesus in Mark's Gospel, words which for Metz are paradigmatic of the mysticism of *Leiden an Gott*. Finally, in a private communication Metz has indicated his general agreement with this way of mapping the difference between himself and Rahner in terms of the different parts of the *Exercises*.

62. For the meditation on sin, see *Spiritual Exercises*, §53 (Ganss, 42).

63. Ignacio Ellacuría, "Las Iglesias latinoamericanas interpelan a la Iglesia de España," *Sal Terrae* 826 (1982), 230. Cited in Jon Sobrino, *Jesus the Liberator: A Historical-Theological Reading of Jesus of Nazareth*, trans. by Paul Burns and Francis McDonagh (Maryknoll: Orbis, 1993), 262f.

64. Metz, "Die Rede von Gott angesichts der Leidensgeschichte der Welt," 313.

65. "Karl Rahner's Struggle for the Theological Dignity of Humankind," *PG*, 119. Earlier he even goes so far as to say that Rahner himself exhibits the mysticism of "suffering unto God," which, in view of the foregoing, is going too far. What can be said is that this Jesuit was able to understand and draw on this particular element of the *Exercises*, although from a different perspective within the *Exercises*.

66. Rahner, "Rede des Ignatius," 400.

67. This is the essence of the rather unsympathetic critique in R. R. Reno, "Christology in Political and Liberation Theology," *The Thomist* 56/2 (April 1992): 291–322, esp. 296–303, 313–18. Reno falls victim to the difficulties of Metz's style enumerated above. He also, his caveats notwithstanding, unfairly conflates Moltmann's thought with Metz's, and either is not aware of or refuses to accept those places where Metz speaks of the narrative and practical mediations of the Christian hope in redemption. Reno also accuses Metz of failing to follow the doctrinal principles that govern predication of the one person, Jesus Christ, as these principles are derived from the Chalcedonian formula. I would suggest that Metz's insistence on the dual mystical-political structure of following Christ—without division, confusion, or separation—expresses his own distinctive awareness of the Christological mystery.

68. This is particularly evident in the second part of Metz's *Faith in History and Society*, "Themes," which discusses everything from soteriology and ecclesiology to apocalyptic eschatology.

69. One can get a good idea of what Metz's Christology would look like by reading his *Followers of Christ*—a text which Reno does not consult.

70. See, for instance, *FHS*, 90.

71. See Gutiérrez's provocative, mutually illuminating correlation in *We Drink from Our Own Wells*, 83–89, 129–31 between the favorite liberation theology text for articulating the *political* character of Scripture, *Exodus*, with the mystical account by John of the Cross of the three "nights" of the soul.

72. Sobrino, *Jesus the Liberator*, 12–14, 17–22.

73. *GGG*, 201; *FHS*, 226. On the importance of the doctrine of the Trinity for any Christian theology, see Catherine Mowry LaCugna, *God for Us: The Trinity and Christian Life* (San Francisco: HarperSanFrancisco, 1991).

74. See Jürgen Moltmann, *The Trinity and the Kingdom: The Doctrine of God*, trans. Margaret Kohl (San Francisco: Harper & Row, 1981), and *History and the Triune God: Contributions to Trinitarian Theology* (New York: Crossroad, 1991).

75. *GGG*, 117f.; *FHS*, 131f.; "Rede von Gott angeschichts der Leidensgeschichte der Welt," 317f. Here, for all of his reservations about his teacher's theology, Metz sides *with* Rahner's approach to the "nontransferable mystery of human suffering": see Metz's essay, "Karl Rahner's Theological Struggle for the Theological Dignity of Humankind," in *PG*, 116–120. For Moltmann's response, specifically to Rahner, see "The Question of Compassion and God's Impassibility," in *History and the Triune God*, 122–24.

76. See E. Peterson, *Der Monotheismus als politisches Problem* (Leipzig: Jakob Hegner, 1935). For an instance of this work of refutation, see Metz's recent work on political theology, in which he also addresses the "political theology" of Carl Schmidt: "Monotheism and Democracy: On Religion and Politics on Modernity's Ground," chap. 9 of *A Passion for God*. It may well be that Metz is here trying to defend monotheism, *together with* Judaism, rather than moving to an explicitly Trinitarian, and thereby non-Jewish, response.

77. For an example of this criticism, from a more sympathetic and careful reader, see Rebecca Chopp, *The Praxis of Suffering: An Interpretation of Liberation and Political Theologies* (New York: Orbis, 1986), 78–81. In the initial stages of writing this work I learned a great deal from Chopp's brief but penetrating analysis of Metz's theology (pp. 64–81).

78. Besides Chopp, see also Don Browning, "Practical Theology and Political Theology," *Theology Today* 42 (April 1985): 15–33.

79. A fact that Metz has himself noted in "Die Verantwortung der Theologie in der gegenwärtigen Krise der Geisteswissenschaften," 113–25. See also Juan Luis Segundo's similarly critical (if perhaps now dated) remarks on the lack of a critical-liberative sociology, in *The Liberation of Theology*, trans. John Drury (Maryknoll: Orbis, 1976), 39–68.

80. As Metz has noted in "Anamnestic Reason: A Theologian's Remarks on the Crisis in the *Geisteswissenschaften*," in Thomas McCarthy et al., *Cultural-Political Inverventions in the Unfinished Project of Enlightenment* (Cambridge: MIT Press, 1992). See also, David Tracy, "Theology, Critical Social Theory, and the Public Realm," in *Habermas, Modernity, and Public Theology*, ed. Don Browning and Francis Schüssler Fiorenza (New York: Crossroad, 1992), 19–42, esp. 37–42.

81. See here the groundbreaking work of Stephen Toulmin, in, inter alia, *Cosmopolis: The Hidden Agenda of Modernity*. Metz has shown himself appreciative of some of these changes, for instance with regard to the new philosophy and history of science and its concept of paradigm and paradigm shift, which Metz has taken over in his own reflections on theology and theological method: see his "Theology in the New Paradigm" and "On the Way to a Post-Idealist Theology." For an analysis of the relationship between Metz's political theology and the new philosophy of science, see Steven Ostovich, *Reason in History: Theology and Science as Community Activities* (Atlanta: Scholars Press, 1990).

82. This is particularly important if political theology is to continue in the countries of its birth, which are quite different from the birthplace of liberation theology. Metz rightly praises liberation theology and finds in it in many ways the fruition of what he has been laboring for in his own theology. Many of the concrete recommendations he makes derive from that theology, particularly his advocacy of the ecclesial structure of base Christian communities. Nevertheless, liberation theology cannot simply be imported without any further ado to the First World. As Francis Schüssler Fiorenza noted early on, the quite different social and political contexts of liberation and political theology require not only careful theological reflection but also the sort of detailed description and analysis that only the social sciences can provide. See Francis Fiorenza, "Political Theology and Liberation Theology: An Inquiry into Their Fundamental Meaning," in *Liberation, Revolution, and Freedom: Theological Perspectives*, ed. Thomas McFadden (New York: Seabury, 1975), 3–29. Metz himself has recognized this. He has recently admitted that there are cultural and social reasons for the success of base Christian communities in Latin America that do not obtain in Central Europe: see his *Trotzdem Hoffen*, 14–16.

83. This is fortunately being remedied by some of Metz's own students. See for example Helmut Peukert's careful analysis and critique of the work of Jürgen Habermas and Karl-Otto Apel, *Science, Action, and Fundamental Theology: Toward a Theology of Communicative Action*, trans. James Bohman (Cambridge: MIT Press, 1986); or, Edmund Arens, *Christopraxis: A Theology of Action* (Minneapolis: Fortress, 1995).

84. See Metz, "Theology versus Polymythicism," *PG*, 78–81.

85. See Michael Buckley, *At the Origins of Modern Atheism* (New Haven: Yale University Press, 1987), 9–25.

86. Metz articulates this sort of argument in "Die Verantwortung der Theologie." For a sustained and compelling philosophical elaboration of this sort of approach, see Richard Bernstein, *The New Constellation: The Ethical-Political Horizons of Modernity/Postmodernity* (Cambridge: MIT Press, 1991).

87. Buckley, *At the Origins of Modern Atheism*, 66f.

88. This is true despite the otherwise admirable and important contribution of papal encyclicals, as Metz himself has observed: see *FHS*, 29f.

89. *Theology and Social Theory: Beyond Secular Reason* (Cambridge, Mass.: Blackwell, 1990).

90. The transpositions and shifts in meaning in moving from *theoria* and *praxis* to the *vita contemplativa* and *vita activa* provide a case in point (see literature cited above, n. 22). See also, Jaroslav Pelikan, *Christianity and Classical Culture: The Metamorphosis of Natural Theology in the Christian Encounter with Hellenism,* (New Haven: Yale University Press, 1993).

91. See Josef Pieper, *The Silence of St. Thomas* (New York: Pantheon, 1957), 38–71.

92. Baron Friedrich Von Hügel, *The Mystical Element of Religion as Studied in Saint Catherine of Genoa and Her Friends,* 2 vols. (London: Clark & Dent, 1961), chaps. 1 and 2.

93. Hadot, *Philosophy as a Way of Life,* 272.

94. J. B. Metz and Hans-Eckard Bahr, *Augen für die Anderen: Lateinamerika—eine theologische Erfahrung* (Munich: Kindler, 1991), 14f.

95. See my comments in "The New Evangelization: Toward an *Ecclesia semper Evangelizanda*" in *The Ecumenist,* 3/3 (July-September 1996), 53–58.

96. Thus, if von Hügel names his third element the mysticial-*volitional* element of religion, Metz offers the important emendation, mystical-*political*.

BIBLIOGRAPHY

I. WORKS BY JOHANN BAPTIST METZ

A. Lexica Articles

In *Handbuch theologischer Grundbegriffe*. 2 vols. Edited by Heinrich Fries. Munich: Kösel Verlag, 1962:

"Freiheit," 1:403–14;
"Konkupiszenz," 1:843–51;
"Leiblichkeit," 2:29–37.

In *Lexicon für Theologie und Kirche*. 10 vols. Edited by Karl Rahner. Freiburg: Herder, 1957–65:

"Gespräch," 2:836–37;
"Leib," 6:902–5;
"Mitsein," 7:492–93;
"Theologie," 10:62–71;
"Unglaube," 10:496–99;
"Welt," 10:1023–26.

In *Sacramentum Mundi*. 4 vols. Edited by Karl Rahner. Freiburg: Herder, 1967–69:

"Apologetik," 1:266–76;
"Politische Theologie," 3:1232–40.

B. Books, Articles, and Addresses

"Heidegger und das Problem der Metaphysik." In *Scholastik* 28 (1953): 1–22.
"Die 'Stunde Christi': Eine geschichtstheologische Erwägung." In *Wort und Wahrheit* 12 (1957): 5–18.
"Zur Metaphysik der Leiblichkeit." In *Arzt und Christ* 4 (1958): 78–84.

257

"Theologische und metaphysische Ordnung." In *Zeitschrift für katolische Theologie* 83 (1961): 1–14.

Christliche Anthropozentrik: Über die Denkform des Thomas von Aquin. Munich: Kosel-Verlag, 1962.

"Freiheit als philosophische-theologische Grenzproblem." In *Gott in Welt: Festgabe für Karl Rahner,* 2 volumes, edited J. B. Metz, et al. Freiburg: Herder, 1964.

"Gott vor uns statt eines theologisches Argument." In *Ernst Bloch zu ehren,* edited by Siegfried Unseld. Frankfurt: Suhrkamp, 1965.

Metz, J. B., with Francis Fiorenza. "Der Mensch als Einheit von Leib und Seele." In *Mysterium Salutis: Grundriss heilsgeschichtlicher Dogmatik,* 6 vols., edited by Johannes Feiner and Magnus Löhrer. Benziger, 1967.

"The Controversy about the Future of Man: An Answer to Roger Garaudy." *Journal of Ecumenical Studies* 4/2 (1967): 223–34.

Poverty of Spirit. Translated by John Drury. New York: Newman Press, 1968.

Zur Theologie der Welt. Mainz: Matthias-Grünewald Verlag, 1968. Translated by William Glen-Doepel as *Theology of the World.* New York: Herder and Herder, 1969.

"'Politische Theologie' in der Diskussion." In *Diskussion zur "Politischen Theologie,"* edited by Helmut Peukert. Mainz: Matthias-Grünewald, 1969.

"Kirchliche Autorität im Anspruch der Freiheitsgeschichte." In *Kirche im Prozess der Aufklärung,* edited by J. B. Metz, J. Moltmann, and W. Oelmüller. Munich: Kaiser Verlag, 1970. Translated by David Kelly and Henry Vander Goot as "Prophetic Authority." In *Religion and Political Society,* translated and edited by the Institute of Christian Thought. New York: Harper Forum Books, 1974.

"Zu einer interdisziplinär orientierten Theologie auf bikonfessioneller Basis." In *Die Theologie in der interdisziplinären Forschung,* edited by J. B. Metz and T. Rendtorff. Düsseldorf: Bertelsmann Universitätsverlag, 1971.

Glaube in Geschichte und Gesellschaft. Mainz: Matthias-Grünewald, 1977. Translated by David Smith as *Faith in History and Society: Toward a Practical Fundamental Theology.* New York: Seabury, 1980.

Metz, J. B., with Karl Rahner. *Ermütigung zum Gebet.* Freiburg: Herder, 1977. Translated by Sarah O'Brien Twohig as *The Courage to Pray.* New York: Crossroad, 1980.

"Vergebung der Sünden." *Stimmen der Zeit* 195/2 (February 1977): 119–28.

Zeit der Orden? Zur Mystik und Politik. Freiburg: Herder, 1977. Translated by Thomas Linton as *Followers of Christ: The Religious Life and the Church.* New York: Paulist Press, 1978.

Metz, J. B, and I. Kogon, eds. *Gott nach Auschwitz: Dimensionen des Massenmordes am jüdischen Volk*. Freiburg, 1979.

Jenseits bürgerliche Religion: Reden über die Zukunft des Christentums. Munich/Mainz: Kaiser-Grünewald, 1980. Translated by Peter Mann as *The Emergent Church: The Future of Christianity in a Postbourgeois World*. New York: Crossroad, 1987.

Unterbrechungen. Gütersloh: Gütersloher Verlagshaus, 1981.

"An Identity Crisis in Christianity? Transcendental and Political Responses." In *Theology and Discovery: Essays in Honor of Karl Rahner, S.J.*, edited by William Kelly, S.J. Milwaukee: Marquette University Press, 1980.

"Facing the Jews: Christian Theology after Auschwitz." In *The Holocaust as Interruption* (*Concilium*, 175), edited by David Tracy and Elisabeth Schüssler Fiorenza. Edinburgh: T. & T. Clark, 1984.

"Productive Noncontemporaneity." In *Observations on "The Spiritual Situation of the Age,"* edited by Jürgen Habermas, translated with an introduction by Andrew Buchwalter. Cambridge: MIT Press, 1984.

"Theology in the Modern Age, and Before Its End." In *Different Theologies, Common Responsibility* (*Concilium*, 171). Edinburgh: T. & T. Clark, 1984.

"Unterwegs zu einer nachidealistischen Theologie." In *Entwürfe der Theologie*, edited by J. B. Bauer. Cologne: Styria, 1985.

"Thesen zum theologischen Ort der Befreiungstheologie." Introduction to *Die Theologie der Befreiung: Hoffnung oder Gefahr für die Kirche*, edited by J. B. Metz. Düsseldorf: Patmos, 1986.

"Politische Theologie und die Herausforderung des Marxismus: Ein Gespräch des Herausgebers mit Johann Baptist Metz." In *Theologie der Befreiung und Marxismus*, edited by Peter Rottländer. Munich: Edition Liberación, 1986.

"Communicating a Dangerous Memory." In *Communicating a Dangerous Memory: Soundings in Political Theology*, edited by Fred Lawrence. Atlanta: Scholars Press, 1987.

"Wider die zweite Unmündigkeit: Zum Verhältnis von Aufklärung und Christentum." In *Die Zukunft der Aufklärung*, edited by Rüssen, Lämmert, Glotz. Frankfurt: Suhrkamp, 1988.

"Theologie versus Polymythie oder kleine Apologie des biblischen Monotheismus." In *Einheit und Vielheit, XIV deutscher Kongreß*, edited by Odo Marquard. Hamburg: Felix Meiner, 1990.

"Theologie gegen Mythologie: Kleine Apologie des biblischen Monotheismus." *Herder Korrespondez* 42/4 (April 1988): 187–93.

"Anamnetische Vernunft: Anmerkungen eines Theologen zur Krise der Geisteswissenschaften." In *Zwischenbetrachtungen: Im Prozess der Aufkärung*. Frankfurt: Suhrkamp, 1989. Translated by Barbara Fultner as "Anamnestic Reason: A Theologian's Remarks on the Crisis in the *Geisteswissenschaften.*" In *Cultural-Political Interventions in the Unfinished Project of Enlightenment*, edited by Axel Honneth, Thomas McCarthy, et al. Cambridge: MIT Press, 1992.

"Theology in the New Paradigm: Political Theology." In *Paradigm Change in Theology*, edited by Hans Küng and David Tracy. New York: Crossroad, 1989.

"Theology in the Struggle for History and Society." Translated by Dinah Livingstone. In *The Future of Liberation Theology: Essays in Honor of Gustavo Gutiérrez*, ed. M. Ellis and O. Maduro. New York: Orbis, 1989.

"Fehlt uns Karl Rahner?" In *Freiburger Akademiearbeiten: 1979–1989*, edited by Dietmar Bader. Munich, 1989.

"Das Konzil—der Anfang eines Anfangs?" *Orientierung* 54/22 (November 1990): 245–50.

"Theologie als Theodizee." In *Theodizee—Gott vor Gericht*, edited by Willi Oelmüller. Munich: Wilhelm Fink, 1990.

"Die Verantwortung der Theologie in der gegenwärtigen Krise der Geisteswissenschaften." In *Wissen als Verantwortung: Ethische Konsequenzen des Erkennens*, edited by Hans-Peter Müller. Stuttgart: Kohlhammer, 1991.

"Ende der Zeit." *Frankfurter Allgemeine Zeitung* 160 (July 13, 1991).

Metz, J. B., with Dorothee Sölle. *Welches Christentum Hat Zukunft? Dorothee Sölle und Johann Baptist Metz im Gespräch mit Karl-Josef Kuschel*. Stuttgart: Kreuz, 1990.

"Gotteszeugenschaft in einer Welt der religionsfreundliche Gottlosigkeit." Address given to superiors of religious orders in Vienna, November 1991.

Metz, J. B., with Tiemo Peters. *Gottespassion: Zur Ordensexistenz Heute*. Freiburg: Herder, 1991.

Metz, J. B., with H-E. Bahr. *Augen für die Anderen: Lateinamerika—eine theologische Erfahrung*. Munich: Kindler, 1991.

"Die Rede von Gott angesichts der Leidensgeschichte der Welt." In *Stimmen der Zeit* 117/5 (May 1992): 311–20.

Trotzdem Hoffen: mit Johann Baptist Metz und Elie Wiesel im Gespräch. Interviews by Ekkehard Schuster and Reinhold Boschert-Kimmig. Mainz: Matthias-Grünewald, 1993.

"Suffering Unto God." Translated by J. Matthew Ashley. In *Critical Inquiry* 20/4 (Summer 1994), 611–22.

Metz, Johann Baptist, with Jürgen Moltmann. *Faith and the Future: Essays on Theology, Solidarity, and Modernity*, with an Introduction by Francis Schüssler Fiorenza. Maryknoll: Orbis, 1995 (this volume collects the most important of Metz's essays from the journal *Concilium*).

"The Last Universalists." In *The Future of Theology: Essays in Honor of Jürgen Moltmann*, ed. Miroslav Volf, Carmen Krieg, and Thomas Kucharz. Grand Rapids: Eerdmans, 1996.

A Passion for God: The Mystical-Political Dimension of Christianity. Translated and edited, with an introduction, by J. Matthew Ashley. Mahwah, N.J.: Paulist Press, 1997.

Zum Begriff der neuen Politischen Theologie: 1967–1997. Mainz: Matthias-Grünewald, 1997.

II. OTHER WORKS

Abraham, K. C., and Bernadette Mbuy-Beya, eds. *Spirituality of the Third World: A Cry for Life.* Maryknoll: Orbis, 1994.

Adorno, Theodor. *Negative Dialectics.* Translated by E. B. Ashton. New York: Continuum, 1973.

Adorno, Theodor, and Max Horkheimer. *Dialectic of Enlightenment.* Translated by John Cumming. New York: Continuum, 1989.

Ancic, Nedjeljko. *Die "politische Theologie" von Johann Baptist Metz als Antwort auf die Herausforderung des Marxismus.* Frankfurt: Peter Lang, 1981.

Arato, A., with E. Gebhardt, eds. *The Essential Frankfurt School Reader.* New York: Continuum, 1988.

Arens, Edmund, John Ottmar, Peter Rottländer. *Erinnerung, Befreiung, Solidarität: Benjamin, Marcuse, Habermas und die politische Theologie.* Düsseldorf: Patmos, 1991.

Ashley, J. Matthew. "The Defense of the Subject: The Problem of Anthropology in Johann Baptist Metz." Ph.D. diss., University of Chicago, 1993.

———. "The Turn to Spirituality? The Relationship between Theology and Spirituality." *Christian Spirituality Bulletin* 3/2 (Fall 1995).

Baum, Gregory. *Religion and Alienation: A Theological Reading of Sociology.* New York: Paulist Press, 1975.

Baumer, Franklin. *Modern European Thought: Continuity and Change in Ideas, 1600–1950.* New York: Macmillan, 1977.

Bellah, Robert, et al., eds. *Habits of the Heart: Individualism and Commitment in American Life.* San Francisco: Harper & Row, 1985.

Benhabib, Seyla. *Critique, Norm, and Utopia: A Study of the Foundations of Critical Theory.* New York: Columbia University Press, 1986.

————. *Situating the Self: Gender, Community, and Postmodernism in Contemporary Ethics.* New York: Routledge, 1992.

Benjamin, Walter. *Illuminations.* Edited and with an introduction by Hannah Arendt; translated by Harry Zohn. New York: Schocken Books, 1968.

Bernstein, Richard. *The New Constellation: The Ethical-Political Horizons of Modernity/ Postmodernity.* Cambridge: MIT Press, 1992.

Bloch, Ernst. *Thomas Münzer als Theologe der Revolution.* Munich: Kurt Wolff, 1921.

————. *Man on His Own: Essays in the Philosophy of Religion.* Translated by E. B. Ashton. New York: Herder and Herder, 1970.

————. *Atheism in Christianity: The Religion of the Exodus and the Kingdom.* Translated by J. T. Swann. New York: Herder and Herder, 1972.

Blumenberg, Hans. *The Legitimacy of the Modern Age.* Translated by Robert Wallace. Cambridge: MIT Press, 1983.

Bradley, J. M. "Rahner's *Spirit in the World:* Aquinas or Hegel?" *The Thomist,* 4/12 (April 1977): 167–99.

Browning, Don, "Practical Theology and Political Theology." *Theology Today* 42 (April 1985): 15–33.

————, and Francis Schüssler Fiorenza, eds. *Habermas, Modernity, and Public Theology.* New York: Crossroad, 1992.

Buckley, Michael. *At the Origins of Modern Atheism.* New Haven: Yale University Press, 1987.

Buck-Morss, Susan. *The Origin of Negative Dialectics: Theodor W. Adorno, Walter Benjamin, and the Frankfurt Institute.* New York: The Free Press, 1977.

Burr, David. "Mendicant Readings of the Apocalypse." In *The Apocalypse in the Middle Ages,* edited by Richard Emerson and Bernard McGinn. Ithaca: Cornell University Press, 1992, 89–102.

Bynum, Caroline Walker. *Jesus as Mother: Studies in the Spirituality of the High Middle Ages.* Berkeley: University of California Press, 1982.

Capra, Fritjof, and David Steindl-Rast. *Belonging to the Universe: Explorations on the Frontier of Science and Spirituality.* San Francisco: HarperSanFrancisco, 1995.

Caputo, John D. *Heidegger and Aquinas: An Essay on Overcoming Metaphysics.* New York: Fordham University Press, 1982.

————. *The Mystical Element in Heidegger's Thought.* Second edition with new introduction by the author. New York: Fordham University Press, 1990.

Carr, Anne. *The Theological Method of Karl Rahner.* Missoula: Scholars Press, 1977.

Casanova, José. *Public Religions in the Modern World*. Chicago: University of Chicago Press, 1994.

Cassirer, Ernst. "Kant und das Problem der Metaphysik: Bemerkungen zu Martin Heidegger's Kant-Interpretation." In *Kant-Studien 36/1*.

Chopp, Rebecca. *The Praxis of Suffering: An Interpretation of Liberation and Political Theologies*. Maryknoll: Orbis Books, 1986.

Cohen, Arthur. *The Tremendum: A Theological Interpretation of the Holocaust*. With a foreword by David Tracy. New York: Crossroad, 1988.

Collingwood, R. G. *The Idea of History*. New York: Oxford University Press, 1946.

Colombo, Joseph. *An Essay on Theology and History: Studies in Pannenberg, Metz, and the Frankfurt School*. Atlanta: Scholars Press, 1990.

———. "Rahner and His Critics: Lindbeck and Metz." *The Thomist 56/1* (January 1992): 71–96.

Cone, James. *The Spirituals and the Blues*. Maryknoll: Orbis, 1972.

———. *My Soul Looks Back*. Maryknoll: Orbis, 1992.

Constable, Giles. "The Interpretation of Martha and Mary." In *Three Studies in Medieval Religious and Social Thought*. Cambridge: Cambridge University Press, 1995.

Coreth, Emerich. "Heidegger und Kant." In *Kant und die Scholastik Heute*, edited by J. B. Lotz, vol. 1 of *Pullacher philosophische Forschungen*, edited by W. Bruegger and J. B. Lotz. Munich: Verlag Berchmanskolleg, 1955.

———. *Metaphysik*. 2nd ed. Innsbruck: Tyrolia Verlag, 1964.

Cousins, Ewert. "Francis of Assisi: Christian Mysticism at the Crossroads." In *Mysticism and Religious Traditions*, edited by Steven Katz. New York: Oxford University Press, 1983.

———. "The Humanity and Passion of Christ." In *Christian Spirituality II: High Middle Ages and Reformation*, edited by Jill Raitt. New York: Crossroad, 1989.

Cunningham, Lawrence. "A Decade of Research on the Saints." *Theological Studies* 53 (1992): 517–33.

———. "*Extra Arcam Noe*: Criteria for Christian Spirituality." *Christian Spirituality Bulletin* 3/1 (Spring 1995).

de Certeau, Michel. *The Mystic Fable*. Translated by Michael B. Smith. Chicago: University of Chicago Press, 1992.

Despland, Michel. *Kant on History and Religion*. Montreal: McGill-Queen's University Press, 1973.

Dreyfus, Hubert. *Being-in-the-World: A Commentary on Heidegger's Being and Time, Division I*. Cambridge: MIT Press, 1991.

Dupré, Louis. *Passage to Modernity.* New Haven: Yale University Press, 1993.

Egan, Harvey. "The Devout Christian of the Future Will . . . Be a 'Mystic': Mysticism and Karl Rahner's Theology." In *Theology and Discovery: Essays in Honor of Karl Rahner, S.J.,* edited by William J. Kelly. Milwaukee: Marquette University Press, 1980.

Elizondo, Virgilio. *The Future Is Mestizo: Life Where Cultures Meet.* New York: Crossroad, 1988.

Espín, Orlando O. "Tradition and Popular Religion: An Understanding of the *Sensus Fidelium.*" In *Frontiers of Hispanic Theology in the United States,* edited by Allan Figueroa Deck. Maryknoll: Orbis, 1992.

Ferré, Frederick. *Hellfire and Lightning Rods: Liberating Science, Technology and Religion.* Maryknoll: Orbis, 1993.

Fiorenza, Francis. "Political Theology and Liberation Theology: An Inquiry into Their Fundamental Meaning." In *Liberation, Revolution, and Freedom,* edited by Francis McFadden. New York: Seabury, 1975.

———. "The Thought of J. B. Metz." *Philosophy Today* 10/4 (1966).

Foucault, Michel. *The Order of Things: An Archaeology of the Human Sciences.* New York: Vintage Books, 1970.

Gay, Peter. *The Enlightenment: An Interpretation.* 2 volumes. New York: Norton, 1969.

Geffré, Claude and Gustavo Gutiérrez, eds. *The Mystical and Political Dimension of Christian Faith (Concilium 96).* New York: Herder and Herder, 1974.

Gelvin, Michael. *A Commentary on Heidegger's Being and Time,* revised edition. Dekalb: Northern Illinois University Press, 1989.

George, Timothy. "The Spirituality of the Radical Reformation." In *Christian Spirituality II: High Middle Ages and Reformation.* World Spirituality: An Encyclopedic History of the Religious Quest, no. 17. Edited by Jill Raitt in collaboration with Bernard McGinn and John Meyendorff. New York: Crossroad, 1989.

Geuss, Raymond. *The Idea of a Critical Theory: Habermas and the Frankfurt School.* New York: Cambridge University Press, 1981.

Guenther, Titus. *Rahner and Metz: Transcendental Theology as Political Theology.* New York: University Press of America, 1994.

Gutiérrez, Gustavo. *A Theology of Liberation: History, Politics and Salvation.* 2d rev. edition. Translated and edited by Sister Caridad Inga and John Eagleson. Maryknoll: Orbis, 1988.

———. *We Drink from Our Own Wells: The Spiritual Journey of a People.* Translated by Matthew J. O'Connell, with an introduction by Henri Nouwen. Maryknoll: Orbis, 1984.

———. *The Truth Shall Make You Free: Confrontations*. Translated by Matthew O'Connell. Maryknoll: Orbis, 1990.

Habermas, Jürgen. *The Philosophical Discourse of Modernity*. Translated by Fred Lawrence, with an introduction by Thomas McCarthy. Cambridge: MIT Press, 1987.

Hadot, Pierre. *Philosophy as a Way of Life: Spiritual Exercises from Socrates to Foucault*. Edited with an introduction by Arnold I. Davidson, translated by Michael Chase. Chicago: University of Chicago Press, 1995.

Haight, Roger. *Dynamics of Theology*. Mahwah, N.J.: Paulist, 1990.

Heidegger, Martin. *Being and Time*. Translated by John Macquarrie and Edward Robinson. San Francisco: Harper & Row, 1966.

———. *Martin Heidegger: Basic Writings*. Edited with introductions by David Farrell Krell. SanFrancisco: HarperSanFrancisco, 1977.

Held, David. *Introduction to Critical Theory: Horkheimer to Habermas*. Berkeley: University of California Press, 1980.

Hennelly, Alfred. *Liberation Theologies: The Global Pursuit of Justice*. Mystic, Conn.: Twenty-Third Publications, 1995.

Hiley, David, James Bohman, and Richard Shusterman, eds. *The Interpretive Turn: Philosophy, Science and Culture*. Ithaca: Cornell University Press, 1991.

Honneth, Axel, et al., eds. *Philosophical Interventions in the Unfinished Project of Modernity*. Translated by William Rehg. Cambridge: MIT Press, 1992.

Horkheimer, Max. *The Eclipse of Reason*. New York: Oxford University Press, 1947.

———. *Critical Theory: Selected Essays*. Translated by Matthew O'Connell and others. New York: Continuum, 1986.

Ignatius of Loyola. *The Spiritual Exercises of Saint Ignatius: A Translation and Commentary*, translated with a commentary by George Ganns, S.J. St. Louis: Institute of Jesuit Sources, 1992.

Jay, Martin. *The Dialectical Imagination: A History of the Frankfurt School and the Institute of Social Research, 1923–1950*. Boston: Little, Brown, 1973.

———. *Adorno*. Cambridge: Harvard University Press, 1984.

Johns, Roger Dick. *Man in the World: The Political Theology of Johannes Baptist Metz*. Missoula: Scholars Press, 1976.

Johnson, Elizabeth. *She Who Is: The Mystery of God in Feminist Theological Discourse*. New York: Crossroad, 1992.

Kant, Immanuel. *Perpetual Peace and Other Essays*. Edited and translated by Ted Humphrey. Indianapolis: Hackett, 1983.

———. *Religion Within the Limits of Reason Alone.* Translated with an introduction and notes by T. M. Greene and H. H. Hudson. New York: Harper & Row, 1960.

———. *The Critique of Judgment.* Translated with an introduction by Werner Pluhar. Indianapolis: Hackett, 1987.

Katz, Stephen, ed. *Mysticism and Religious Traditions.* New York: Oxford University Press, 1983.

Kelly, William, ed. *Theology and Discovery: Essays in Honor of Karl Rahner, S.J.* Milwaukee: Marquette University Press, 1980.

Kerr, Fergus. *Theology after Wittgenstein.* Oxford: Basil Blackwell, 1986.

Kuhn, Thomas S. *The Structure of Scientific Revolutions,* 2d edition, enlarged with a postscript. Chicago: University of Chicago Press, 1970.

Küng, Hans, and David Tracy, eds. *Paradigm Change in Theology: A Symposium for the Future.* New York: Crossroad, 1989.

LaCugna, Catherine Mowry. *God for Us: The Trinity and Christian Life.* San Francisco: HarperSanFrancisco, 1991.

Lamb, Matthew. *History, Method, and Theology: A Dialectical Comparison of Wilhelm Dilthey's Critique of Historical Reason and Bernard Lonergan's Meta-Methodology.* Atlanta: Scholars Press, 1978.

———. *Solidarity with Victims.* New York: Crossroad, 1982.

Leclercq, Jean. *The Love of Learning and the Desire for God: A Study of Monastic Culture.* 2d rev. edition. Translated by Catherine Misrahi. New York: Fordham University Press, 1974.

Little, Lester. *Religious Poverty and the Profit Economy in Medieval Europe.* Ithaca: Cornell University Press, 1978.

Lobkowicz, Nicholas. *Theory and Practice: The History of a Concept from Aristotle to Marx.* New York: University Press of America, 1967.

Lonergan, Bernard. *Insight: A Study of Human Understanding.* London: Philosophical Library, 1958.

Löwith, Karl. *Meaning in History.* Chicago: University of Chicago Press, 1949.

Maher, Mary. "Historicity and Christian Theology: Johannes Baptist Metz's Critique of Karl Rahner's Theology." Ph.D. diss., Catholic University of America, 1988.

Marcuse, Herbert. *One-Dimensional Man: Studies in the Ideology of Advanced Industrial Society.* Boston: Beacon Press, 1964.

Marsden, George. *Fundamentalism and American Culture: The Shaping of Twentieth-Century Evangelicalism: 1870–1925.* Oxford: Oxford University Press, 1980.

McCool, Gerald. *Catholic Theology in the Nineteenth Century: The Search for a Unitary Method.* New York: Seabury, 1977.

————. *From Unity to Pluralism: The Internal Evolution of Thomism*. New York: Fordham University Press, 1989.

McGinn, Bernard. "The God beyond God: Theology and Mysticism in the Thought of Meister Eckhart." *Journal of Religion* 60 (1981): 1–19.

————. *The Calabrian Abbot: Joachim of Fiore in the History of Western Thought*. New York: Macmillan, 1985.

————. *The Foundations of Mysticism: Origins to the Fifth Century*. New York: Crossroad, 1992.

————. "The Letter and the Spirit: Spirituality as an Academic Discipline." *Christian Spirituality Bulletin* 1/2 (Fall 1993).

————. *The Growth of Mysticism: Gregory the Great through the 12th Century*. New York: Crossroad, 1994.

————. "Meister Eckhart and the Beguines in the Context of Vernacular Theology." In *Meister Eckhart and the Beguine Mystics: Hadewijch of Brabant, Mechthild of Magdeburg, and Marguerite Porete,* edited by Bernard McGinn. New York: Continuum, 1994.

McIntosh, Mark. *Christology from Within: Spirituality and the Incarnation in Hans Urs Von Balthasar*. Studies in Spirituality and Theology, no. 3. Notre Dame: University of Notre Dame Press, 1996.

Mieth, Dietmar. *Die Einheit von Vita activa und Vita contemplativa in den deutschen Predigten und Traktaten Meister Eckharts und bei Johannes Tauler*. Regensburg: Friedrich Pustet, 1969.

Milbank, John. *Theology and Social Theory: Beyond Secular Reason*. Cambridge: Blackwell, 1990.

Moltmann, Jürgen. *Theology of Hope*. Translated by James Leitch. New York: Harper & Row, 1967.

————. *The Crucified God*. Translated by R. A. Wilson and J. Bowden. New York: Harper & Row, 1974.

————. *The Trinity and the Kingdom: The Doctrine of God*. Translated by Margaret Kohl. San Francisco: Harper & Row, 1981.

————. *History and the Triune God: Contributions to Trinitarian Theology*. New York: Crossroad, 1991.

Mosse, George L. *Germans and Jews*. Detroit: Wayne State University Press, 1970.

————. *German Jews Beyond Judaism*. Cincinnati: Hebrew Union College Press, 1985.

Muck, Otto. *The Transcendental Method*. Translated by William Seidensticker. New York: Herder and Herder, 1968.

Nuth, Joan. *Wisdom's Daughter: The Theology of Julian of Norwich*. New York: Crossroad, 1991.

Olafson, Frederick. *Heidegger and the Philosophy of Mind*. New Haven: Yale University Press, 1987.

O'Meara, Thomas F. *Romantic Idealism and Roman Catholicism: Schelling and the Theologians.* Notre Dame: University of Notre Dame Press, 1982.

———. *Church and Culture: German Catholic Theology, 1860–1914.* Notre Dame: University of Notre Dame Press, 1991.

O'Murchu, Diarmuid. *Quantum Theology: Spiritual Implications of the New Physics.* New York: Crossroad, 1997.

Ostovich, Steven. *Reason in History: Theology and Science as Community Activities.* Atlanta: Scholars Press, 1990.

Pelikan, Jaroslav. *Christianity and Classical Culture: The Metamorphosis of Natural Theology in the Christian Encounter with Hellenism.* New Haven: Yale University Press, 1993.

Peterson, Erik. *Der Monotheismus als politisches Problem.* Leipzig: Jakob Hegner, 1935.

Peukert, Helmut. *Science, Action, and Fundamental Theology: Toward a Theology of Communicative Action.* Translated with an introduction by James Bohmann. Cambridge: MIT Press, 1986.

Pieper, Joseph. *The Silence of St. Thomas.* New York: Pantheon, 1957.

Pöggeler, Otto. *Martin Heidegger's Path of Thinking.* Translated by Daniel Magurshak and Sigmund Barber. Atlantic Highlands: Humanities Press, 1989.

Principe, Walter. "Toward Defining Spirituality." *Sciences Religieuses* 12/2 (Spring 1983).

Rahner, Hugo. "Die Gottesgeburt: Die Lehre der Kirchenvätern von der Geburt Christi aus dem Herzen der Kirche und der Gläubigen." In *Symbole der Kirche: Die Ekklesiologie der Vätern.* Salzburg: Müller, 1964.

Rahner, Karl. *Hörer des Wortes: Zur Grundlegung einer Religionsphilosophie.* Munich: Kösel, 1941. Translated by Joseph Donceel, edited with an introduction by Andrew Tallon, as *Hearer of the Word: Laying the Foundation for a Philosophy of Religion.* New York: Continuum, 1994.

———. *Geist in Welt: zur Metaphysik der endlichen Erkenntnis bei Thomas von Aquin.* Neu bearbeitet von J. B. Metz. Munich: Kösel, 1957. Translated by William Dych as *Spirit in the World.* New York: Herder and Herder, 1968.

———. *Hörer des Wortes: Zur Grundlegung einer Religionsphilosophie.* Neu bearbeitet von J. B. Metz. Munich: Kösel, 1963. Translated by Michael Richards as *Hearers of the Word.* New York: Herder and Herder, 1969.

———. *The Dynamic Element in the Church.* Translated by W. J. O'Hara. London: Burns & Oates, 1964.

———. "The Incomprehensibility of God in Thomas Aquinas," *Journal of Religion, Supplement* 58 (1978).

———. Introduction to James Bacik. *Apologetics and the Eclipse of Mystery: Mystagogy According to Karl Rahner.* Notre Dame: University of Notre Dame Press, 1980.

———. "Rede des Ignatius von Loyola an einen Jesuiten von Heute." In *Schriften zur Theologie XV: Wissenschaft und christlischer Glaube.* Zürich: Benziger. 1984.

———. *Foundations of Christian Faith: An Introduction to the Idea of Christianity.* Translated by William V. Dych. New York: Seabury, 1978.

———. *Theological Investigations.* 23 volumes. New York: Crossroad, 1992.

———. *The Practice of Faith.* Ed. Karl Lehman and Albert Raffelt. New York: Crossroad, 1986.

Reinharz, Jehuda, and Walter Schatzber, eds. *The Jewish Response to German Culture: From the Enlightenment to the Second World War.* Hanover: University Press of New England, 1985.

Reno, R. R. "Christology in Political and Liberation Theology." *The Thomist* 56/2 (April 1992): 291–322.

Ricoeur, Paul. *Lectures in Ideology and Utopia.* Edited by George Taylor. New York: Columbia University Press, 1986.

———. *Oneself as Another.* Translated by Kathleen Blamey. Chicago: University of Chicago Press, 1992.

Rieff, Philip. *The Triumph of the Therapeutic: Uses of Faith after Freud.* Chicago: University of Chicago Press: 1987.

Roberts, Louis. *The Achievement of Karl Rahner,* with a foreword by Karl Rahner. New York: Herder, 1967.

Roberts, Richard. *Hope and Its Hieroglyph: A Critical Decipherment of Ernst Bloch's "Principle of Hope."* Atlanta: Scholars Press, 1990.

Rorty, Richard M., ed. *The Linguistic Turn: Essays in Philosophical Method with Two Retrospective Essays.* Chicago: University of Chicago Press, 1992.

Rose, Gillian. *The Melancholy Science: An Introduction to the Thought of Theodor W. Adorno.* New York: Columbia University Press, 1979.

Schillebeeckx, Edward, ed. *Mystik und Politik, Theologie im Ringen um Geschichte und Gesellschaft: Johann Baptist Metz zu Ehren.* Mainz: Matthias-Grünewald, 1988.

Schindler, David, ed. *Hans Urs von Balthasar: His Life and Work.* San Francisco: Ignatius Press, 1991.

Schneiders, Sandra. "Spirituality in the Academy." *Theological Studies* 50 (1988):676–97.

———. *The Revelatory Text: Interpreting the New Testament as Sacred Scripture.* San Francisco: Harper Collins, 1991.

Schner, George. "The Appeal to Experience." *Theological Studies* 53 (1992):40–59.

Scholem, Gershom. "Mysticism and Society." *Diogenes* 58 (1967): 1–24.

———. *On the Kabbalah and Its Symbolism.* Translated by Ralph Manheim. New York: Schocken, 1965.

———. *On Jews and Judaism in Crisis: Selected Essays.* Edited by Werner Dannhauser. New York: Schocken, 1976.

———. *Walter Benjamin: The Story of a Friendship.* London: Faber & Faber, 1982.

Segundo, Juan Luis. *The Liberation of Theology.* Translated by John Drury. Maryknoll: Orbis, 1976.

Sheldrake, Philip. *Spirituality and History: Questions of Interpretation and Method.* New York: Crossroad, 1992.

Smart, Ninian, et al., eds. *Nineteenth Century Religious Thought in the West.* 3 volumes. New York: Cambridge University Press, 1985.

Sobrino, Jon. *Christology at the Crossroads.* Translated by John Drury. New York: Crossroad, 1978.

———. "The Crucified Peoples: Yahweh's Suffering Servant Today." In *1492–1992: The Voice of the Victims* (*Concilium* Special Edition). Edited by Leonardo Boff and Virgil Elizondo, and translated by Dinah Livingstone. London: SCM Press, 1990.

———. *Jesus the Liberator: A Historical-Theological Reading of Jesus of Nazareth.* Translated by Paul Burns and Francis McDonagh. Maryknoll: Orbis, 1993.

———. *The Principle of Mercy: Taking the Crucified People from the Cross.* Maryknoll: Orbis, 1994.

Sölle, Dorothee. *Political Theology.* Translated with an introduction by J. Shelley. Philadelphia: Fortress Press, 1974.

Tallon, Andrew. "Personal Becoming: Karl Rahner's Christian Anthropology." *The Thomist* 43 (January 1979): 1–177.

Taylor, Charles. *Sources of the Self: The Making of the Modern Identity.* Cambridge: Harvard University Press, 1989.

Thompson, William. *Fire and Light: The Saints and Theology.* New York: Crossroad, 1987.

———. *Christology and Spirituality.* New York: Crossroad, 1991.

Tickle, Phyllis. *Re-discovering the Sacred: Spirituality in America.* New York: Crossroad, 1995.

Toulmin, Stephen. "The Historicization of Natural Science: Its Implications for Theology." In *Paradigm Change in Theology: A Symposium for the Future,* edited by Hans Küng and David Tracy. New York: Crossroad, 1989.

———. *Cosmopolis: The Hidden Agenda of Modernity.* New York: The Free Press, 1990.

Tracy, David. *Blessed Rage for Order: The New Pluralism in Theology.* Minneapolis: Winston-Seabury Press, 1975.

———. *The Analogical Imagination: Christian Theology and the Culture of Pluralism.* New York: Crossroad, 1986.

———. "Theology, Critical Social Theory, and the Public Realm." In *Habermas, Modernity, and Public Theology,* ed. Don Browning and Francis Schüssler Fiorenza. New York: Crossroad, 1992.

———. *Dialogue with the Other: The Inter-religious Dialogue.* Grand Rapids: Eerdmans, 1990.

———. "Conversation with David Tracy." An interview conducted by Todd Breyfogle and Thomas Levergood. *Cross Currents* 44/3 (Fall 1994).

Vickers, Brian, ed. *Arbeit Musse Meditation: Betrachtungen zur Vita activa und Vita contemplativa.* Zürich: Verlag der Fachvereine, 1985.

Von Hügel, Friedrich. *The Mystical Element of Religion as Studied in Saint Catherine of Genoa and Her Friends.* 2 volumes. London: Clark & Dent, 1961.

Vorgrimler, Herbert. *Understanding Karl Rahner: An Introduction to His Life and Thought.* Translated by John Bowden. New York: Crossroad, 1986.

Welch, Claude. *Protestant Theology in the Nineteenth Century.* 2 volumes. New Haven: Yale University Press, 1972.

Wiesel, Elie. *The Night Trilogy.* New York: Noonday Press, 1988.

Wolin, Richard. *Walter Benjamin: An Aesthetic of Redemption.* New York: Columbia University Press, 1982.

Wuthnow, Robert. *God and Mammon in America.* New York: The Free Press, 1994.

INDEX

Abraham, K. C., 4
absurdity, presence of, for Metz,
144–45
academic theology, 8–9, 10–11,
20, 24
action: interruption as prelude to,
195; radical, 120, 124,
239n. 78; realm of, for
Rahner, 73–76; relationship
to spirituality, x–xi, 176–78,
187
Adorno, Theodor, 33, 97, 100,
109–15, 116, 221n. 58;
Habermas's turn away from,
43; influenced by the
Holocaust, 123; influence on
Metz, 28, 43, 103, 149; Jay's
summary of work, 29–30
anamnesis. *See* memory
Ancic, Nedjeljko, 217n. 26
Angelus Silesius, 242n. 17
anthropocentricity, 99, 101, 105–6;
of Aquinas's thought-form,
90–91; of Augustine's
response to theodicy question,
126
anthropology, 8–9, 22, 39–40, 59
(*see also* theological
anthropology)
of Heidegger, 65, 135–40
of Kant, 38–39, 48, 51, 64–65;
Metz's treatment of, 54–56,
72
of Rahner, 81–82, 135–40
Thomist, 84–85

transcendental, 135–40, 166,
184
anticipatory resoluteness, of
Heidegger, 230n. 82; Metz's
alternative to, 86
anxiety, for Heidegger, 155,
225n. 19
apocalyptic eschatology, 105–6,
108, 118–21, 145, 187–88,
238n. 71
imagery and language, viii, 124,
129–30, 163–67; as divisive
issue for Metz and Rahner,
172, 187–88, 251n. 58
messianic wisdom of Judaism,
122–23
as response to the theodicy
question, 126, 243n. 24
apocalyptic mysticism/spirituality,
xii, 26, 34, 180–81, 184, 187;
of the Middle Ages, 180,
249nn. 31, 32; Trinitarian
speculation in traditions of,
194
apophatic tradition, 26, 178–79,
210n. 15, 247n. 23
Aquinas. *See* Thomas Aquinas
argument: place in theology, 132;
primacy of narrative over,
121, 239n. 82
Aristotelianism, 229n. 61
Aristotle, 9
atheism, 33, 138, 197–201,
214n. 52, 240n. 95
Augustine, 126, 178, 184

273